THE BREAD BOOK

THE BREAD BOOK

Linda Collister & Anthony Blake

Sedgewood® Press
New York, New York

TO ALAN AND KYLE

U.S. edition published by
Sedgewood® Press
150 East 52nd Street
New York, NY 10022

Sedgewood® Press is an imprint of Meredith® Books:
President, Book Group: Joseph J. Ward
Vice-President, Editorial Director: Elizabeth P. Rice

For Sedgewood® Press
Executive Editor: Maryanne Bannon
Americanization Project Editors: Miriam Rubin, David Ricketts
Recipe Testers: Carol Prager, Louise Burbidge, Rebecca Adams,
Sandra Rose Gluck, Georgia Chan Downard, Susan McQuillan

All correspondence should be addressed to Sedgewood® Press.

ISBN: 0-696-02564-7
Library of Congress Number: 93-077499

Distributed by Meredith Corporation
Des Moines, Iowa

Printed in Italy

CONTENTS

FRIED DOUGHS 90

SAVORY BREADS 102

FRUIT AND NUT BREADS 120

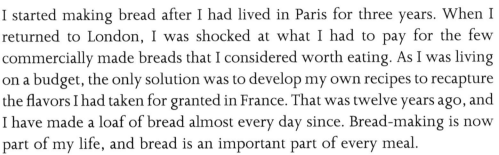

INTRODUCTION

I started making bread after I had lived in Paris for three years. When I returned to London, I was shocked at what I had to pay for the few commercially made breads that I considered worth eating. As I was living on a budget, the only solution was to develop my own recipes to recapture the flavors I had taken for granted in France. That was twelve years ago, and I have made a loaf of bread almost every day since. Bread-making is now part of my life, and bread is an important part of every meal.

Yes, family and work do keep me busy, but baking a loaf a day is not difficult. For our daily needs, I usually bake French Sourdough Loaf (page 162), which allows me great flexibility in preparation and rising times. Also, I frequently make my family Herb Rolls (page 82), which again are neither demanding nor time-consuming. I serve these with a bowl of soup for a nourishing, light meal.

Anthony Blake and I share a passion for well-made bread, but we have come together to work on this book from different backgrounds. I had a classical training as a cook and have worked in Paris and Italy, while Anthony has had a life-long interest in food, which was enhanced as he photographed some of the world's greatest chefs at work.

I was greatly helped and inspired in my bread-making by Pierre Koffmann, chef and owner of La Tante Claire, currently London's only restaurant with three Michelin stars. Pierre is fascinated by bread-making, and in turn fascinates with his knowledge and enthusiasm. His expertise is such that each day he bakes rolls flavored to complement the dishes he serves. Anthony and I both thank him for sharing his wisdom with us.

In the year-and-a-half we traveled about in America, Ireland, Britain, France, Italy, and Germany, seeking out both the famous and unsung bread bakers, we met all sorts of bread enthusiasts. They generously shared with us their secrets and tips. We were welcomed by bakers and millers of all ages and experience in a host of private and professional kitchens. Bread-

In the kitchens of La Tante Claire, Chef Pierre Koffmann enthusiastically explains his philosophy of bread-making.

making has introduced us to a warm international community, with each member sharing his or her own way of making a perfect loaf. So many breads, so many recipes!

The first lesson I learned was that you can not make good bread without good flour. It amazes me how many skilled bakers spend time producing impressive-looking loaves that only disappoint on the palate. More often than not this is because they have used mass-produced, bleached, and highly refined flour. Yet, high-quality, flavorful flour is easily available from small, independent millers. Check your local health-food store or see the list of mail-order suppliers on page 187. Once you have started baking with well-produced flours, you will find the flavor and texture of your loaves vastly superior to those made with most ordinary, supermarket flours.

The advantage of stone-ground flours is that they add texture as well as flavor to your breads. The grains are not as finely crushed as they are when mass producers put them through large steel rollers. The traditional, slower method of milling grain between two stone disks does not heat the grains as the modern, rapid techniques do. This means that flour milled in the old-fashioned way retains its good flavor. If the wheat has been organically grown, your loaf will have even more goodness.

The second important lesson of bread-making I have learned is that haste makes waste, not taste. Most bread-baking books instruct you to make the dough with very warm liquid and let it rise in a warm place. A quickly made loaf does have the merit of being homemade but to my mind, it will not have the best flavor or texture.

You will see that most of my recipes are made with cool or lukewarm liquid and then left to rise at cool to normal room temperatures. This is because a slowly risen dough produces a loaf with a fuller flavor. I also prefer this loaf's texture because it is chewier and not filled with air holes. All in all, a slowly risen dough makes a more satisfying loaf than one made with a speedy rising. There is the added advantage that slowly-made bread stays fresher longer.

I am always surprised when people tell me they think bread-making requires great skill. This is not true especially with the basic, everyday loaves; some enriched breads, with their flaky layers, do take a bit of practice. But for the most part, working with yeast doughs is actually simple and straightforward. As long as you do not kill the yeast with too much heat before the loaf is baked, there is very little that can go wrong. Unlike making pastry or cakes, which requires a light touch, kneading dough only requires time and effort. Even a child can successfully knead dough and shape a loaf.

Once you begin baking bread, you will soon discover that you are

Home-baked bread is included in a simple lunch for a farm worker in an oast house in Kent, England. Large, circular oast houses were where hops were traditionally dried after harvesting.

absorbed by the endless variety. Breads come in all shapes and sizes, with different textures and tastes. Remember, too, that simple, basic loaves may be considered peasant food in one part of the world while elsewhere, they are found only on sophisticated gourmet tables.

This book contains my favorite bread recipes, as well as the ones given to Anthony and me by enthusiastic bakers around the world. This is not intended to be an encyclopedia of all the world's bread, or even a technical manual, although, I do, from time to time, illustrate techniques with step-by-step photographs. My hope is that this collection of breads we enjoy eating as well as making will inspire you to bake breads for yourself, your family, and your friends.

BASIC BREADS

It is immensely satisfying to bake an honest, flavorful loaf of bread with a rich, tantalizing aroma. Good, nourishing bread has been held in high esteem since the age of the Pharaohs, and rightly so. The bread you eat today is a slice of social history. The basic ingredients, used by those ancient Egyptians, have remained unchanged – flour, salt, water, and usually leavening – although today we can choose from a dozen different flours, enrich the water with milk, eggs, or fat, and use fresh or dried yeasts, chemical leavening agents, or the natural yeasts produced in a sourdough. Our modern bread can be as fancy or simple, sophisticated or rustic as we choose.

This chapter contains complete instructions and photographs for each stage in the recipe for making a basic loaf of bread. Although bread making is neither complex nor tricky, you do have to take many variables into account. I bake bread every day, yet I can never be absolutely sure of the result. Much depends on the weather and the kitchen temperature, the kind of flour, the type and age of the yeast, and even the hardness of the water. My aim is that you learn what looks, tastes, smells, and feels right.

OPPOSITE AND ABOVE
Baguettes are a traditional bread for the French

To the old saying that all you need to make good bread is time, warmth, and love, I would add practice. Once you have mastered a basic recipe – and it will take three or four batches to get the correct feel – you can experiment. Take risks – play around with various shapes, change the flavor and texture of the crumb by mixing flours and grains, or vary the crust with different toppings and glazes. The classic French baguette, for example, has a high proportion of crust to crumb, yet the crust is thin and razor-sharp, the crumb moist and light. You will soon learn that this result is achieved in the shaping, finishing, and baking of the loaf, and that a similar bread dough handled in a different manner is used to make soft, floury baps, a favorite Scottish breakfast roll.

Anthony Blake and I have watched many fine bakers in several countries make bread, and each has a special, individual method. Some bakers start with a "sponge" – yeast, liquid, and some of the flour – while others add all the liquid to the flour at once, and others add all the flour to the liquid. Some bakers swear by ice water; others use quite warm water. Some like hot conditions, while others prefer the refrigerator for the fermentation and rising of the dough. I prefer a loaf made with very little fresh yeast, flavorful flour, cool water, a fair amount of sea salt, and a long rising time in a cool spot. It is this slow fermentation of the dough that produces a well-flavored, chewy, even sturdy loaf that, as it matures, assumes a rich, complex flavor and is slow to stale.

Try the recipes and find what works best for you.

POINTS TO REMEMBER

Before you begin, read these points and The Basic Loaf recipe. These points explain why some of my recipes are made differently than recipes found in other books. For information on the chemistry of bread-making, read Harold McGee's *On Food and Cooking: The Science and Lore of the Kitchen* (Charles Scribner's Sons, 1984).

– Yeast is an organism that needs moisture, warmth, and sugar or flour to stimulate its growth. As it multiplies, it produces carbon dioxide, which makes dough rise.

– Temperature is crucial to yeast; if the water or liquid you add to it is too hot the yeast will be killed, too cool and its growth will be inhibited – which is actually often desirable if you want a slow rising. According to conventional wisdom, the ideal temperature is between 95F and 105F, termed lukewarm.

– The yeast will grow quickly if the dough is left to rise in a warm, draft-free spot. In a cool place, however, the dough will rise slower. Therefore rising times can vary from about 1 hour to overnight. I find that the cooler rising temperature gives a much better-tasting bread, which is why most of my recipes leave the dough to rise at cool to normal room temperature. Choose a spot which is about 60F, such as an unheated pantry.

– The quantity of liquid and flour you add varies depending on the flour and conditions, such as the heat and humidity in the kitchen. You may need a little more or a little less than the recipe states to achieve the desired dough consistency. In many recipes I've given a range for the amount of flour.

– To measure flour, scoop a dry-measure cup directly into the bag or canister. Level off the excess. If you prefer to weigh the flour, one cup will weigh five ounces.

– I prefer fresh yeast to active dry yeast because it gives loaves a deeper flavor and I find the fresh easier to use. However, most recipes will work with active dry yeast and recipes usually include directions for both types (for detailed instructions; see page 18).

– My recipes call for either flaked (not crystal) sea salt or kosher salt because I prefer the flavor. If you use regular fine table salt, decrease the amount by half.

– Kneading (page 16) is vital for good, even-textured, well-shaped bread. Kneading helps to develop the gluten in the flour, which is necessary to support the carbon dioxide produced by the yeast. Kneading also incorporates air into the dough and ensures that the yeast is evenly distributed throughout so the loaf rises evenly.

– Dough is usually kneaded by hand for 10 minutes, or in a large, stationary mixer using a dough hook. However, I have never found that kneading dough in a food processor does it much good – and, as with all mechanical methods of kneading, it is easy to over-knead which does more harm than good by breaking down gluten strands.

– The dough should be left to rise covered with a damp linen or cotton (but not terry-cloth) dish towel, or sheet of plastic wrap to prevent a dry crust forming, which can leave hard lumps in the finished loaf. The loaf will be heavy if it is not left to rise for long enough, though over-rising is more of a problem than slight under-rising. If a dough is seriously distended by being left to rise too long, it collapses when baked.

– Punching down the risen dough disperses the gas bubbles for uniform texture and crumb.

– I do not usually specify what to use for greasing pans and baking sheets. Some bakers use melted lard, vegetable oil or non-stick sprays; I prefer melted unsalted butter because doughs do not absorb butter as they do oil, and the loaf is less likely to stick as it bakes.

– Baking in a hot, preheated oven (usually 400F or higher) kills the yeast quickly (which is what you want to have happen at this point) and prevents over-rising. The hotter the oven, the crisper the crust will be.

– Bread is baked through when it sounds hollow when tapped on the underside. Most breads are turned out of the baking pans onto wire racks to cool, which prevents the steam from the loaf making the crust soggy underneath.

THE BASIC LOAF

INGREDIENTS

Makes one large loaf.

- $2\frac{1}{2}$ cups white bread flour (preferably unbleached and stone-ground)
- 2 to $2\frac{1}{2}$ cups whole-wheat bread flour (preferably stone-ground)
- $2\frac{1}{2}$ teaspoons kosher salt or flaked sea salt
- 1 cake compressed fresh yeast (0.6 ounce), or 1 envelope active dry yeast ($2\frac{1}{2}$ teaspoons) plus $\frac{1}{2}$ teaspoon granulated sugar
- $1\frac{3}{4}$ cups lukewarm water (95F to 105F)

a large baking sheet, greased, or a greased $9 \times 5 \times 3$-inch loaf pan

This is how to make a fine-tasting, good-looking loaf of bread. The combination of white bread flour (preferably stone-ground and unbleached) and whole-wheat flour (preferably stone-ground) makes a loaf that is easy to work, but with great flavor and a good texture. It is shaped into an oval and simply baked on a cookie sheet, rather than in a loaf pan. Although you may use a loaf pan if you like (see instructions for shaping in A Plain White Loaf, page 24), I find this free-form shape easier and more attractive.

This basic method, which first creates a "sponge," is the same for most yeast doughs. Many of the recipes in this book will refer back to the techniques illustrated and explained below and overleaf. This loaf will keep for up to five days, and can be frozen for one month.

In very cold weather, warming the bowl of flour in a 250F oven for 5 to 8 minutes, or microwaving on high for $\frac{1}{2}$ to $1\frac{1}{2}$ minutes (be sure to use a microwave-safe bowl), depending upon the amount of flour, helps the yeast start working.

Fresh Yeast Method

Professional bakers use the sponge method shown in steps 1 through 7 on page 16 to test whether the yeast is alive and working – growing and multiplying rapidly – before they add large quantities of flour, which will be wasted if the yeast is dead. If the batter does not become spongy, throw it out and begin again; the yeast is probably too old, or was killed by too hot water.

This sponge technique also has the advantage of lightening the heavier loaves. It is a time-consuming technique, so many experienced home bakers prefer to skip this step, but I think it is a good idea for anyone new to bread-making to use this technique until your knowledge of yeast's characteristics becomes second nature.

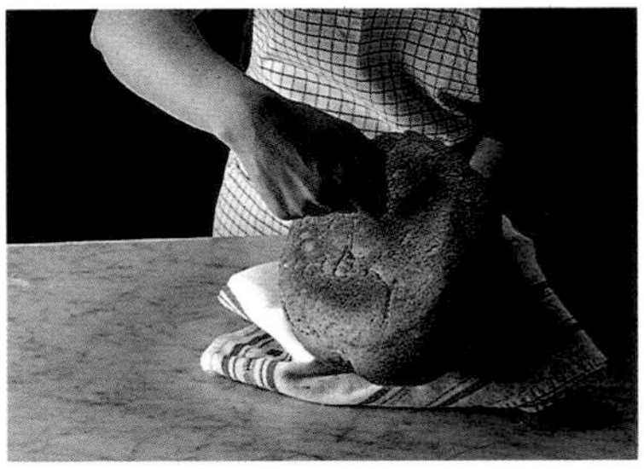

TO TEST IF THE LOAF IS BAKED THROUGH, CAREFULLY TURN IT UPSIDE DOWN AND TAP IT WITH YOUR KNUCKLES; A THOROUGHLY BAKED LOAF SOUNDS HOLLOW. IF THE LOAF SOUNDS DENSE OR HEAVY, BAKE IT FOR 5 MINUTES LONGER AND TEST AGAIN. TRANSFER THE BREAD TO A WIRE RACK TO COOL COMPLETELY.

The aroma of freshly baked bread will fill the kitchen when the loaf comes out of the oven. This perfectly baked loaf has a good crisp crust and a well-flavored, chewy crumb.

The Basic Loaf Step-by-Step Directions

MIX TOGETHER THE *WHITE* FLOUR, 2 CUPS OF THE *WHOLE*-*WHEAT* FLOUR, *AND* THE SALT IN *A* LARGE BOWL. IN *VERY* COLD *WEATHER WARM* THE BOWL OF FLOUR (SEE PAGE 15). THIS *WILL* HELP THE YEAST START *WORKING*.

1 CRUMBLE THE CAKE OF FRESH YEAST INTO *A* SMALL BOWL *WITH* YOUR FINGERS. (IF USING *ACTIVE* DRY YEAST, SEE PAGE 18.)

2 MIX ABOUT $\frac{1}{4}$ CUP OF THE MEASURED LUKE*WARM WATER WITH* THE YEAST UNTIL SMOOTH.

3 MAKE *A WELL* ABOUT 6 INCHES *WIDE* IN THE CENTER OF THE FLOUR. *ADD* THE YEAST MIXTURE.

4 POUR THE REST OF THE LUKE*WARM WATER* INTO THE *WELL*.

5 *DRAW A* LITTLE FLOUR INTO THE *WELL AND* MIX THOROUGHLY *WITH* THE LIQUID. GRADUALLY MIX IN MORE FLOUR UNTIL YOU *HAVE A* THICK, SMOOTH BATTER IN THE *WELL*.

6 SPRINKLE THE BATTER *WITH A* LITTLE *WHITE* FLOUR TO PREVENT *A* SKIN FROM FORMING.

7 LET THE BATTER STAND FOR ABOUT 20 MINUTES TO SPONGE. IT *WILL* BECOME *AERATED AND* FROTHY *AND* EXPAND NEARLY TO FILL THE *WELL* IN THE FLOUR.

8 GRADUALLY MIX THE REST OF THE FLOUR IN THE BOWL INTO THE BATTER *WITH* YOUR *HAND*.

9 GATHER THE DOUGH INTO *A* BALL. IT SHOULD BE FIRM *AND* LEAVE THE SIDE OF THE BOWL CLEANLY. IF DRY, *ADD* LUKE*WARM WATER*, 1 TABLESPOON *AT A* TIME; IF STICKY, *ADD* FLOUR, 1 TABLESPOON *AT A* TIME.

10 TURN DOUGH OUT OF THE BOWL ONTO *A* LIGHTLY FLOURED *WORK* SURFACE *AND* KNEAD FOR 10 MINUTES. TO KNEAD, FIRST STRETCH THE DOUGH *AWAY* FROM YOU.

11 THEN GATHER THE DOUGH BACK INTO *A* BALL.

12 GIVE THE DOUGH A QUARTER TURN, THEN CONTINUE REPEATING THESE THREE MOVEMENTS.

13 AS DOUGH IS KNEADED, IT GRADUALLY CHANGES TEXTURE TO BECOME VERY SMOOTH AND ELASTIC. IT LOOKS ALMOST GLOSSY. SHAPE THE DOUGH INTO A SMOOTH BALL.

14 WASH, DRY, AND OIL THE BOWL. RETURN DOUGH TO BOWL AND TURN IT OVER SO THE TOP IS OILED TO PREVENT STICKING. COVER THE BOWL WITH A DAMP DISH TOWEL.

15 LET THE DOUGH RISE, OR PROOF, AT ROOM TEMPERATURE (ABOUT 70F), AWAY FROM DRAFTS, UNTIL DOUBLED IN SIZE, WHICH USUALLY TAKES 1½ TO 2 HOURS.

16 THE DOUGH IS PROPERLY RISEN WHEN YOU CAN PRESS THE TIP OF YOUR FINGER INTO IT AND THE DOUGH DOES NOT SPRING BACK.

17 PUNCH DOWN THE DOUGH WITH YOUR KNUCKLES. THIS BREAKS UP LARGE CARBON DIOXIDE POCKETS AND REDISTRIBUTES THE GAS SO YOU GET AN EVEN-TEXTURED LOAF.

18 TO MAKE A FREE-FORM LOAF, ON A LIGHTLY FLOURED SURFACE, SHAPE THE DOUGH BY GENTLY KNEADING IT INTO AN OVAL 8 × 4 INCHES.

19 WITH THE EDGE OF YOUR HAND, MAKE A DEEP CREASE LENGTHWISE DOWN THE CENTER OF THE DOUGH.

20 ROLL THE SIDES OF THE DOUGH OVER TO MAKE A FAT SAUSAGE-SHAPE. TUCK THE SHORT ENDS UNDER AND PINCH ALL SEAMS TOGETHER TO SEAL THEM.

21 ROLL THE DOUGH OVER ON THE WORK SURFACE SO THE SEAM IS UNDERNEATH AND THE TOP LOOKS SMOOTH AND EVENLY SHAPED. (THE OVAL WILL MEASURE ABOUT 9 × 4 INCHES.)

22 PUT LOAF, SEAM DOWN, ONTO A GREASED BAKING SHEET. MAKE ½-INCH DEEP DIAGONAL SLASHES ON TOP. COVER WITH A DAMP DISH TOWEL; LET RISE UNTIL DOUBLED IN SIZE, 1½ TO 2 HOURS.

Baking Instructions

DURING THE LAST 15 MINUTES OF THE RISING TIME, HEAT THE OVEN TO 425F. UNCOVER THE LOAF AND SPRINKLE THE TOP WITH ABOUT 1 TABLESPOON OF WHOLE-WHEAT FLOUR. BAKE THE LOAF FOR 15 MINUTES, THEN REDUCE THE OVEN TEMPERATURE TO 375F AND CONTINUE BAKING FOR ANOTHER 20 TO 30 MINUTES, UNTIL THE LOAF SOUNDS HOLLOW WHEN TAPPED UNDERNEATH (PAGE 15).

Method for *Active* Dry Yeast

If you are using active dry yeast, it must be reconstituted before it will work. Reconstitute the yeast by sprinkling it over a small bowl containing $\frac{1}{4}$ cup warm water (105F to 115F), or an amount specified in a recipe, and $\frac{1}{2}$ teaspoon granulated sugar.

STIR THE YEAST, SUGAR AND WATER UNTIL THE YEAST IS DISSOLVED.

YOU SHOULD HAVE A LUMP-FREE LIQUID. LEAVE IT TO BECOME FOAMY.

This is how reconstituted active dry yeast looks when it is foamy and ready to use. If your yeast does not look like this after 15 minutes, throw it out and begin with another, fresher envelope of yeast. It is a good idea to check the yeast's expiration date before beginning.

After 5 to 10 minutes, the mixture should look very foamy. (If after 15 minutes the yeast is not foamy, it is inactive, either because it was too old or because it was killed by water that was too hot. Throw the mixture out and start again with another, fresher envelope of yeast.) Dry yeast that is near its expiration date or taken from an open container will be slow to work, if it works at all, and the dough may take longer to rise than the times given in specific recipes. Add the foamy yeast mixture to a well in the flour and make the sponge as described in the fresh yeast method. Continue making the dough from step 8 of the fresh yeast method (see page 16).

WHAT WENT WRONG? COMMON PROBLEMS IN BREAD-MAKING

CRUST IS SOFT, PALE AND SOGGY.

– Not baked long enough, or the oven temperature was too low.

– If a loaf does not sound hollow when tapped underneath, return it to the oven for 5–10 minutes longer. To make the crust crisper, place the loaf directly on the oven rack.

LOAF IS CRUMBLY AND DRY.
– Baked for too long, or the oven temperature was too high.
– Too much flour was used in the dough.

LOAF HAS UNINTENDED, LARGE HOLES.
– Over-kneaded in a food processor or electric mixer.
– If made by hand, the dough was under-kneaded (page 16).
– Risen dough was not punched down thoroughly before shaping (page 17).

CRUST IS DETACHED FROM CRUMB.
– Risen dough was not punched down thoroughly before shaping (page 17).
– Dough was not rolled tight enough while being shaped for a loaf pan (page 26).

DOUGH DIDN'T RISE, OR ROSE POORLY.
– Yeast was used past the expiration date on the envelope (page 18).
– Liquids to be mixed with yeast were too hot and killed the yeast. Liquid must be lukewarm (95F–105F), which is often described as blood heat or hand-hot.
– Dough was left to rise in a spot that was too hot. This is a particular danger with dough left to rise in a stainless steel bowl, especially when it is placed in an oven with a pilot light or on a stovetop.

BREAD TASTES YEASTY AND DAMP.
– Too much yeast was used. Take particular care measuring fresh yeast.
– Not baked long enough. If the loaf does not sound hollow when unmolded and tapped underneath, return it to the oven for 5–10 minutes longer. You can put the bread directly on the oven rack.

BREAD IS SOGGY, FLAT, AND DENSE.
– Too much liquid was added when making the dough and there was not enough flour to absorb it.
– Dough was not kneaded long enough, nor thoroughly enough (page 16).

LOAF COLLAPSED IN OVEN.
– Dough was left too long during second rising and it became over-risen. Dough should only double in size, or as specified in the recipe.

FREE-FORM LOAVES (page 17) AND SHAPED LOAVES (page 24) SPREAD DURING BAKING.
– Dough was too soft or too warm when it was shaped. Dough can be too soft if it is made with too much liquid, or not enough flour. Softness can also be caused by the dough being left to rise in a spot that is too warm. This is especially true for enriched doughs (see Chapter 9, page 168).

LOAF CRACKED ALONG ONE SIDE OR ROSE UNEVENLY.
– Loaf was subjected to uneven heat. It was placed too far to one side, or too near a hot spot in the oven. Check the oven manufacturer's handbook for correct rack and position (usually the middle of the oven).
– If you have an "eccentric" oven, turn loaf regularly while it bakes. Check the evenness of the temperature throughout the oven with an oven thermometer.
– Too much dough in the loaf pan, or the pan was too small.

TYPES OF FLOUR

Organic corn ready for grinding at Philipsburg Manor (page 69).

Although wheat flour is the most common variety used for making bread, you should familiarize yourself with the wide range of flours ground from other grains – these are the flours that can vary the flavor and add more texture to your loaves.

Whatever flour you buy, I urge you to search out both the stone-ground and unbleached varieties whenever possible. Your breads will have a deeper, fuller flavor.

In the following glossary, I have included other grain products important to bread-making, as well as flour storage tips (see right).

ALL-PURPOSE FLOUR is a blend of high-gluten hard wheat and low-gluten soft wheat, and is suitable for a wide range of baking needs. The flour is milled from the endosperm of the wheat berry, and contains neither the bran nor the germ. U.S. law requires that any flour not containing the germ of the wheat must have certain nutrients added back in, resulting in a flour labeled "enriched."

BARLEY FLOUR, ground from pearl barley (the grain stripped of husks and germ), imparts to breads a moist, cakelike quality with a malty aftertaste. Low in gluten, it needs to be combined with wheat flour. Adding 10 to 15 percent barley flour to sourdough, rye, and plain whole-wheat doughs makes for especially robust loaves.

BARLEY FLAKES can be cooked as a breakfast cereal or added to wheat flour for bread doughs (see Barley flour above).

BRAN is the outer layer or husk of the wheat berry. It is what gives whole-wheat flour its characteristic color. Unprocessed bran, or miller's bran, is often added to bread doughs, as well as muffin or pancake batters for extra fiber.

BULGHUR (some times spelt bulgur) is wheat berries that have been first steamed, then dried and cracked into either coarse, medium, or fine pieces, the latter often used in bread-making.

UNBLEACHED BREAD FLOUR, or bleached, formulated with practically all hard-wheat flour, has a high proportion of protein to starch. As the dough is kneaded, the protein develops into gluten, the firm, elastic structure that allows breads to rise. Available in whole-wheat or white.

BUCKWHEAT flour does not come from a true cereal but rather from a grass belonging to the sorrel family. The speckled gray-brown flour, ground from the buckwheat groat, has a distinct, slightly bitter flavor, and when mixed with wheat flour produces bread with a pungent, earthy flavor, a soft crust, and a moist, fine crumb. Buckwheat flour is also used in blinis, pancakes, and Japanese soba noodles.

CAKE FLOUR is a fine-textured, soft-wheat flour, with little gluten, and is used where a tender, delicate crumb is desired, as in cakes.

CORNMEAL is ground from dried whole kernels of yellow, white, or blue field corn, and can be milled fine or coarse. Stone-ground is preferable. Degerminated cornmeal has been sieved to remove the germ for longer shelf life. When incorporated into doughs, cornmeal creates a loaf with a grainy, somewhat dry crumb, and a slightly sweet flavor.

COARSE YELLOW CORNMEAL is the key ingredient in the well-known Italian polenta.

CORN FLOUR is finely ground cornmeal from the whole corn kernel and can be mixed with wheat flour for bread-making.

CORNSTARCH is ground from the heart or the endosperm of the corn kernel. Silky in texture, it's used as a thickener and in small quantities, to lighten flour for pastry-making.

MASA HARINA is cornmeal finely ground from white corn kernels that have been soaked in lime water before being dried. It is a major ingredient in tortilla making.

VITAL WHEAT (also known as gluten flour) is made from wheat flour and contains pure gluten, ranging from 70 to 100 percent. Gluten gives bread dough its elasticity and

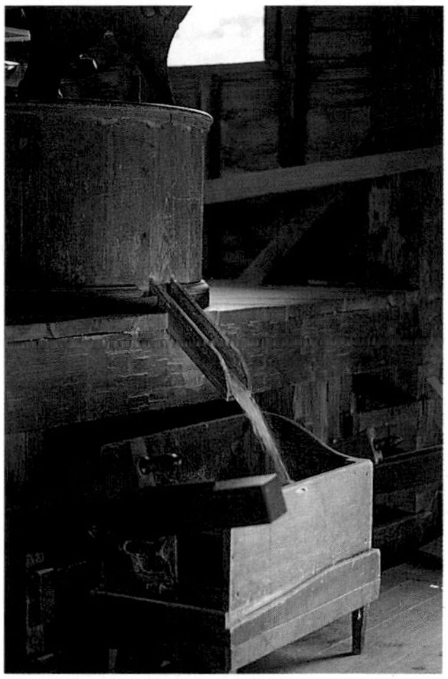

Fresh stone-ground cornmeal.

allows it to rise. Added to a dough, vital wheat gluten gives it additional resiliency.
MILLET FLOUR is ground from whole millet and is rich in protein, vitamins, and minerals, but lacking gluten. It is used for making flat breads and griddle cakes, and when mixed with wheat flour, produces bread with a buttery, slightly sweet taste, a smooth, thin crust, and a moist, dense crumb.
ROLLED OATS, known commonly as oatmeal, are oat groats that have been hulled, steamed, and flattened into flakes. They can be ground into a coarse meal, or can be added as they are to bread doughs for extra fiber and nutrients.
STEEL-CUT OATS, often called Scotch or Irish oatmeal, are made by cutting the groats (hulled whole oat kernels) into pieces with steel rollers. Used for Scottish Griddle Oatcakes (page 72), they may also be added to bread doughs.
OAT FLOUR, finely ground from oat groats, contains no gluten. When mixed with wheat flour for bread-making, it contributes a firm crust, chewy texture, and a sweet, nutty flavor. Not widely available.
RYE FLAKES are cooked, rolled rye berries (the whole grain), similar to rolled oats. A small amount mixed into bread doughs adds a chewy texture and a slightly tangy flavor.
RYE FLOUR adds a distinctive tangy, slightly sour flavor to breads, as well as a chewy texture. Since it contains little gluten, it is usually combined with higher protein flours (usually wheat) to increase elasticity and lighten the dough.
SELF-RISING FLOUR is a blend of all-purpose flour, baking powder, and salt, and is often used in the southern U.S. for corn bread and biscuits.
SEMOLINA FLOUR is finely ground from the endosperm of hard durum wheat. It is not the same as semolina meal which is coarsely ground from spring or winter wheat. Semolina flour adds texture and a strong wheat flavor to breads, and is also used for making pasta.
SOY FLOUR is high in protein and fat, contains no gluten, and is fifteen times richer in calcium and iron than wheat. Ground from toasted soybeans, it is used as a nutrition booster in many foods. For bread-making, a small amount mixed with wheat flour adds a mild almond flavor, a spongy crust, and a moist, fine crumb. Soy flour will cause baked goods to brown faster, so baking times or temperatures may need to be adjusted.
SPELT FLOUR is not a modern hybrid wheat, but rather its ancient ancestor. Although it can be substituted for regular wheat flour in any recipe, the usual rule is to use about 25 percent less liquid since the hydration rate of spelt flour is much higher than wheat. Also, the gluten in spelt flour is fragile, so over-mixing or kneading will produce a flat loaf.
STONE-GROUND flours have higher nutritional value and better taste than those ground by high-speed steel rollers or hammers. The slow-moving stones crush the grain without tearing the germ and without generating heat that destroys vitamins and enzymes. The texture of stone-ground flour can range from coarse to powdery, depending on the amount of sieving the flour receives at the mill.
WHEAT GERM, the seed or embryo of the wheat kernel or berry, is high in nutrients, especially B vitamins. Its high oil content causes rancidity if it is not refrigerated. Available raw or toasted, wheat germ provides a nutrition boost to baked goods.
WHOLE-WHEAT FLOUR makes excellent breads because of its high gluten content and sweet, nutty taste. It includes the fibrous bran and nutritious germ oil from the wheat kernel or berry.
81% WHOLE-WHEAT FLOUR has had 19% of the husk and bran removed from the wheat berry, leaving only a very small amount of the germ and bran in the flour. This flour is not available retail in the U.S., although some specialty mills may be able to grind it to specification. Whole-wheat flour available in this country is labelled simply whole-wheat and includes all of the bran and germ.
CRACKED WHEAT can be fine, medium, or coarse cut, and is made by cracking the dried wheat berry between rollers. It is an excellent addition to bread doughs.
WHEAT FLAKES are cooked, rolled wheat berries, and can be used in the same ways as rolled oats.

FLOUR STORAGE

All flours should be kept in airtight containers or place the bag of flour in a plastic bag. If you remove the flour from its bag, be sure to label and date the container. All-purpose and white bread flour can be stored at 70F for up to six months. Any flour, wheat or otherwise, that contains part of the germ from the grain will easily turn rancid because of the oil content. Tightly wrap these flours and refrigerate or freeze for up to three months. Let the flour come to room temperature before using.

TOPPINGS

Dough can be rolled in seeds or nuts after the first shaping and before the second rising, or glazed and then sprinkled with a topping just before baking. Some toppings scorch easily, so be ready to lower the oven temperature or cover the bread with foil after 15 to 20 minutes baking if the top is browning too quickly.

Fried sweet doughs (Chapter 4) are usually sprinkled with or rolled in confectioners' sugar, granulated or superfine sugar, or a ground cinnamon and sugar mixture after draining on paper towels.

1 Cornmeal
2 *Wheat flakes*
3 Fresh herbs, such as rosemary
4 Sunflower seeds
5 Barley flakes
6 Sea salt (kosher salt)
7 Sesame seeds
8 Cracked wheat
9 Linseeds (flaxseeds)
10 Oats
11 Caraway seeds
12 Grated cheese
13 Rye flakes
14 Poppy seeds
15 Plain top

GLAZES

Applied to the dough just before or just after baking, a glaze changes the appearance and taste of the crust, as well as its texture. A good, wide pastry brush (one that doesn't shed) is essential, and two thin coats of glaze give a better result than one thick one.

If you glaze the dough before baking, take care that you do not glue the dough to the rim of the loaf pan or to the baking sheet; this will not only give you a problem when you turn out the baked bread, but will hinder the "spring" as the bread tries to expand in the oven. You will get a cracked or strangely shaped result.

1 Unglazed plain loaf
2 Brushed with 1 egg white beaten with ¼ teaspoon sea salt before baking
3 Dusted with flour before baking
4 Brushed with water before baking
5 Brushed with whole milk before baking
6 Dusted with granulated sugar before baking
7 Brushed with 2 teaspoons sea salt dissolved in 1 cup water before baking
8 Brushed with half-and-half before baking
9 Brushed with olive oil after baking
10 Brushed with 1 whole egg beaten with ¼ teaspoon sea salt before baking
11 Brushed with light or heavy cream before baking
12 Rubbed with a butter wrapper after baking
13 Brushed with 1 egg yolk beaten with a large pinch of sea salt before baking
14 Brushed with olive oil before baking
15 Brushed with a sweet glaze (3 tablespoons granular sugar dissolved in 3 tablespoons hot milk) after baking

A PLAIN WHITE LOAF

INGREDIENTS

Makes two medium-size loaves.

- 4 to $4\frac{3}{4}$ cups white bread flour (preferably unbleached and stone-ground)
- 4 teaspoons kosher salt or flaked sea salt
- 1 cake compressed fresh yeast (0.6 ounce), or 1 envelope active dry yeast ($2\frac{1}{2}$ teaspoons) plus $\frac{1}{2}$ teaspoon granulated sugar
- $1\frac{3}{4}$ cups cold water from the tap

two $8\frac{1}{2} \times 4\frac{1}{2} \times 2\frac{3}{4}$-inch loaf pans, greased

This basic recipe for white bread can be used to make puffy loaves, or formed into some traditional English styles of loaves – for example, a large cottage, Coburg, porcupine, or rumpy loaf – or divided into rolls. (See page 26 for shaping breads.) You can also try the toppings and glazes on pages 22 and 23 to alter the taste and appearance of the baked loaf. This loaf will keep for four days and can be frozen for one month.

Prepare the sponge and then the dough as for The Basic Loaf (page 16), using 4 cups of the white flour. If the dough is sticky, work in small amounts of the remaining flour. Knead the dough, place it in a clean, lightly greased bowl, turn the dough over so the top is oiled, then cover it with a damp dish towel and let it rise at room temperature, away from drafts. Because of the cool temperature of the water, the dough will take longer to double in size than does the dough for The Basic Loaf – up to $2\frac{1}{2}$ hours.

Punch down the risen dough and turn it out onto a lightly floured work surface. Cut the dough in half. Gently knead the dough, then pat or, with a floured rolling pin, roll it into a rectangle as wide as the pans are long, about $\frac{1}{2}$ inch thick. Beginning with a short side, tightly roll up the pieces of dough, pinching the edges together as you roll, then pinch the seam closed. Tuck the ends under. Place the dough, seam sides down, in the prepared pans. The pans should be half filled.

Cover the pans with damp dish towels and let the doughs rise at room temperature until doubled in size – about 1 hour. (Do not let the doughs overproof and become enormous, however, or they will collapse during baking.) During the last 15 minutes of rising, heat the oven to 450F.

Uncover the loaves and sprinkle the tops lightly with flour. Using a very sharp knife or razor blade, either make one deep slash lengthwise down the center of the loaves to form a split, or make two diagonal slashes across the tops.

Bake for 15 minutes. Reduce the oven temperature to 400F. Bake for another 20 to 30 minutes. To test if a loaf is baked, turn it out of the pan and tap it with your knuckles; a thoroughly baked loaf sounds hollow when tapped underneath. Unmold the bread onto wire racks and cool completely.

TO SHAPE THE DOUGH TO FIT THE PAN, ROLL IT UP, PINCHING THE EDGES.

PINCH THE SEAM CLOSED AND TUCK THE ENDS UNDER.

PLACE THE LOAF, SEAM SIDE DOWN, INTO THE PAN. THE PAN SHOULD BE HALF-FULL.

FOR A SPLIT-LOAF SHAPE, MAKE A DEEP SLASH LENGTHWISE DOWN THE CENTER.

OATMEAL ROLLS

INGREDIENTS

Makes sixteen rolls.

2½ cups old-fashioned rolled oats
1⅔ cups milk
1 to 1⅓ cups whole-wheat bread flour (preferably stone-ground)
¼ cup white bread flour (preferably unbleached and stone ground, see Note)
2 teaspoons kosher salt or flaked sea salt
1 cake compressed fresh yeast (0.6 ounce), or 1 envelope active dry yeast (2½ teaspoons) plus ½ teaspoon granulated sugar
2 tablespoons lukewarm water (95F to 105F)
beaten egg, light or heavy cream, or half-and-half, to glaze
additional old-fashioned rolled oats

two baking sheets, lightly greased

Oats add texture and a distinct mealy taste that you either like or loathe. Oat bread is in vogue on both sides of the Atlantic as I write this, due to the possible connection between a diet high in oat bran and lowered blood cholesterol levels. However, many commercial oat breads taste soapy or cakelike. I suggest you use organic oats for the best flavor. In England, I buy either Jordan's or Mornflake oats.

These rolls are good with soup and are excellent toasted. Eat them the day they're baked, or freeze when cooled. The dough can also be shaped into one medium-size loaf and baked free-form. (For shaping, see The Basic Loaf, page 17.) Allow more time for a single loaf to bake.

Soak the oats in the milk in a large, covered bowl for 2 hours. In a second large bowl, mix together 1 cup of the whole-wheat flour, the white flour, and salt. After the oats have soaked, crumble the fresh yeast into a small bowl and mix with the lukewarm water until smooth. If using dry yeast, mix the granules and the sugar with 2 tablespoons lukewarm water, and let stand until foamy, 5 to 10 minutes (see page 18).

Stir the yeast mixture into the soaked oats and stir this mixture into the flour. Mix well to make a soft dough. If the dough is slightly crumbly, add more water, 1 tablespoon at a time, until the dough comes together. If the dough is sticky, gradually knead in the remaining whole-wheat flour, 1 tablespoon at a time, until the dough leaves your hands and the sides of the bowl cleanly. The amount of liquid and flour needed in this recipe varies, depending on the kind of oats and the type of flours you use.

Turn out the dough onto a lightly floured work surface and knead for 10 minutes, or until smooth and elastic. Put the dough into an oiled bowl, and turn the dough over so the top is oiled. Cover with a damp dish towel. Let rise at room temperature, away from drafts, until doubled in size, about 1 hour.

Punch down the risen dough. Turn out the dough onto a lightly floured work surface. Weigh the dough and divide it into sixteen equal pieces, or roll it into a fat rope and cut into sixteen even pieces. Shape each piece into a roll by making a rough ball of dough and cupping your hand over the ball so your fingertips and wrist touch the work surface. Gently rotate your hand so the dough is rolled around and smoothed into a neat roll.

Space the rolls well apart on the prepared baking sheets. Cover lightly with damp dish towels and let rise at room temperature until almost doubled in size, 30 to 45 minutes. During the last 15 minutes of rising, heat the oven to 425F.

Remove the dish towels. Lightly brush the rolls with the chosen glaze. Sprinkle with oats. Bake the rolls for 20 minutes, or until they are browned and sound hollow when tapped underneath. Transfer to a wire rack and cool completely.

NOTE: A mixture of half whole-wheat bread flour and half white bread flour can be substituted for the proportions in the recipe.

THE OATS WILL LOOK VERY SLOPPY AND SOFT AFTER THEY HAVE SOAKED IN THE MILK FOR 2 HOURS.

ROTATE YOUR HAND SO THE DOUGH IS ROLLED AROUND AND SMOOTHED INTO A NEAT ROLL.

TRADITIONAL BRITISH SHAPES

Most of these shapes are typically British and have a long and colorful history. Whenever possible, I'll provide a bit of background material. To make these shapes, use the dough for The Basic Loaf (page 15) or A Plain White Loaf (page 24) and let it rise once, then punch down the dough.

Appealing to the eyes as well as the palate, these homemade breads have been shaped into traditional British-style loaves. The basket includes a Sesame Snail, a Bloomer loaf, two Coburg loaves, and two Porcupine loaves. The round Coburg loaf, baked free-form with a cross cut in the top, was, according to Elizabeth David, originally a four-cornered bread, sometimes called a skull. The porcupine shape is really self-explanatory. The directions for making each shape are explained and illustrated here and on the following two pages.

Bloomer

Makes one large loaf.

Considerable controversy surrounds the origin of this shape, according to the late food writer Elizabeth David. It may have gotten its name because it was baked without a pan, and was thus allowed to "bloom" unhindered in the oven. Another version tells us that the loaf resembled the pantaloons worn by Mrs. Amelia Bloomer, an American, who brought them to England and made them popular as the practical garb for bicycling. Stories aside, the bloomer is shaped into a long, fat loaf with flat ends and deep crosswise slashes on the top.

Roll out the punched-down dough with a floured rolling pin into a large rectangle, about 1 inch thick. Starting with a short side, tightly roll up the dough like a jelly roll, pinching it together after each roll. Push the ends of the roll of dough toward the center to make a short, thick roll. Pinch the seam to seal and tuck the ends under neatly. These fiddly measures help prevent air pockets from forming in the loaf.

Slide a lightly greased baking sheet under the loaf, cover with a damp dish towel, and let rise at room temperature, away from drafts, until doubled in size, 1 to $1\frac{1}{2}$ hours. During the last 15 minutes of rising, heat the oven to 450F.

Using a very sharp knife, make six deep slashes across the top of the loaf, being careful not to drag the knife. Dust the loaf with white flour, then brush the slits with salt water (page 23). Bake for 15 minutes. Lower the oven temperature to 400F and bake for another 25 to 35 minutes, or until the loaf sounds hollow when tapped underneath.

ROLL OUT THE DOUGH ON A LIGHTLY FLOURED WORK SURFACE WITH A LIGHTLY FLOURED ROLLING PIN TO A RECTANGLE 1 INCH THICK.

STARTING FROM A SHORT END, ROLL UP THE DOUGH LIKE A JELLY ROLL, PINCHING IT TOGETHER AFTER EACH ROLL.

AFTER DUSTING THE LOAF WITH WHITE FLOUR, BRUSH THE SLITS WITH SALT WATER (PAGE 23).

MAKE ONE DEEP CUT THROUGH THE MIDDLE, THEN MAKE TWO SHORT CUTS INTO THE CENTER.

OR, USE KITCHEN SCISSORS TO MAKE FOUR DEEP CUTS AT RIGHT ANGLES.

Coburg

Makes two medium-size loaves.

On a lightly floured work surface, quickly knead the punched-down dough for a few seconds. Divide the dough in half. Shape each piece into a neat ball. Place each ball on a greased baking sheet. Cover with a damp dish towel and let rise at room temperature, away from drafts, until doubled in size, 1 to $1\frac{1}{2}$ hours.

During the last 15 minutes of rising, heat the oven to 450F. Using a very sharp knife, slash a deep cross through the top of each ball of dough, making one deep cut through the middle, then two short ones into the center. (Or, using kitchen scissors, make four cuts at right angles.) Brush with salt water (page 23), then dust with flour. Bake for 25 to 30 minutes, or until the loaves sound hollow when tapped underneath. If the loaves are browning too quickly, lower the oven temperature to 400F.

Porcupine or Rumpy

Makes two medium-size loaves.

Shape the punched-down dough into two balls, as for the Coburg (above). Place on greased baking sheets, cover with damp dish towels, and let rise at room temperature, away from drafts, until doubled in size, about 1 to $1\frac{1}{2}$ hours. During the last 15 minutes of rising, heat the oven to 450F.

Using a very sharp knife, slash the top of the dough several times to make a checkerboard pattern. You could also snip the dough using kitchen scissors. Brush the dough with a glaze (page 23).

Bake for 25 to 30 minutes, or until the loaves sound hollow when tapped underneath. If the loaves brown too quickly, lower the oven temperature to 400F.

WITH A SHARP KNIFE, SCORE A CHECKERBOARD PATTERN ON TOP OF THE RISEN LOAF.

OR, USE KITCHEN SCISSORS TO MAKE NEAT ROWS OF SNIPS.

Sesame Snail

Makes one large loaf.

Once again, punch down the risen dough – usually white (page 24) for this loaf, but there is no reason why you cannot use any other shade of dough. With your hands, roll the dough on a lightly floured work surface into a rope about 3 inches thick and 25 inches long. Coil the dough into a snail shape, twisting the rope as you lift it, and tuck the ends under. Slide a greased baking sheet under the dough, pressing it back into shape if necessary. Cover with a damp dish towel and let rise, away from drafts, until almost doubled in size, about 1 hour. During the last 15 minutes, heat the oven to 450F.

Brush the dough with water, then sprinkle with 1 to 2 tablespoons black or white sesame seeds, or a mixture of both. Gently prick the loaf around the sides with a fork. Bake for 15 minutes. Reduce the oven temperature to 400F. Bake another 25 to 30 minutes, or until the loaf sounds hollow when tapped underneath.

In a North African bakery I found a similar loaf flavored with star anise; it was unusual and very good. To make that version, use a spice mill or clean coffee grinder to grind 2 whole star anise and 1 tablespoon black or white sesame seeds to a fine powder. This should give you a total of 2 tablespoons, which you add to the flour along with the salt. Make the white dough as (page 15) directed, then let rise and shape as for the Sesame Snail. After brushing with water and sprinkling with sesame seeds, gently prick the loaf around the sides with a fork, then bake as for the Sesame Snail.

USING YOUR HANDS, ROLL OUT THE DOUGH ON A LIGHTLY FLOURED WORK SURFACE TO A ROPE ABOUT 3 INCHES THICK AND 25 INCHES LONG.

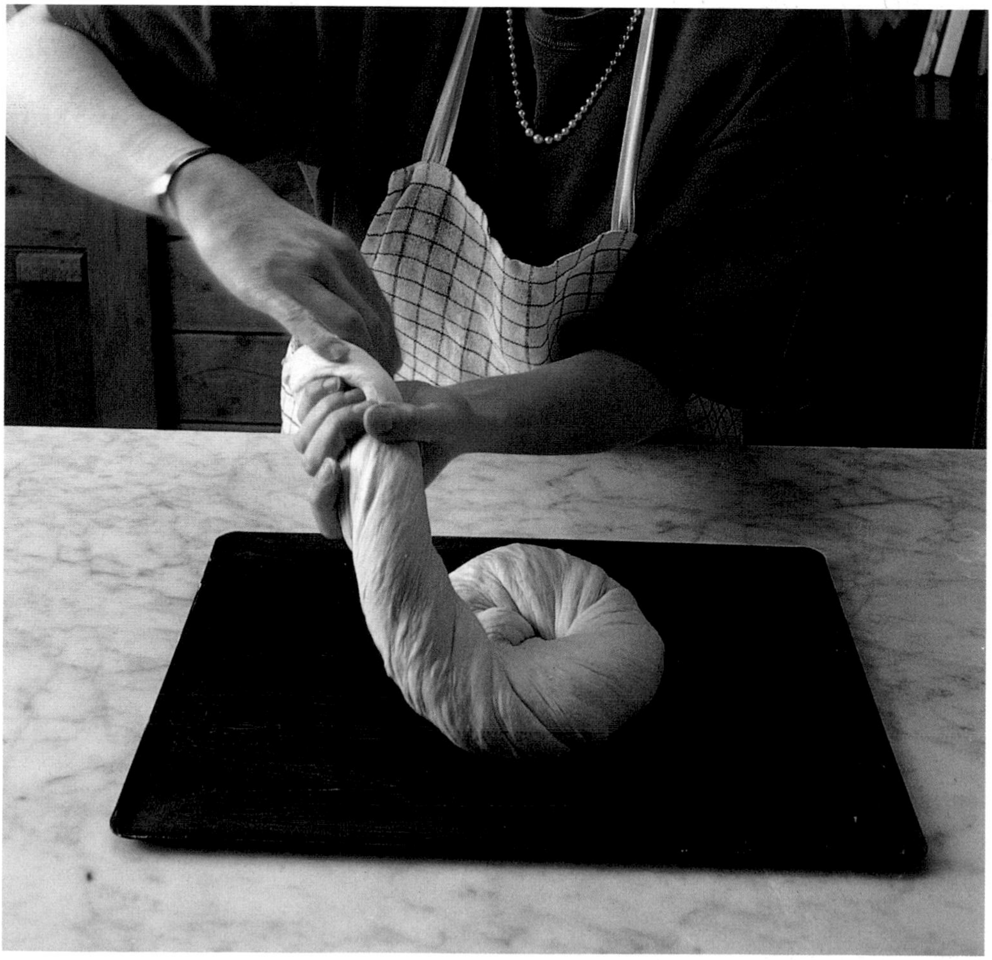

Right COIL THE DOUGH INTO A SNAIL SHAPE, TWISTING THE ROPE AS YOU LIFT IT. TUCK THE ENDS UNDER.

COTTAGE LOAF

INGREDIENTS

Makes one large loaf.

2 to 3 cups whole-wheat bread flour (preferably stone-ground)
2 cups white bread flour (preferably unbleached and stone-ground)
or: use 3 to 4 cups whole-wheat and $\frac{3}{4}$ cup white bread flour
4 teaspoons kosher salt or flaked sea salt
1 cake compressed fresh yeast (0.6 ounce), or 1 envelope active dry yeast ($2\frac{1}{2}$ teaspoons) plus $\frac{1}{2}$ teaspoon granulated sugar
$1\frac{2}{3}$ cups cold water from the tap
salt water or 1 beaten egg to glaze

a large baking sheet, lightly greased

SECURE THE BALLS OF DOUGH BY PUSHING TWO FINGERS AND A THUMB THROUGH THE MIDDLE.

CAREFULLY BRUSH THE LOAF WITH THE CHOSEN GLAZE.

SCORE ALL AROUND THE BOTTOM BALL OF DOUGH. REPEAT ALL AROUND THE TOP BALL.

RIGHT Freshly baked cottage loaves at Wreford's Bakery (page 177).

This very distinctive bread is always a round loaf with a smaller ball of dough pressed into the center, like a topknot. For the best taste I like to use a dough with at least 50 percent whole-wheat flour, but if you are after a "purer" look, the dough for A Plain White Loaf (page 24) is fine, too.

For the best shape the dough must be quite firm, so be ready to work in a little extra flour if necessary. It is also worth remembering that as the yeast multiplies it produces carbon dioxide and liquid (alcohol), so the dough will become softer after rising. It is best to do the final rising at cool room temperature to preserve the shape.

There are different methods for assembling this bread. Home bakers tend to fashion the loaf by shaping the dough into two balls, putting the smaller on top, then fixing them together by pushing a finger through the middle of both balls before leaving the loaf to rise. Professional bakers, however, prefer to shape the balls and let them rise separately. They then gently flatten both balls and attach them by pushing two fingers and a thumb joined together through the middle. This technique produces the most reliable shape. Finish the loaf with either an egg glaze or a saltwater glaze (page 23) before baking. This loaf keeps for four days and can be frozen for one month.

Prepare the sponge as for The Basic Loaf (page 16), using the smaller amount of whole-wheat flour to begin with, the white flour, salt, yeast, and water. Mix in the remaining flour from the bowl and, if the dough is sticky, work in small amounts of the remaining whole-wheat flour. Knead the dough, place in a clean, greased bowl, turn the dough over, then cover it with a damp dish towel and let rise at room temperature, away from drafts, until doubled in size, $1\frac{1}{2}$ to 2 hours.

Punch down the risen dough and turn it out onto a lightly floured work surface. Cut off one-third, then shape both the small and larger pieces of dough into balls. Place the balls well apart on the prepared baking sheet and cover with a damp dish towel. Let rise at room temperature until puffy but not quite doubled in size, usually 30 to 45 minutes. Heat the oven to 450F.

Gently flatten each ball and put the smaller ball on top of the larger one. Push two fingers and a thumb joined together into the middle of the dough to join the pieces. Let stand for 5 to 10 minutes; if left for much longer, the loaf takes on a "drunken" look.

Brush the loaf with the chosen glaze, then vertically score around the edges of the top and bottom balls with a small sharp knife or razor blade. Bake for 15 minutes. Lower the oven temperature to 400F. Bake for another 20 to 30 minutes, or until the loaf sounds hollow when tapped underneath. Transfer to a wire rack and cool completely.

BRAIDED LOAF

INGREDIENTS

Makes one large loaf.

- $4\frac{3}{4}$ cups white bread flour (preferably unbleached and stone-ground)
- 1 teaspoon granulated sugar
- 1 cake compressed fresh yeast (0.6 ounce), or 1 envelope active dry yeast ($2\frac{1}{2}$ teaspoons) plus $\frac{1}{2}$ teaspoon granulated sugar
- $1\frac{3}{4}$ cups lukewarm milk (95F to 105F)
- 2 teaspoons salt
- 2 tablespoons cold unsalted butter, diced
- 1 large egg, beaten
- light or heavy cream, half-and-half, or beaten egg, to glaze
- 2 tablespoons poppy seeds

a large baking sheet, greased

Although you can use a basic all-white dough (page 24) or a dough made with a combination of whole-wheat and white flours (page 15), this slightly richer white dough, made with milk and an egg and sprinkled with poppy seeds, is the one that made my mother's Irish cook Annie famous before the Second World War.

To keep a good, even shape, the dough should not be too soft, and do not be tempted to put the dough to rise in a warm spot. This loaf will stay fresh for two to three days at room temperature, and it can be frozen for one month.

Mix together about $1\frac{1}{4}$ cups of the flour with the sugar in a large bowl. Make a well in the center of the flour and crumble in the fresh yeast. Pour the lukewarm milk over the yeast and mix until combined. If using dry yeast, mix the granules and the additional $\frac{1}{2}$ teaspoon sugar with the milk in a separate bowl and let stand until frothy, 5 to 10 minutes (see page 18). Then pour the yeast mixture into the well in the flour.

Using your hand, work the flour in the bowl into the milk and yeast mixture to make a smooth batter (page 16). Cover with plastic wrap and let stand at room temperature for about 30 minutes until spongy.

Mix most of the remaining flour with the salt in another large bowl. Rub in the butter with your fingertips until the mixture looks like coarse crumbs. Stir the egg into the yeast sponge, then add the sponge to the flour mixture. Mix to form a fairly firm, rather than a soft or sticky, dough, adding as much of the remaining flour as is necessary, about 1 tablespoon at a time.

Turn out the dough onto a lightly floured work surface and punch down with your knuckles. Knead for 10 minutes, until the dough is quite firm, silky-smooth, and elastic. Put the dough into the washed and lightly greased bowl and turn the dough over so the top is oiled. Cover with a damp dish towel and let stand at room temperature, away from drafts, until doubled in size, 1 to $1\frac{1}{2}$ hours.

Punch down the risen dough and turn it out onto the lightly floured work surface. The dough should be quite pliable, but not soft. It should hold its shape well – if not, work in

AFTER ABOUT 30 MINUTES THE BATTER WILL BE SPONGY (FOREGROUND). THEN MIX MOST OF THE REMAINING FLOUR WITH THE SALT IN A LARGE BOWL. RUB IN THE BUTTER WITH YOUR FINGERTIPS.

WHEN THE BUTTER IS RUBBED IN THE FLOUR MIXTURE WILL LOOK LIKE COARSE CRUMBS.

AFTER THE DOUGH HAS RISEN, TURN IT OUT OF THE BOWL AND PUNCH IT DOWN.

DIVIDE THE DOUGH INTO THREE EQUAL PIECES. ROLL EACH PIECE OF DOUGH INTO A LONG ROPE.

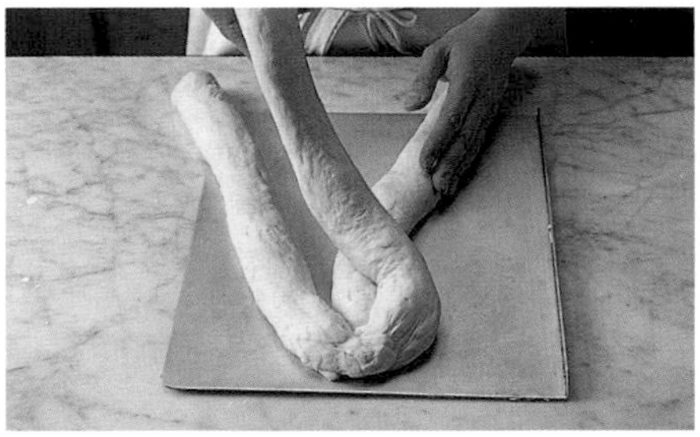

TO BRAID THE DOUGH, ARRANGE THE ROPES SIDE BY SIDE AND SLIGHTLY APART ON THE BAKING SHEET. PINCH THE ENDS TOGETHER FIRMLY. LIFT THE LEFT STRAND OVER THE CENTER STRAND.

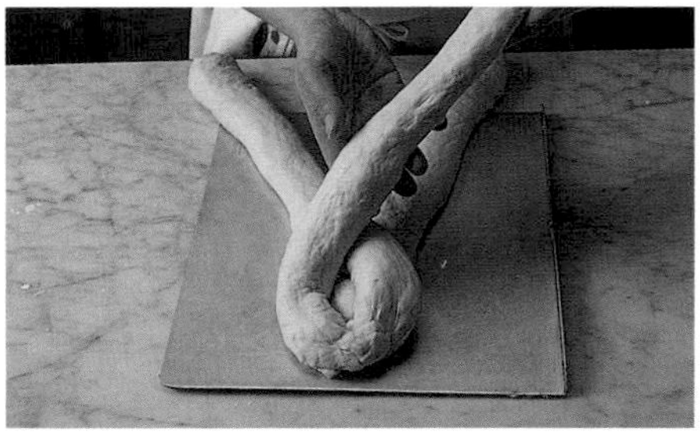

LIFT THE RIGHT STRAND OVER THE NEW CENTER STRAND.

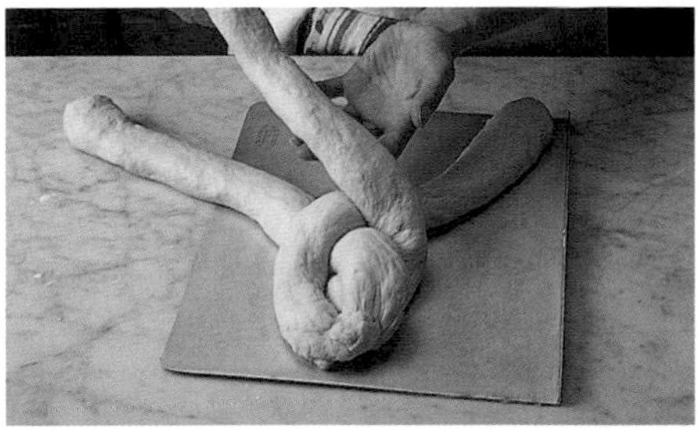

THEN LIFT THE NEW LEFT STRAND OVER THE NEW CENTER STRAND. REPEAT THIS PROCESS UNTIL ALL THE STRANDS ARE BRAIDED.

PINCH THE ENDS TOGETHER TO SEAL THEM. TUCK UNDER BOTH ENDS FOR A NEAT FINISH.

CAREFULLY BRUSH THE RISEN LOAF WITH LIGHT OR HEAVY CREAM, HALF-AND-HALF, OR BEATEN EGG TO GLAZE IT.

a little more flour. Weigh the dough and divide it into three equal pieces, or roll it into a fat rope and cut into thirds.

Using your hands, roll each piece into a rope 16 inches long. Lay the three ropes on the prepared baking sheet, then braid the strands together neatly, but not too tightly. Take care not to stretch the dough unduly. Tuck the ends under and pinch to seal.

Cover with a damp dish towel and let stand at room temperature until almost doubled in size, about 1 hour. It is important not to overproof this loaf. During the last 15 minutes of rising, heat the oven to 450F.

Carefully brush the loaf with the chosen glaze, then sprinkle with the poppy seeds. Bake for 15 to 20 minutes or until golden. Reduce the oven temperature to 400F. Bake for another 20 minutes, or until the loaf sounds hollow when tapped on the bottom. Transfer to a wire rack and cool completely.

BAGUETTES

INGREDIENTS

Makes three loaves.

4 to 5 cups white bread flour (preferably unbleached and stone-ground)
$\frac{3}{4}$ cup cake flour
4 teaspoons kosher salt or flaked sea salt
1 cake compressed fresh yeast (0.6 ounce) (see Note)
$1\frac{3}{4}$ cups water
saltwater to glaze (2 teaspoons kosher salt or flaked sea salt dissolved in 1 cup water)

a large dish towel, floured
a large baking sheet, lightly greased

The traditional French stick loaf – with a shiny crust so crisp it breaks into razor-sharp shards and a fine-tasting, chewy interior with irregular holes – is rapidly disappearing. It is becoming difficult to find even in France, let alone anywhere else. It is also difficult to reproduce at home. In fact, you should probably not attempt this recipe unless you are an experienced bread maker. The best flour for baguettes is French and imported in bulk for bakeries and restaurants, rather than for home bakers. The oven temperature is crucial, too – domestic ovens are rarely hot enough – and, for a crunchy crust, jets of steam are also vital. The best homemade loaves are made with a blend of stone-ground unbleached white bread flour and cake flour, and the oven is misted with water during baking.

Chef Pierre Koffmann, from the Michelin three-starred La Tante Claire restaurant in London, taught me how to achieve the correct temperature for the ingredients. He says the room temperature, the flour temperature (usually the same as the room temperature), and the water temperature must all total the number 190. This means if the kitchen is 72F (a usual kitchen temperature), and the flour the same, the water must be chilled to 46F. On a warm day it is best to use ice water. Pierre also showed me how to make the dough using what French bakers call the Polish method. The yeast and water mixture is made into a thin batter with an equal quantity of flour. It is then left to rise before continuing with the dough.

You can buy metal baguette pans, but good bakers regard them with contempt: "Avoid the loaf with that pattern of little dots underneath." Large dish towels are cheaper to use and work better for shaping the loaves. It is best to eat these loaves on the day they are made, and they do not freeze well.

A sliced baguette, with its soft, irregular crumb, and a country-style loaf ready for the start of a simple meal. Even though the baguette has lost some of its flavor, it still appears on most tables every day in France.

Combine 4 cups of the bread flour, the cake flour, and the salt in a large bowl. Calculate the room and flour temperatures (see above) and chill the $1\frac{3}{4}$ cups of water so all the numbers add up to 190. Crumble the fresh yeast into a small bowl. Add 2 tablespoons of the chilled water, stir until smooth, then stir in the remaining water. Put 3 cups of the flour and salt mixture in another large bowl. Make a well in the center of the flour mixture and add the yeast mixture. Gradually work the flour into the liquid, using your hand, to make a sloppy batter (page 16).

Cover with a damp dish towel, or put the bowl into a large plastic bag and tie closed. Let stand for 4 to 5 hours at room temperature, away from drafts. The batter will become frothy, rise up in the bowl, then collapse back down.

Work in the rest of the flour mixture, plus as much of the remaining bread flour (about $\frac{1}{4}$ cup at a time) as is necessary to form a very soft dough. Turn out the dough onto a lightly floured work surface and knead for 10 minutes, or until the dough becomes firmer and springy, adding more bread flour if needed.

Wash, dry, and oil the bowl. Place the dough in the bowl and turn the dough over so the top is oiled. Cover with a damp dish towel and let rise at cool room temperature until doubled in size, $1\frac{1}{2}$ to 2 hours.

Punch down the dough. Weigh the dough and divide it into three equal pieces, or roll

RIGHT Pedal power has transported a baguette fresh from the local baker's.

USE YOUR HAND TO MIX THE YEAST MIXTURE AND FLOUR TO MAKE A SLOPPY BATTER.

WHEN LEFT TO RISE, THE BATTER WILL BECOME FROTHY AND RISE UP IN THE BOWL.

AFTER 3 TO 5 HOURS RISING, THE BATTER WILL COLLAPSE BACK DOWN.

WORK IN THE REMAINING FLOUR MIXTURE PLUS THE REMAINING BREAD FLOUR TO FORM A SOFT DOUGH.

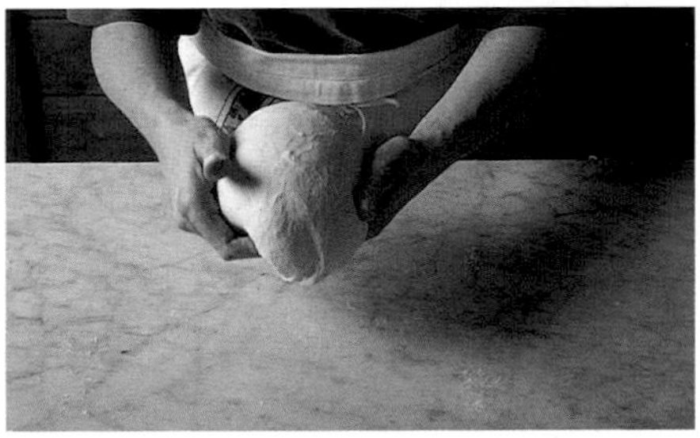

KNEAD THE DOUGH ON A LIGHTLY FLOURED WORK SURFACE FOR 10 MINUTES UNTIL IT BECOMES FIRMER AND SPRINGY.

ROLL OUT EACH PIECE OF DOUGH ON A LIGHTLY FLOURED WORK SURFACE INTO A CYLINDER, ABOUT 12 × 3 INCHES.

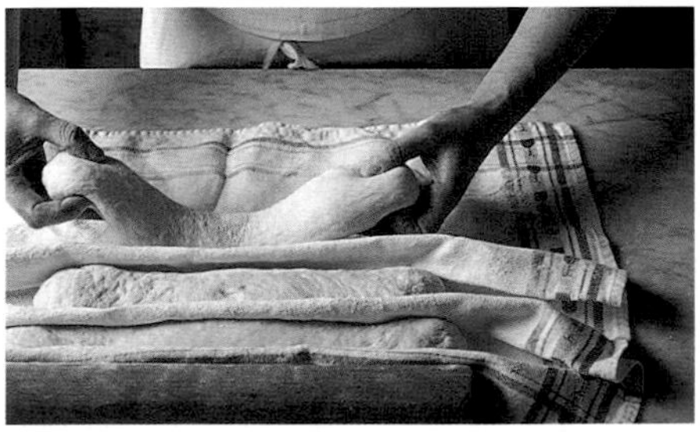

ARRANGE THE SHAPED LOAVES BETWEEN THE FOLDS OF THE FLOURED DISH TOWEL.

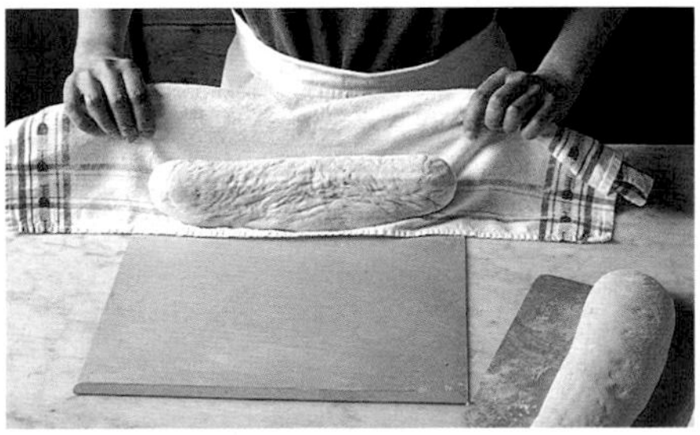

USE THE DISH TOWEL TO HELP ROLL THE LOAVES ONTO THE LIGHTLY GREASED BAKING SHEET.

USING A SHARP KNIFE, QUICKLY SLASH THE TOP OF EACH LOAF SEVERAL TIMES.

it into a fat rope and cut it into thirds. Roll each piece into a cylinder, about 12 × 3 inches. Fold the floured dish towel lengthwise to make three accordion-like creases or pleats. Arrange the pieces of dough between the folds so the loaves will keep their traditional baguette shape while they rise. Cover with a damp dish towel and let rise at cool room temperature until doubled in size, about 1 hour.

During the last 15 minutes of rising, place the baking sheet on an oven rack in the lowest position and heat the oven to 450F.

Remove the damp dish towel and roll or lift the loaves onto the prepared baking sheet without crowding. It is best to bake the last loaf after the first two come out of the oven. Using a sharp knife or razor blade, quickly slash the top of each loaf several times, then brush with the salt water glaze.

Put the loaves in the oven, then spray the oven sides and bottom with water. Bake the loaves for 20 minutes, brushing them with salt water and spraying the oven sides and bottom with water after 10 minutes. At the end of 20 minutes, spray the oven again with water and reduce the oven temperature to 400F.

Bake for another 5 to 10 minutes, until the loaves are crisp and they sound hollow when tapped underneath. Cool the loaves on a wire rack. Increase the oven temperature to 450F, and bake the third loaf as described.

NOTE: You can use 1 envelope active dry yeast (2½ teaspoons), but fresh yeast gives a noticeably better result. For the dry yeast method, see page 18.

BRIDGE ROLLS

INGREDIENTS

Makes thirty-six rolls.

4 to $4\frac{3}{4}$ cups white bread flour (preferably unbleached and stone-ground)
4 teaspoons granulated sugar
4 teaspoons kosher salt or flaked sea salt
4 tablespoons cold unsalted butter, diced
1 cake compressed fresh yeast (0.6 ounce), or 1 envelope active dry yeast ($2\frac{1}{2}$ teaspoons) plus $\frac{1}{2}$ teaspoon granulated sugar
$2\frac{3}{4}$ cups warm milk (105F to 115F)
1 large egg, beaten
additional milk for brushing

two large baking sheets, lightly greased

These are the small, soft-crusted finger rolls with a sweetish, light crumb that I remember from children's parties. They are an ideal sandwich roll filled and packed for picnics and lunch boxes. Eat within twenty-four hours of baking or freeze for up to one month.

On a vacation in Maine, I made the rolls a little larger than in this recipe and filled them with the local lobster meat mixed with mayonnaise for "Maine lobster rolls" – sheer heaven!

Mix together the 4 cups flour, sugar, and salt in a large bowl. Using your fingertips, rub the butter into the flour until the mixture looks like fine crumbs. Make a well in the center of the flour.

Crumble the fresh yeast into a small bowl. Add $\frac{1}{4}$ cup of the milk and mix until smooth. If using dry yeast, mix the granules and the additional $\frac{1}{2}$ teaspoon sugar with $\frac{1}{4}$ cup milk and let stand until foamy, 5 to 10 minutes (see page 18).

Add the yeast mixture to the well in the flour, then mix in the remaining milk and the beaten egg. Work in the flour that is in the bowl to make a soft, but not sticky dough, adding as much of the remaining flour as is necessary, about $\frac{1}{4}$ cup at a time.

Turn out the dough onto a well-floured work surface and knead for 10 minutes, or until smooth and elastic. Return the dough to the washed and greased bowl, and turn the dough over so the top is oiled. Cover the bowl with a damp dish towel or plastic wrap and let rise at room temperature, away from drafts, until doubled in size, about 2 hours. (It is the milk and slow rising time that give the rolls a fine, light crumb.)

Punch down the risen dough, roll it into a fat rope, and divide it into thirty-six equal

USING YOUR FINGERTIPS, RUB THE BUTTER INTO THE FLOUR UNTIL THE MIXTURE LOOKS LIKE FINE CRUMBS.

WORK IN THE FLOUR IN THE BOWL TO MAKE A SOFT, BUT NOT STICKY DOUGH, ADDING AS MUCH OF THE REMAINING FLOUR AS NECESSARY.

SHAPE EACH PIECE OF DOUGH INTO AN OVAL BY FIRST ROLLING IT INTO A CYLINDER.

SQUEEZE EACH PIECE WITH THE EDGES OF YOUR HANDS TO MAKE THE ENDS SLIGHTLY POINTED. ARRANGE APART ON THE LIGHTLY GREASED BAKING SHEETS.

LIGHTLY BRUSH THE RISEN ROLLS WITH THE MILK. IT IS BETTER TO BRUSH THE ROLLS LIGHTLY TWICE, THAN ONCE HEAVILY.

TRANSFER THE BAKED ROLLS TO WIRE RACKS. COVER WITH DRY DISH TOWELS SO THE CRUSTS REMAIN SOFT. LET THE ROLLS COOL COMPLETELY.

pieces. Shape each piece into an oval by first rolling it on the work surface into a cylinder, then roll the dough on the work surface with both of your hands to make pointed ends. Place the rolls slightly apart on the prepared baking sheets. Cover with damp dish towels and let the rolls rise at room temperature until doubled in size, 30 to 45 minutes. During the last 15 minutes of rising, heat the oven to 450F.

Lightly brush the rolls with milk. Bake for 5 minutes. Lower the oven temperature to 400F. Bake for another 5 to 10 minutes, or until the rolls are browned and sound hollow when tapped underneath.

Transfer the rolls to a wire rack. Cover with dry dish towels to keep the crusts soft and let cool completely.

For my wedding reception, I served guests small bridge rolls with a selection of fillings. I think you will find these rolls delicious with any filling you use.

BAPS

INGREDIENTS

Makes twelve rolls.

- $3\frac{3}{4}$ to $4\frac{3}{4}$ cups white bread flour (preferably unbleached and stone-ground)
- 4 teaspoons kosher salt or flaked sea salt
- 2 ounces ($\frac{1}{4}$ cup) lard, diced
- 1 cake compressed fresh yeast (0.6 ounce) or 1 envelope active dry yeast ($2\frac{1}{2}$ teaspoons)
- $\frac{1}{2}$ teaspoon granulated sugar
- $1\frac{3}{4}$ cups half milk and half water, warmed to lukewarm (95F to 105F)
- milk for glazing
- additional flour for dusting

two baking sheets, lightly greased

Traditional Scottish scenes.

RIGHT Flour-topped baps and shiny softies ready for a traditional Scottish breakfast.

Breakfast and afternoon tea are the best meals of the day in Scotland. Breakfast is my idea of a superb feast, with oatmeal porridge, Loch Fyne kippers, good tea, homemade marmalade, plus floury, white, soft-crusted oval baps, warm from the oven, and Aberdeen Butteries (page 180).

When I worked in Scotland, I enjoyed the baps from Leiths in Ballater, Aberdeenshire, and they are still my favorite. The shape, size, and crumb of baps vary from baker to baker in Scotland, but the basic mixture and the techniques are the same. They use equal quantities of milk and water to give a fine, soft crumb, dust the baps with flour, then cover them with a cloth after baking to produce a soft top, rather than a tough or crisp crust. Many bakers add a little lard to the dough, too, to add extra flavor and improve the texture.

For hill walkers and stalkers, baps are wonderful, filled with grilled strips of bacon and a fried egg, then wrapped in plastic wrap or foil, ready for a fresh-air breakfast. Baps should be eaten warm when they are baked, but can be frozen for one month.

Mix together $3\frac{3}{4}$ cups of the flour and the salt in a large bowl. Using your fingertips, rub the lard into the flour until the mixture looks like fine crumbs. Make a well in the center of the flour.

Crumble the fresh yeast into a small bowl. Stir in the sugar and 2 tablespoons of the lukewarm milk and water mixture until smooth. If using dry yeast, mix the granules and the sugar with 2 tablespoons of the liquid and let stand until foamy, 5 to 10 minutes (see page 18).

Add the yeast mixture and remaining milk and water to the well and mix in the flour in the bowl to make a very soft dough, adding as much of the remaining flour as is necessary, about $\frac{1}{4}$ cup at a time. If necessary, add a little more water, but the dough should not stick to your fingers or the sides of the bowl.

Turn out the dough onto a lightly floured work surface and knead for 10 minutes or until it looks and feels smooth and silky, adding a little more flour if necessary to prevent sticking. Put the dough back in the washed and lightly greased bowl, and turn the dough so the top is oiled. Cover with a damp dish towel or plastic wrap and let rise, away from drafts, until doubled in size, about 1 hour in a warm kitchen, or $1\frac{1}{2}$ hours at room temperature, or overnight in a cold pantry or in the refrigerator.

PAT EACH PIECE OF DOUGH INTO AN OVAL ABOUT $4\frac{1}{2} \times 3$ INCHES. PLACE EACH BAP ON THE BAKING SHEET AS IT IS SHAPED.

SIFT A FINE LAYER OF FLOUR OVER THE BAPS. THEN, LET THEM RISE UNTIL DOUBLED IN SIZE, ABOUT 30 MINUTES.

JUST BEFORE BAKING, SIFT A SECOND LAYER OF FLOUR OVER THE BAPS, THEN PRESS YOUR THUMB INTO THE CENTER OF EACH.

ABOVE RIGHT A hearty stalker's breakfast of a freshly baked bap filled with a fried egg and bacon.

Punch down the risen dough. Turn out the dough onto a lightly floured work surface and knead it for a few seconds.

Weigh the dough and divide it into twelve equal pieces, or roll it into a fat rope and cut it into twelve even pieces. With floured fingers, pat each piece of dough into an oval, about $4\frac{1}{2} \times 3$ inches. Place well apart on the prepared baking sheets. Lightly brush the baps with milk, then sift a fine layer of flour over them. Let rise at room temperature until doubled in size, about 30 minutes, taking care not to let the baps over-proof. While the baps are rising, heat the oven to 425F.

Sift another fine layer of flour over the baps, then press your thumb into the center of each. This technique makes the surface flattish, rather than domed. Bake immediately for 15 minutes, until golden and cooked underneath. Transfer to wire racks, cover with dry dish towels, and let cool for a few minutes before eating.

VARIATION: SOFTIES OR MORNING ROLLS

Use the same dough as for baps to make the soft rolls known as softies or morning rolls. Shape into smooth rolls by rolling each ball on the work surface under your cupped hand. Then cover and let rise as directed above. Before baking, brush with a little light or heavy cream. Bake in a 425F oven for 20 minutes, or until golden brown. Brush again with cream after removing from the oven. Transfer to wire racks, cover with dry dish towels, and leave to cool. Serve warm or leave to cool completely.

LIGHTLY BRUSH THE RISEN SOFTIES WITH CREAM JUST BEFORE BAKING.

AS SOON AS THE SOFTIES COME OUT OF THE OVEN, BRUSH AGAIN WITH CREAM.

CORNISH OR DEVONSHIRE SPLITS

INGREDIENTS

Makes twenty-two buns.

- 5 cups white bread flour (preferably unbleached and stone-ground)
- 4 teaspoons kosher salt or flaked sea salt
- 1 cake compressed fresh yeast (0.6 ounce) or 1 envelope active dry yeast ($2\frac{1}{2}$ teaspoons)
- 1 teaspoon granulated sugar
- $1\frac{3}{4}$ cups lukewarm milk (95F to 105F)
- 1 stick (8 tablespoons) cold unsalted butter, diced
- confectioners' sugar for dusting

one baking sheet, floured

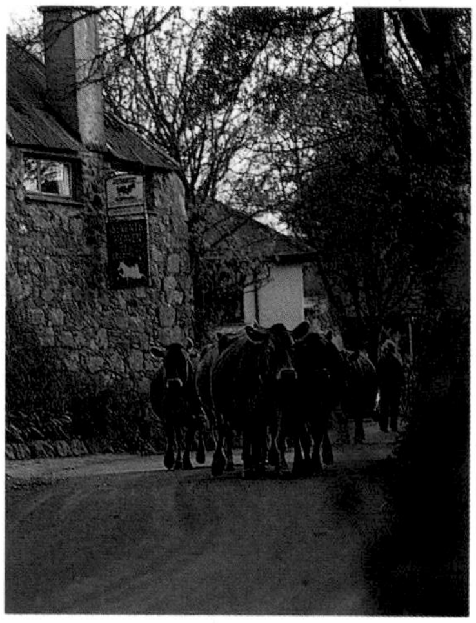

Joe Roskilly drives the family's herd of Jersey and Guernsey cows to the milking parlor.

In England, these buns, with their soft, sweet crust and light, moist crumb, are eaten warm, split open and spread with clotted cream and treacle, raspberry jam, or golden syrup. The cream and treacle combination, favored by Rachel Roskilly, who makes the best clotted cream I have ever tasted from her Jersey/Guernsey herd at St. Kevern, on The Lizard in Cornwall, is called "thunder and lightning." Clotted cream isn't readily available in the U.S., nor is treacle, but you could make an approximation of this wonderful combination by blending crème fraîche with dark molasses to taste.

Serve splits after they have cooled to warm. Eat within one day or freeze for up to one month.

Mix together the flour and salt in a large bowl. If it is a chilly day, gently warm the flour (page 15). Crumble the fresh yeast into a medium-size bowl. Mix with the sugar and 2 tablespoons of the milk until smooth. If using dry yeast, mix the granules and the sugar with 2 tablespoons of the milk and let stand until foamy, 5 to 10 minutes (see page 18).

Stir the rest of the milk into the yeast mixture, followed by $1\frac{1}{4}$ cups of the flour mixture, until smooth. Cover with plastic wrap and let stand at room temperature until frothy, about 30 minutes.

Using your fingertips, rub the diced butter into the remaining flour mixed with the salt until the mixture looks like fine crumbs. Mix in the frothy yeast sponge to make a soft, but not too sticky, dough. If the dough is dry and crumbly, add a little more milk or water, 1 tablespoon at a time, until the dough comes together. If the dough sticks to your fingers, work in extra flour, 1 tablespoon at a time.

MIX THE BUTTER AND FLOUR MIXTURE WITH THE FROTHY YEAST SPONGE UNTIL THE DOUGH IS SOFT BUT NOT STICKY. IF THE DOUGH STICKS TO YOUR FINGERS, WORK IN ABOUT 1 TABLESPOON FLOUR.

CUP YOUR HAND OVER A BALL OF DOUGH SO YOUR FINGERTIPS AND WRIST TOUCH THE WORK SURFACE. ROTATE YOUR HAND, SHAPING THE DOUGH INTO A SMOOTH ROLL.

ARRANGE THE ROLLS ON THE FLOURED BAKING SHEETS SO THEY ALMOST TOUCH EACH OTHER.

AS SOON AS THE ROLLS COME OUT OF THE OVEN, SIFT CONFECTIONERS' SUGAR OVER THEM. TRANSFER TO WIRE RACKS AND COVER WITH DRY DISH TOWELS. COOL TO WARM.

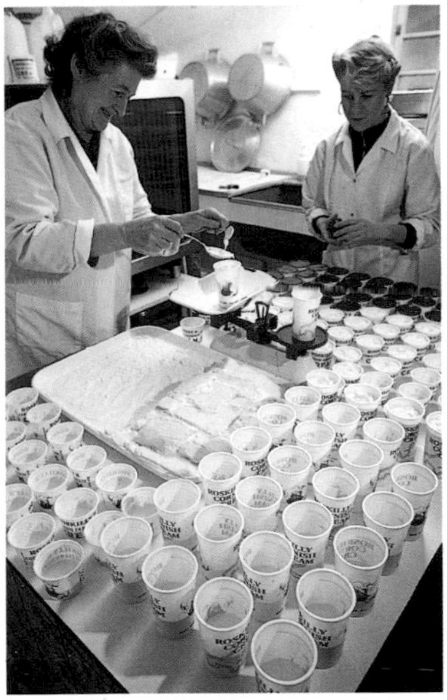

Rachel Roskilly (left) and an assistant fill pots with rich, thick clotted cream from her family dairy. Rachel's clotted cream is an essential ingredient in local cream teas.

RIGHT A mouth-watering Cornish split filled with Rachel's clotted cream and homemade strawberry jam is a Cornish specialty. Neighboring Devonians also claim this rich treat as their own, calling it a Devonshire split.

Turn out the dough onto a lightly floured work surface and knead for 10 minutes until smooth and elastic. Put the dough into an oiled bowl, and turn the dough over so the top is oiled. Cover with a damp dish towel. Let rise at room temperature, away from drafts, until doubled in size, 1 to 1½ hours.

Punch down the risen dough with your knuckles. Turn out the dough onto a floured surface and knead for about 10 seconds only. Weigh the dough and divide it into twenty-two equal pieces, or roll it into a fat rope and cut it into twenty-two even pieces. Shape each piece into a smooth roll by rolling it on the work surface under your cupped hand. Arrange the rolls on the prepared baking sheets so they almost touch each other. Cover lightly with damp dish towels and let rise at room temperature until almost doubled in size, about 45 minutes. During the last 15 minutes of rising, heat the oven to 425F. Bake the splits for 15 to 20 minutes, or until golden. Remove the sheets from the oven and immediately sift confectioners' sugar over the splits. Transfer to wire racks and cover with dry dish towels to keep the crust soft until cooled to lukewarm, then serve.

SPELT BREAD

The flour made from spelt, an ancient wheat grain (page 21), has a distinct, nutty flavor quite different from the wheat flour with which we are familiar. Clare Marriage (left), who has experimented with sacks upon sacks of different flours in more than twenty years of bread making at Doves Farm, is emphatic in her claim that spelt flour "makes the tastiest bread I've ever eaten." It certainly makes a loaf with a nuttier, wheatier taste than most. The flour seems to benefit from the very wet dough of the Grant method (page 44); the flavor develops, and the open texture with plenty of air pockets is very appealing. It also means fewer crumbs when the loaf is sliced.

This recipe is adapted from Clare's Doves Farm Spelt Bread recipe. It tastes best the day after baking and keeps for up to five days. It can also be frozen for one month.

INGREDIENTS

Makes two large loaves.

$10\frac{1}{2}$ cups spelt flour
2 cakes compressed fresh yeast (0.6 ounce each), or 2 envelopes active dry yeast ($2\frac{1}{2}$ teaspoons each) plus 1 teaspoon granulated sugar
about 5 cups lukewarm water (95F to 105F)
2 tablespoons kosher salt or flaked sea salt
2 tablespoons sunflower or light olive oil
3 tablespoons sesame seeds (optional)

two 13 × 4 × 4-inch Pullman loaf pans, greased (see Note)

Michael and Clare Marriage of Doves Farm, near Hungerford in Oxfordshire, England, with the organically grown grains they use for their stone-ground flours.

MIX THE DOUGH FOR 5 MINUTES. IT WILL BECOME SMOOTH AND ELASTIC.

Put the flour into a large bowl and make a well in the center. Crumble the fresh yeast into a medium-size bowl. Pour half the water into the yeast and stir until smooth. If using dry yeast, mix the granules and the sugar with half the water and let stand until foamy, 5 to 10 minutes (see page 18).

Dissolve the salt in the remaining water, then stir in the oil. Pour the yeast mixture into the well in the flour and roughly mix the flour from the bowl into the yeast mixture, using your hand. Add the remaining liquid and mix vigorously with your hand for 5 minutes. Although the dough starts out soft and sticky, it will become smooth and elastic as you work it and will leave the sides of the bowl cleanly. (If not, mix in a little additional flour.) Divide the dough between the two prepared pans. They should be half full. Smooth each top with a damp pastry brush or with moistened fingers, gently easing the dough into the corners. Sprinkle with the sesame seeds, if desired.

Cover each pan with plastic wrap or a damp dish towel and let rise at warm room temperature, away from drafts, for 35 to 45 minutes, until the dough rises to just below the top of the pans. During the last 15 minutes of rising, heat the oven to 400F.

Bake for 45 to 50 minutes, until the loaves sound hollow when unmolded and tapped underneath. The loaves will have flattish tops. Turn them out onto wire racks to cool.

NOTE: This bread can also be baked in four greased $8\frac{1}{2} \times 4\frac{1}{2} \times 2\frac{3}{4}$-inch loaf pans. Or, use one Pullman pan and two of the smaller pans. The baking time is about the same.

WHOLE-WHEAT LOAF

INGREDIENTS

Makes one large loaf.

- $3\frac{3}{4}$ to $4\frac{3}{4}$ cups whole-wheat bread flour (preferably stone-ground)
- 4 teaspoons kosher salt or flaked sea salt
- 1 cake compressed fresh yeast (0.6 ounce), or 1 envelope active dry yeast ($2\frac{1}{2}$ teaspoons) plus $\frac{1}{2}$ teaspoon granulated sugar
- 2 cups lukewarm water (95F to 105F)
- 2 teaspoons olive oil, vegetable oil, or melted unsalted butter
- a baking sheet, lightly greased

Stone-ground whole-wheat flour makes a very good bread – slightly dense, with plenty of flavor and a chewy crust. You know when you have eaten a slice that you will not feel hungry for a while. This bread is ideal for always-starving teenagers, as it really does fill them up – and healthfully!

This is not, however, a bread for an absolute beginner to try, since whole-wheat flour is difficult to work and knead. But once you get used to the heavy texture, it is not at all scary. If you are new to bread making and want to try a whole-wheat loaf, I suggest you bake The Grant Loaf (page 44) first for a very easy whole-wheat bread. Another alternative is to use The Basic Loaf recipe (page 15) and gradually increase the quantity of stone-ground whole-wheat bread flour each time you make the recipe, simultaneously decreasing the amount of white bread flour, until you are using only whole-wheat flour.

The oil or melted butter makes the loaf less crumbly, and also helps it keep longer. As with many breads in this chapter, this loaf improves on keeping and tastes best the day after it is baked. It can also be frozen for one month.

THIS DOUGH WILL BE HEAVY, SLIPPERY-WET AND DIFFICULT TO WORK WHEN IT IS FIRST TURNED OUT FOR KNEADING.

SHAPE THE DOUGH INTO A SMOOTH BALL. PLACE ON THE LIGHTLY GREASED BAKING SHEET AND LET RISE A SECOND TIME AT ROOM TEMPERATURE UNTIL DOUBLED IN SIZE, $1\frac{1}{2}$ TO 2 HOURS.

Prepare the dough as for The Basic Loaf (page 16), using $3\frac{3}{4}$ cups of the flour, the salt, yeast, and water, and adding the oil or melted butter with the last of the water. If using dry yeast, mix the granules and the sugar with $\frac{1}{4}$ cup of the water and let stand until foamy, 5 to 10 minutes (see page 18). Pour the yeast mixture into the well in the flour.

The dough will seem heavy and slippery-wet at first, but do not be tempted to add more flour at this stage. As you knead the dough and the water is absorbed by the flour, it will gradually become less sticky, although kneading will be hard work at first.

Knead for 10 minutes, until the dough becomes softer and very elastic and pliable, but not sticky or crumbly. If the dough is crumbly, add 1 tablespoon of water at a time, until the dough comes together. If the dough is very sticky after the 10 minutes, knead in additional flour, 1 tablespoon at a time, thoroughly working in each addition before adding more.

Put the dough into a lightly greased bowl and turn the dough over so the top is oiled. Cover with a damp dish towel and let rise at room temperature, away from drafts, until doubled in size, $1\frac{1}{2}$ to 2 hours.

Punch down the dough. Turn out the dough onto a floured work surface and knead for 1 minute, then shape the dough into a ball. Put the ball of dough on the prepared baking sheet and cover with a damp dish towel. Let rise at room temperature until doubled in size, about 1 hour. During the last 15 minutes of rising, heat the oven to 425F.

Uncover the loaf and snip the top with scissors or slash it with a sharp knife or razor blade to make a cross. Bake the loaf for 15 minutes, until lightly browned. Reduce the oven temperature to 350F. Bake for another 20 to 25 minutes, until the loaf sounds hollow when tapped underneath. If the loaf sounds dense or heavy, bake it for another 5 minutes, then test again. Transfer the bread to a wire rack to cool completely.

The water-powered Letheringsett Mill supplied local Norfolk communities with freshly ground flour from 1802 until 1944 when it was abandoned and left to deteriorate. It remained unused until 1982 when a conservation trust undertook the repairs and restoration.

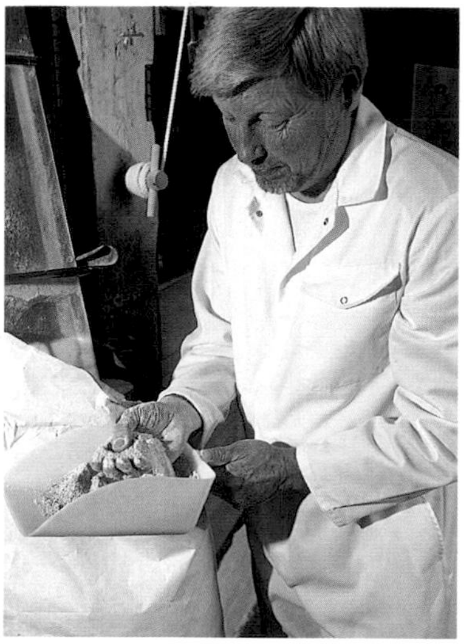

After leaving the Royal Navy, miller Mike Thurlow (above) moved to the mill in 1987 as the tenant-miller and completed the restoration to bring the mill back to working order. The educational demonstrations he gave then for local schoolchildren proved to be a learning experience for him as well because he knew nothing about milling when he first walked into the mill. Today, several London chefs have regular orders for his stone-ground whole-wheat flours.

Local farmers supply many of the grains Mike uses to grind his malted grain and several grades of whole-wheat flours.

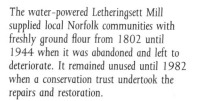

MY FAVORITE LOAD

INGREDIENTS

Makes one large loaf.
- $1\frac{1}{3}$ cups thick wheat flakes
- 1 to $1\frac{2}{3}$ cups whole-wheat bread flour (preferably stone-ground)
- $1\frac{2}{3}$ cups white bread flour (preferably unbleached and stone-ground)
- $4\frac{1}{2}$ teaspoons kosher salt or flaked sea salt
- 1 cake compressed fresh yeast (0.6 ounce) or 1 envelope active dry yeast ($2\frac{1}{2}$ teaspoons)
- $\frac{1}{2}$ teaspoon granulated sugar
- $1\frac{3}{4}$ cups lukewarm water (95F to 105F)
- 2 tablespoons olive oil or melted unsalted butter

a 9 × 5 × 3-inch loaf pan, lightly greased

This is the loaf I come back to time and time again. However much I enjoy making and eating plenty of different styles and types of bread, I find everyone really appreciates the flavor and texture of this loaf. In England, I like to make this bread with a combination of three flours from Letheringsett Mill (left), which miller Mike Thurlow grinds to my specifications. However, the coarse-ground whole-wheat flour he grinds for me is difficult to come by in the States, so I've substituted wheat flakes ground to a medium-coarse meal in a food processor.

Like most whole-wheat breads, this one matures and tastes best one or two days after baking. Store wrapped at room temperature or freeze for up to one month.

Put the wheat flakes and 1 tablespoon of the whole-wheat flour in a food processor. Process 30 to 60 seconds until the flakes are ground to a medium-coarse meal. Put the meal into a large bowl and stir in 1 cup of the whole-wheat flour, the white flour, and the salt. Make a well in the center of the flour mixture.

Crumble the fresh yeast into a small bowl with the sugar. Add $\frac{1}{4}$ cup of the lukewarm water and stir until smooth. Cover with plastic wrap and let stand 5 to 10 minutes, until foamy. If using dry yeast, mix the granules with the $\frac{1}{4}$ cup lukewarm water and sugar and let stand until foamy, 5 to 10 minutes (page 18).

Pour the yeast mixture into the well in the flour. Stir the remaining lukewarm water and the oil or butter into the yeast mixture and draw a little of the flour mixture into the well and mix thoroughly. Gradually mix in enough of the flour that is in the bowl to make a smooth, thick batter. Cover the bowl with a damp dish towel and let stand about 20 minutes to form a frothy sponge.

Mix in the remaining flour that is in the bowl, adding as much of the remaining whole-wheat flour as is necessary, about 1 tablespoon at a time, to form a fairly wet dough. Work the dough until it leaves the sides of the bowl cleanly. Then turn it out onto a lightly floured work surface and, with floured hands, knead the dough for 10 minutes. The dough will gradually become firmer and smoother as the water is absorbed by the wheat-flake meal, so don't be tempted to add more flour than is absolutely necessary.

Place the dough in the washed and lightly greased bowl and turn the dough over. Cover and let rise at room temperature until doubled in size, about 2 hours.

Turn out the dough onto a lightly floured work surface and punch it down. Shape it into a loaf to fit the prepared pan (see A Plain White Loaf, page 24). Cover it with a damp dish towel or plastic wrap and let rise until doubled in size, about $1\frac{1}{2}$ hours. During the last 15 minutes of rising, heat the oven to 450F.

Bake the loaf for 15 minutes. Reduce the oven temperature to 400F. Bake for another 30 to 35 minutes, or until the loaf sounds hollow when unmolded and tapped underneath. Unmold the loaf onto a wire rack to cool completely.

FOR EXTRA FLAVOR AND TEXTURE, ADD 2 TABLESPOONS SHELLED SUNFLOWER SEEDS TO THE FLOURS AND SALT. ROLL THE DOUGH IN EXTRA SHELLED SUNFLOWER SEEDS AFTER IT IS SHAPED.

THE GRANT LOAF

INGREDIENTS

Makes one large loaf.
- 4 to $4\frac{3}{4}$ cups whole-wheat bread flour (preferably stone-ground)
- 2 teaspoons kosher salt or flaked sea salt
- $2\frac{1}{2}$ cups lukewarm water (95F to 105F)
- 1 cake compressed fresh yeast (0.6 ounce) (see Notes)
- 1 teaspoon packed brown sugar or honey

a 13 × 4 × 4-inch Pullman loaf pan, greased and warmed (see Notes)

In 1944, Doris Grant published a simple recipe for a delicious, wholesome bread in her book, Your Daily Bread (Faber & Faber). Ever since, generations of bakers influenced by her have enjoyed making and eating homemade bread. This recipe is the answer to those who claim that bread making is too difficult or too time-consuming. The dough requires no kneading and has just one short rising period, in the pan. The majority of the bakers I have talked to say they caught the bread-making bug from trying the Grant recipe.

Once again, the secret is to start with a good quality stone-ground whole-wheat flour, and to make sure the dough is elastic and slippery when you finish mixing it. The texture of this bread is moist and light, even though it appears quite dense, and the bread keeps well (the taste improves, too). I have halved Mrs. Grant's original quantities and increased the rising time from 20 minutes, as my loaves seem to need 30 to 35 minutes.

Mix together 4 cups of the flour and the salt in a large bowl. In very cold weather, warm the bowl of flour in a 250F oven for 5 to 8 minutes, or microwave on high for 1 to $1\frac{1}{2}$ minutes. Make a well in the center of the flour.

Put 3 tablespoons of the lukewarm water in a small bowl, crumble in the fresh yeast, and mix until smooth. Stir in the sugar or honey. Let stand for 10 to 15 minutes, until the mixture is thick and frothy.

Pour the yeast mixture and the remaining lukewarm water into the well in the flour. Mix vigorously with your hand for 1 to 2 minutes, working in the flour from the sides to the center, until the dough feels elastic and comes cleanly away from the sides of the bowl. Add as much of the remaining flour as is necessary, about $\frac{1}{4}$ cup at a time. Doris Grant described the correct texture as "slippery."

Put the dough into the prepared pan and cover with a damp dish towel. Let stand in a warm place for 20 to 35 minutes, until the dough rises to within $\frac{1}{2}$ inch of the top of the pan. While the dough is rising, heat the oven to 400F.

Bake for 35 to 40 minutes, until the loaf sounds hollow when unmolded and gently tapped underneath. Transfer the bread to a wire rack to cool completely.

NOTES: You can also make this loaf using 1 envelope active dry yeast ($2\frac{1}{2}$ teaspoons), but I have never been happy with the result when I have used it in this recipe. For the method, see page 18.

This bread can also be baked in two $8\frac{1}{2} \times 4\frac{1}{2} \times 2\frac{3}{4}$-inch loaf pans. The baking time is about the same.

MIX THE WET DOUGH VIGOROUSLY IN THE BOWL FOR 1 TO 2 MINUTES, WORKING IN THE FLOUR FROM THE SIDES TO THE CENTER. CONTINUE MIXING UNTIL THE DOUGH FEELS ELASTIC AND COMES CLEANLY AWAY FROM THE SIDES OF THE BOWL.

Award-winning baker Viola Unruh and her husband, Henry, outside their farmhouse.

VIOLA'S LIGHT WHOLE-WHEAT BREAD

INGREDIENTS

Makes three or four medium-size loaves.

- $3\frac{1}{2}$ cups water
- 2 cakes compressed fresh yeast (0.6 ounce each) or 2 envelopes active dry yeast ($2\frac{1}{2}$ teaspoons each)
- 1 large egg, beaten
- 4 tablespoons solid vegetable shortening or softened unsalted butter
- $\frac{1}{3}$ cup granulated sugar
- 2 tablespoons kosher or flaked sea salt
- 2 cups whole-wheat bread flour
- 6 to 7 cups white bread flour (preferably unbleached and stone-ground)
- 3 tablespoons vital wheat gluten (see introduction)

four $8\frac{1}{2} \times 4\frac{1}{2} \times 2\frac{3}{4}$-inch loaf pans, or three $9 \times 5 \times 3$-inch loaf pans, lightly greased

"Just the kind of bread you like to eat," said one of the judges as Viola Unruh beat two hundred other home bakers to win the 1990 Kansas Festival of Breads Contest, sponsored by the Kansas Wheat Commission.

"My recipe was so simple I never thought I would win against some of the fancier breads," said Viola as she rapidly made yet another batch of four loaves. She swears by vital wheat gluten and Hudson Cream Flour (page 48) to produce a light, fine loaf that looks great. Viola started making bread when she married Henry 45 years ago. The quantity of bread, as well as the quality, is important when you live on a remote corn farm with 3,200 head of cattle in Montezuma, Kansas – and you have to feed your sons and farm workers, who can demolish a batch of bread in just one meal.

This recipe uses the sponging technique, which Viola prefers for all her breads. "You get a better loaf," she says, adding that if you mix and knead bread dough by hand, rather than with a dough hook on a machine, "the texture is much finer."

I have made this bread without the vital wheat gluten, and the recipe still works well. Gluten is found at health-food stores or may be purchased by mail order (see List of Suppliers, page 187). Viola keeps her whole-wheat flour in the freezer to prevent it from becoming rancid in the Kansas heat. This loaf keeps for two days, or it can be frozen for one month.

Warm $\frac{1}{2}$ cup of the water to lukewarm (95F to 105F). Crumble the fresh yeast into the lukewarm water in a small bowl and stir until smooth. If using dry yeast, mix the granules and the warmed $\frac{1}{2}$ cup of water in a small bowl, stir in a teaspoon of the sugar, and let stand until foamy, 5 to 10 minutes (see page 18).

Heat the rest of the water to about 150F and pour it over the butter or shortening, sugar, and salt in a large bowl. Stir until melted and slightly cooled.

Stir in the whole-wheat flour, followed by about 3 cups of the white flour and the vital wheat gluten. Mix thoroughly together. (Viola uses a slotted spoon.) Add the yeast mixture and stir well. Beat in the egg. Beat this sloppy batter for 3 minutes, then cover with plastic wrap and let stand until it becomes spongy, about 10 minutes.

Uncover the sponge and gradually work in some of the white bread flour, about ½ cup at a time, until the dough is firm enough to turn out onto a lightly floured work surface. Then knead in enough of the remaining flour, very little at a time, until the dough is no longer sticky. Knead the dough for 10 minutes, until it is firm and pliable enough to flop from hand to hand. The exact amount of flour will depend on the flour itself and the temperature in the kitchen. Put the dough back into the bowl (there is no need to oil the bowl). Cover with plastic wrap or a damp dish towel and let rise until doubled in size, about 1 hour in a warm Kansas kitchen. Turn out the risen dough onto a lightly floured work surface. Punch it down and lightly knead, working the dough from hand to hand for 2 to 3 minutes.

Divide the dough into four (or three) equal pieces. Shape each piece into a rough ball, then place in the prepared pans. Cover with damp dish towels or plastic wrap and let rest for 10 minutes, which makes the dough easier to shape. Flour the work surface. Remove the dough, one piece at a time, and roll out with a lightly floured rolling pin into a rectangle measuring about 11 × 9 inches, and about ½ inch thick. Starting with a short side, roll up tightly like a jelly roll, then pinch the seam to seal tightly. Return to the loaf pan, seam side down, and tuck the ends under, pinching to seal. Repeat with the remaining dough. Cover the loaves again and let rise until doubled in size, about 45 minutes. During the last 15 minutes of rising, heat the oven to 400F. Bake the loaves for 10 minutes, then lower the oven temperature to 350F. Bake the loaves for about 25 minutes longer, or until they sound hollow when unmolded and tapped underneath. Turn out the loaves from the pans onto wire racks. Rub the crusts with a butter wrapper and let cool completely.

Viola recommends serving her delicious bread with homemade apricot jam.

LIKE ALL GOOD BAKERS, VIOLA ASSEMBLES AND MEASURES ALL HER INGREDIENTS BEFORE SHE STARTS MIXING. HERE SHE BEATS THE EGG IN A MUG.

SHE POURS HOT WATER OVER VEGETABLE SHORTENING, SUGAR, AND SALT, STIRRING TO MELT THE SHORTENING AND DISSOLVE THE SUGAR.

SHE ADDS THE EGG TO A MIXTURE OF SHORTENING, WATER, SUGAR, YEAST, AND FLOUR. SHE BEATS IT WITH A SLOTTED SPOON TO MAKE A SLOPPY BATTER.

THE BATTER IS COVERED WITH PLASTIC WRAP AND LEFT FOR ABOUT 10 MINUTES UNTIL IT BECOMES SPONGY.

VIOLA THEN USES HER SLOTTED SPOON TO BEAT IN ENOUGH OF THE REMAINING WHITE FLOUR TO MAKE A FIRM DOUGH.

SHE TURNS OUT THE DOUGH ONTO A LIGHTLY FLOURED WORK SURFACE AND KNEADS IT FOR 10 MINUTES, ADDING ADDITIONAL FLOUR, UNTIL THE DOUGH IS NO LONGER STICKY.

AFTER KNEADING, THE DOUGH BECOMES FIRM AND PLIABLE. THE DOUGH IS RETURNED TO THE BOWL, COVERED WITH PLASTIC WRAP, AND LEFT TO RISE.

AFTER THE DOUGH HAS DOUBLED IN SIZE, VIOLA REMOVES THE PLASTIC WRAP, TURNS OUT THE DOUGH AND WORKS IT FROM HAND TO HAND FOR 2 TO 3 MINUTES.

USING A KNIFE, VIOLA CUTS THE DOUGH INTO QUARTERS.

EACH PORTION OF DOUGH IS THEN SHAPED INTO A ROUGH OVAL, PLACED IN THE GREASED PANS AND LEFT TO REST, COVERED, FOR 10 MINUTES.

WORKING WITH ONE PORTION OF DOUGH AT A TIME, VIOLA ROLLS IT OUT TO A RECTANGLE MEASURING ABOUT 11×9 INCHES, AND ABOUT $\frac{1}{2}$ INCH THICK.

SHE THEN ROLLS UP THE DOUGH LIKE A JELLY ROLL AND PUTS IT IN THE PAN FOR A SECOND RISING. AFTER THE DOUGH DOUBLES IN SIZE, IT IS PUT IN THE OVEN TO BAKE FOR ABOUT 35 MINUTES, OR UNTIL THEY SOUND HOLLOW WHEN TAPPED UNDERNEATH.

HUDSON CREAM WHOLE-WHEAT BREAD

INGREDIENTS

Makes two medium-size loaves.

- 2 cakes compressed fresh yeast (0.6 ounce each) or 2 envelopes active dry yeast ($2\frac{1}{2}$ teaspoons each)
- 1 cup lukewarm water (95F to 105F)
- 1 cup lukewarm milk (95F to 105F)
- $\frac{1}{3}$ cup spun or whipped honey (see Note)
- 6 to 7 cups white-wheat bread flour (preferably Hudson Cream Flour) or whole-wheat bread flour
- 2 large eggs, beaten
- 4 teaspoons kosher salt or flaked sea salt
- 4 tablespoons shortening: softened unsalted butter, diced lard, or solid vegetable shortening

two $8\frac{1}{2} \times 4\frac{1}{2} \times 2\frac{3}{4}$-inch loaf pans, or two $9 \times 5 \times 3$-inch loaf pans, lightly greased

NOTE: Whipped or spun honey is solid and nearly white in color. It is found at most health-food stores, but if not available, use regular liquid honey.

Talking to finalists and prize winners of bread-making competitions in the States, I discovered that many swore by Hudson Cream Flour (see List of Suppliers, page 187). One cook in West Virginia who used it for her prize-winning biscuits said, "I want to pass down to my children good morals, good values, and Hudson Cream Flour."

The printed cambric flour bags sold at the mill and by mail order (the flour comes in paper sacks) are sought after for making aprons like the one Viola Unrah is wearing on page 45. Stafford County Flour Mill in Kansas, where this flour is milled, can be seen three miles away from the road, the silos rising from the farmland like a huge block of apartments. Founded in 1905 by a German immigrant, the mill stayed in the same family until 1986; the current president, Al Brensing, has worked there for more than 55 years. The dairy image (the company logo is a Jersey cow) and "cream" brand name refer not to the color of the flour, available bleached and unbleached, but to the very smooth texture, due to the hard red winter wheat from which it is milled. Their organic unbleached flour and white wheat flours (a new type of whole-wheat flour) are slowly finding a market. Look in grocery stores in Pennsylvania, Indiana, Ohio, Kentucky, Tennessee, and West Virginia, as well as in Kansas.

This recipe, using Hudson Cream whole-wheat flour, has won many prizes. A loaf of this bread disappeared very quickly when I took it to a luncheon with friends. It is a moist loaf that keeps well and improves with age. It can be frozen for up to one month.

Crumble the fresh yeast into a large bowl. Add the lukewarm water and stir until dissolved. Stir in the milk and honey. Using your hand or a wooden spoon, beat in 3 cups of the flour and the eggs. The original recipe says to beat for one hundred strokes, which takes 2 to 3 minutes. Cover with a damp dish towel and let rest at room temperature until spongy, 20 to 30 minutes. If using dry yeast, mix the granules with half the lukewarm water and half the honey, and let stand until foamy, 5 to 10 minutes (page 18). Add the remaining water and honey, plus the milk, and continue to make a sponge.

Uncover the sponge and mix in the salt, followed by the remaining flour, about $\frac{1}{2}$ cup at a time, until the dough is no longer sticky. The exact amount will depend on the flour you use. Turn out the dough onto a lightly floured work surface and knead for 10 minutes, gradually working in the shortening and additional flour, if necessary. When the dough looks and feels smooth and pliable, return it to the washed and lightly greased bowl, and turn the dough over so the top is oiled. Cover with a damp dish towel and let rise at room temperature, away from drafts, until doubled in size, 1 to $1\frac{1}{2}$ hours.

Punch down the risen dough and divide in half. Cover with a damp dish towel and let rest for 10 minutes. Shape the portions into loaves to fit the prepared pans (see A Plain White Loaf, page 24). Cover the pans with damp dish towels and let the dough rise at room temperature until doubled in size, about 1 hour. During the last 15 minutes of rising, heat the oven to 375F.

Bake the loaves for 10 minutes. Reduce the oven temperature to 350F. Bake for another 20 to 30 minutes, or until the loaves sound hollow when unmolded and tapped underneath. Turn out the loaves from the pans and transfer to wire racks and cool.

USING YOUR HAND, BEAT 3 CUPS OF FLOUR AND THE EGGS INTO THE YEAST MIXTURE.

CONTINUE ADDING FLOUR UNTIL THE DOUGH IS NO LONGER STICKY.

FOUR-WHEAT LOAF

INGREDIENTS

Makes one large loaf.

- $\frac{2}{3}$ cup medium bulghur wheat
- 2 cups water
- $\frac{1}{4}$ cup firmly packed light-brown sugar
- 1 tablespoon olive oil
- 1 cake compressed fresh yeast (0.6 ounce), or 1 envelope active dry yeast ($2\frac{1}{2}$ teaspoons)
- 2 cups white bread flour (preferably unbleached and stone-ground)
- $1\frac{1}{2}$ to 2 cups whole-wheat bread flour (preferably stone-ground)
- $\frac{1}{4}$ cup unprocessed bran flakes
- $3\frac{1}{2}$ teaspoons kosher salt or flaked sea salt

a 13 × 4 × 4-inch Pullman loaf pan, lightly greased

The combination of bulghur wheat, whole-wheat bread flour, unprocessed bran flakes, and white bread flour makes a nutty-flavored, yet light-textured loaf that is slightly sweet. This loaf tastes good freshly baked or after one or two days. Store wrapped at room temperature, or freeze for one month.

Place the bulghur wheat in a medium-size bowl. In a small saucepan, combine the water, sugar, and olive oil. Bring to a boil, stirring to dissolve the sugar. Pour the mixture over the bulghur and let stand until lukewarm (95F to 105F), about 30 minutes.

Crumble the fresh yeast into a large bowl and mix with 2 tablespoons of the bulghur mixture. If using dry yeast, sprinkle the granules over 2 tablespoons of the bulghur mixture and stir to mix. Cover and let stand 5 to 10 minutes, or until foamy.

Stir in 1 cup of the white flour and the remaining bulghur mixture and beat to form a grainy batter. Cover with a damp dish towel and let stand 20 to 30 minutes to sponge.

Add the remaining 1 cup white flour, 1 cup of the whole-wheat flour, the bran, and the salt. Mix to form a soft dough, adding as much of the remaining whole-wheat flour as is necessary to prevent sticking until the dough leaves the sides of the bowl cleanly.

Turn out the dough onto a floured surface and knead for 10 minutes, adding any remaining whole-wheat flour as needed, until smooth and elastic. Place the dough in the washed and lightly greased bowl and turn the dough so the top is oiled. Cover with a damp dish towel and let dough rise until doubled in size, about $1\frac{1}{2}$ hours.

Punch down the dough, then turn it out onto a lightly floured work surface. Roll and shape the dough to fit the pan as for A Plain White Loaf (page 24). Cover with a damp dish towel and let rise at room temperature until the dough just reaches the rim of the pan, 1 to $1\frac{1}{2}$ hours. During the last 15 minutes of rising, heat the oven to 425F.

Using a sharp knife, make a deep slash lengthwise along the loaf. Bake the loaf for 15 minutes. Reduce the oven temperature to 375F. Bake for another 20 to 25 minutes, until the bread sounds hollow when unmolded and tapped underneath. Transfer to a wire rack and cool completely.

It is not surprising that cultures around the world start the day with bread for breakfast. Both whole-wheat and white breads made with enriched flour are an excellent source of niacin, riboflavin, and thiamin, vital vitamins necessary for good health. Breads also contain starch, minerals, and varying amounts of roughage. Serve bread fresh or toasted for breakfast.

GERMAN THREE-GRAIN BREAD

INGREDIENTS

Makes two small or one medium loaf.

- $2\frac{1}{2}$ to 3 cups white bread flour (preferably unbleached and stone-ground)
- $1\frac{1}{4}$ cups rye flour
- $\frac{1}{3}$ cup old-fashioned rolled oats
- 3 tablespoons linseeds (flaxseeds) or sesame seeds, preferably black
- 4 teaspoons kosher salt or flaked sea salt
- 1 cake compressed fresh yeast (0.6 ounce), or 1 envelope active dry yeast ($2\frac{1}{2}$ teaspoons) plus $\frac{1}{2}$ teaspoon granulated sugar
- $\frac{1}{2}$ cup milk
- $1\frac{1}{4}$ cups water
- additional milk to glaze
- additional linseeds or sesame seeds

a large baking sheet, lightly greased

This is a flavorful loaf made from wheat and rye flours with oatmeal and linseeds (known in the U.S. as flaxseeds), which are available by mail order or at health-food stores. They are popular in German baking. This loaf is suberb with cured meats, hard cheeses, or smoked fish, and pickles. It tastes best after it has matured for a day and it can be frozen for one month.

In a large, warmed bowl, stir together $2\frac{1}{2}$ cups of the white flour, the rye flour, oats, linseeds, and salt. In a small saucepan, heat the water and milk to lukewarm (95F to 105F). Put $\frac{1}{4}$ cup of this mixture into a small bowl. Crumble in the fresh yeast and mix until smooth. Add 2 tablespoons of the dry ingredients and stir to make a thick paste. Let stand until frothy and spongy-looking, about 10 minutes. (This won't rise as much as other sponges.) If using dry yeast, mix the granules and the sugar with $\frac{1}{4}$ cup of the lukewarm liquid and let stand until foamy, 5 to 10 minutes (see page 18).

Make a well in the dry ingredients and add the yeast mixture and the remaining liquid. Mix to form a firm dough, adding as much of the remaining white flour as is necessary, about 1 tablespoon at a time.

Turn out the dough onto a lightly floured work surface and knead thoroughly for 10 minutes, or until smooth and elastic. Put the dough into a lightly oiled bowl and turn the dough over so the top is oiled. Cover with a damp dish towel. Let rise at room temperature, away from drafts, until doubled in size, 2 to 3 hours.

Punch down the risen dough. Shape into a neat oval, or 2 smaller ovals, if you prefer (page 17). Arrange the loaf or loaves on the prepared baking sheet. Cover with a damp dish towel and let rise at room temperature until doubled in size, about 1 hour. During the last 15 minutes of rising, heat the oven to 425F.

Using a sharp knife or a razor blade, make a slash lengthwise down the center of the loaf or loaves. Brush with milk to glaze, then sprinkle with the additional linseeds. Bake for 30 to 40 minutes, or until the bread sounds hollow when tapped on the underside. Transfer to a wire rack or two racks to cool completely. Wrap tightly in aluminum foil and let rest at room temperature for one day so the flavors mature.

SPRINKLE LINSEEDS OVER THE SLASHED LOAVES JUST BEFORE BAKING.

Traditionally dressed Bavarians take a break from their shopping in a Munich market. Breads made with rye flour and linseeds (flaxseeds) are eaten with full-flavored cured meats and smoked fish.

There are few days when Kansas home economist Cindy Falk does not bake a loaf of bread for her family. Multi-grain Harvest Bread and Pioneer Bread (page 53) are two of her flavor-packed loaves. Both have the nutritional bonus of being high in protein. Cindy teaches bread making in local schools, and her children are following in her footsteps. Here her daughter helps her measure water before starting a fresh batch of dough.

MULTI-GRAIN HARVEST BREAD

Cindy Falk, a home economist with the Kansas Wheat Commission, lives in Onaga, in northeast Kansas, up toward Nebraska. Her house has wonderful views of the hills and of the fields her husband farms in his spare time. In 1826, Cindy's ancestors came to the States from a dairy farm in Neuchâtel, Switzerland, an area famed for its wine and cheese. This area of Kansas, with its rolling green hills and fields, reminded them of home more than any other part of the state.

Cindy has been making bread since she was eleven years old and has won countless awards at state fairs and national cooking contests, which may not be surprising as her mother is another prize-winning baker. Now Cindy's children win competitions, too. Derek, the fourteen year old, cans fruits and vegetables and makes wonderful cakes, while Laura, aged eleven, has won prizes for her Portuguese Sweet Breads (page 136).

This is Cindy's blue-ribbon recipe from the 1992 Kansas State Fair, and it's a flavorful, high-protein loaf. Make the oat flour by processing 5 tablespoons old-fashioned rolled oats in a blender or food processor using the pulse switch until the oats are floury. Eat this blue-ribbon recipe the day it is baked, or the day after; do not refrigerate, or it will go stale more quickly.

INGREDIENTS

Makes two medium-size loaves.

- $1\frac{1}{2}$ cups water
- 4 tablespoons unsalted butter, softened
- 2 tablespoons packed dark-brown sugar
- 2 tablespoons molasses
- $\frac{1}{4}$ cup cracked wheat (not bulghur wheat)
- $\frac{1}{2}$ cup whole-wheat bread flour (preferably stone-ground)
- 2 tablespoons nonfat dry milk powder
- $\frac{1}{4}$ cup soy flour
- $\frac{1}{4}$ cup yellow cornmeal
- $\frac{1}{4}$ cup old-fashioned rolled oats
- $\frac{1}{4}$ cup rye flour
- $\frac{1}{4}$ cup amaranth flour or barley flour
- $\frac{1}{3}$ cup oat flour (see above)
- 4 teaspoons kosher salt or flaked sea salt
- 1 cake compressed fresh yeast (0.6 ounce), or 1 envelope active dry yeast ($2\frac{1}{2}$ teaspoons) plus $\frac{1}{2}$ teaspoon granulated sugar
- 1 large egg, beaten
- $2\frac{1}{2}$ to $3\frac{1}{2}$ cups white bread flour (preferably unbleached and stone-ground)
- vegetable oil, about 2 to 3 tablespoons for kneading

two $8\frac{1}{2} \times 4\frac{1}{2} \times 2\frac{3}{4}$-inch or $9 \times 5 \times 3$-inch bread pans, lightly greased

Heat together the water, butter, brown sugar, and molasses in a medium-size saucepan over moderate heat for about 2 minutes, stirring frequently, until it is very warm (125F to 130F). Stir in the cracked wheat. Remove from the heat and let stand for 10 to 12 minutes, stirring occasionally, until the liquid is lukewarm (95F to 105F).

In a large bowl, stir together the whole-wheat flour, milk powder, soy flour, cornmeal, rolled oats, rye flour, amaranth or barley flour, oat flour, and salt. (Warm the flours if it is a cold day; see page 15). Crumble the fresh yeast into a small bowl. Add 2 tablespoons of the lukewarm cracked-wheat mixture and mix until smooth. If using dry yeast, mix the granules and the granulated sugar with 2 tablespoons of the lukewarm cracked-wheat mixture and let stand until foamy, 5 to 10 minutes (see page 18).

Add the yeast mixture and the cracked-wheat mixture to the flours in the bowl and

This loaf is excellent for slicing and using for sandwiches.

beat with your hand or a wooden spoon for 2 minutes. Add the egg and about $\frac{1}{4}$ cup of the white flour, then beat for 2 minutes more. Gradually mix in enough of the remaining flour as necessary, about $\frac{1}{4}$ cup at a time, to make a soft dough that forms a ball and leaves the sides of the bowl cleanly. The exact amount of flour needed will vary depending on the type of flour and the temperature.

Generously oil your hands and the work surface. Turn out the dough and knead for 10 to 12 minutes until smooth, elastic, but still slightly sticky. The oil stops the dough from sticking as you knead; adding extra flour at this stage would make the loaf tough and dry. Cover the dough with the upturned bowl, or return it to the washed and lightly greased bowl, turn the dough so the top is oiled, and cover with a damp dish towel or plastic wrap. Let the dough rise at room temperature, away from drafts, until doubled in size, 1 to $1\frac{1}{2}$ hours.

Punch down the dough and divide in half. Cover with a damp dish towel or plastic wrap and let rest for 10 minutes. On a lightly floured work surface, shape the loaves by rolling each piece with a lightly floured rolling pin from the center outward into a rectangle, about 15 × 7 inches. The dough should be about $\frac{1}{4}$ inch thick. Starting from a short end, roll up the dough tightly – pushing the dough together and pinching the seams after each roll – so you have a short, fat roll. Seal the ends of the roll with the edge of your hand, pushing down to the counter. Fold the ends under, and pinch to seal.

Put one roll seam side down into each prepared pan to ensure a loaf with an even shape and no large pockets of air or "floating" crust. (Cindy has a quick method for shaping loaves not intended for competitions: Press the lump of punched-down dough into a heavily greased pan. Turn the dough out, then slide it back into the pan so that the side that was underneath is now on top. Cindy covers the second piece of dough with a damp dish towel or plastic wrap while shaping the first to prevent it from drying out.) Cover the pans with damp dish towels or plastic wrap and let the dough rise at room temperature until doubled in size, about 1 hour. During the last 15 minutes of rising, heat the oven to 375F.

Bake the loaves for 25 to 30 minutes, until they are golden and sound hollow when unmolded and tapped underneath. Transfer the loaves to wire racks and cool completely.

CINDY ROLLS OUT EACH PORTION OF DOUGH, ROLLING FROM THE CENTER OUTWARD INTO A RECTANGLE.

STARTING FROM A SHORT END, SHE THEN ROLLS UP THE DOUGH, SEALING AND PINCHING THE EDGES TOGETHER AFTER EACH ROLL.

PIONEER BREAD

This is Cindy Falk's recipe for "a healthy daily bread dating from Kansas's settler days." Baked in round cake pans, this is a delicious loaf, very nutritious, with a light, but chewy texture. It is best on the day it is baked, or the day after. It toasts and freezes well.

Cindy uses this recipe to teach local schoolchildren just how good homemade bread tastes, as well as to illustrate

INGREDIENTS

Makes two medium-size loaves.

$\frac{1}{2}$ cup yellow cornmeal
$\frac{1}{4}$ cup packed dark-brown sugar
4 teaspoons kosher salt or flaked sea salt
$\frac{1}{4}$ cup vegetable oil
1 cup boiling water
2 cakes compressed fresh yeast (0.6 ounce each), or 2 envelopes active dry yeast ($2\frac{1}{2}$ teaspoons each) plus $\frac{1}{2}$ teaspoon granulated sugar
$\frac{1}{2}$ cup lukewarm water (95F to 105F)
1 cup cold water from tap
1 cup whole-wheat bread flour (preferably stone-ground)
$\frac{1}{2}$ cup rye flour
$3\frac{1}{2}$ to $4\frac{1}{2}$ cups white bread flour (preferably unbleached and stone-ground)
3 tablespoons sunflower seeds
additional vegetable oil
additional cornmeal

two 8-inch-round cake pans, or two 9-inch pie pans, heavily greased (if possible, use pans that have a nonstick finish)

how American settler history is bound with the land and cultivation. This recipe reflects Kansas's nickname – the Sunflower State – as well as its reputation as America's breadbasket.

Cindy also teaches the children how to measure accurately, and sets a timer for the kneading, rising, and baking times.

Combine the cornmeal, brown sugar, salt, oil, and boiling water in a large bowl to soften the cornmeal and dissolve the sugar and salt. The oil prevents the loaf from being crumbly when sliced.

Crumble the fresh yeast into a small bowl and stir in the lukewarm water until smooth. If using dry yeast, mix the granules and the $\frac{1}{2}$ teaspoon granulated sugar with the lukewarm water and let stand until foamy, 5 to 10 minutes (see page 18).

Add the cold tap water to the cornmeal mixture, then add the yeast mixture and stir well. Using your hand or a wooden spoon, beat in the whole-wheat and rye flours, mixing well. Gradually stir in the white flour, a handful at a time, adding just enough to make a dough that is moderately stiff and leaves the sides of the bowl cleanly. (Cindy prefers a dough that is slightly too soft, rather than too stiff, as "you get a nicer bread.")

Turn out the dough onto a lightly floured work surface and knead for at least 10 minutes until smooth and elastic, only using enough additional flour to prevent sticking. (Cindy says she kneads her bread for 25 minutes for competitions, to improve the volume and texture.)

Sprinkle the sunflower seeds over the dough and knead for a couple of minutes to incorporate them evenly throughout the dough.

Put the dough into the washed and lightly greased bowl, turning the dough so the top is oiled. Cover with a damp dish towel or plastic wrap and let rise in a warm place, away from drafts, until doubled in size, about 1 hour.

Punch down the risen dough with your fist. Lightly oil your hands and the work surface to avoid needing extra flour, which can make streaks in the finished loaf. Sprinkle the greased pans with a little extra cornmeal. Turn out the dough and divide it into two equal pieces. Shape each piece into a ball. Then roll it into a pear-shaped oval so one end is narrower than the other.

Put a loaf in each pan, putting the narrow end in first and letting the wider end form the top. Cover with damp dish towels or plastic wrap and let rise at room temperature, away from drafts, until almost doubled in size, about 1 hour. During the last 15 minutes of rising, heat the oven to 375F.

Using a sharp knife or razor blade, slash the top of each loaf in a star pattern, or use kitchen scissors to snip a star pattern. Bake the loaves for 35 to 45 minutes, or until they are well browned and sound hollow when unmolded and tapped underneath. If the loaves stick to the pans, let them stand for 5 minutes so the steam loosens the bottom, then try again. Transfer the loaves to wire racks and cool completely.

Pioneer Bread has a soft crust and a well-textured crumb. Cindy recommends serving it with a salad and, in fact, she often serves it with her mother's award-winning meatball, pasta, and red pepper salad.

FLAT BREADS

The international collection of breads in this chapter includes the oldest and simplest of all breads to make. Leavened or unleavened, flat breads can be crisp or chewy, plain or rich. They are generally quick to make and cook in minutes, if not seconds, either on top of the stove or in a red-hot oven.

Traditionally cooked on a hot, flat iron plate over a flame, many of these breads have been made for centuries by travelers and nomads, linking the cultures of the world. Pita Bread (page 62) and Lavash (page 63), both from the Middle East, for example, are close cousins of the Naan (page 61) and Chapati (page 56) of India; Branch Bread (page 64) from Scandinavia is a second cousin to Griddle Oatcakes (page 72) of Scotland, Maddybenny Fadge (page 70) of Northern Ireland and Manx Potato Cakes (page 70).

In some cultures in the Middle East, and in parts of Asia, flat breads have the dual purpose of being a basic dietary staple and of replacing plates and silverware, making them essential for every meal. For example, grilled meat kabobs and koftas are enclosed in pita breads so they can be eaten out of hand. Naan and chapatis have been designed to scoop food from the plate to the mouth.

OPPOSITE *Making an Indian flat bread.* ABOVE *Enjoying a stuffed pita-bread.*

Flat breads cooked on top of the stove traditionally require a griddle, a large, flat cast-iron round, although you can use a heavy aluminum, or even a nonstick griddle, or a tava, a slightly concave, heavy iron cooking pan used throughout India. (Look for this pan in stores selling Indian foods and cookware.) Even a shallow, cast-iron frying pan works well. Good, heavy-duty baking sheets that will not buckle in extreme heat are essential for flat breads which are to be baked in the oven, such as pitas.

The recipes for Hoe Cakes (page 69), Pita Bread (page 62), Maddybenny Fadge (page 70), and Manx Potato Cakes (page 70) are ideal for new bread makers because they do not require any special equipment or skill. They are also "fun" recipes to make.

One point to remember when making flat breads is to make sure the oven is free from grease and debris before heating it to the maximum setting for pitas and the like. I forgot to check this once and when I opened the door to put in a batch of pitas I was greeted by clouds of smoke.

So if you are as dismayed as I am by the flat breads available in the supermarket, try your hand at the recipes here; I know the results will please.

INDIAN FLAT BREADS

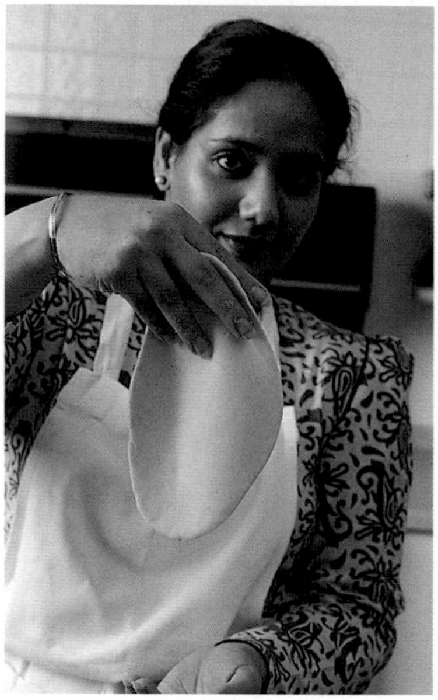

Jagdessh Sohal demonstrates her fail-proof technique for making Indian flat breads.

Whether it is the oval, white naan from the Punjab, the flat, chewy, unleavened chapati, or the flaky, rich paratha of northern India, a flat bread is eaten with every meal in India.

Although I cook a lot of Indian food, I had never thought of making Indian flat breads at home until I met Jagdessh Sohal. Jagdessh was born in Bombay and came to England in 1976, when she married. For the past few years she has been a consultant to Sharwood, a company specializing in Asian foods, making sure their large range of Indian prepared dishes and products is authentic. Jagdessh explained to me that these breads are purposely kept simple in flavor to act as a foil for the rich or spicy dishes in the meal. She also explained which bread to serve with which type of dish; for example, chapatis, pooris, parathas are best served with lentil dishes, and naans best with dry-cooked meat or vegetable dishes, such as tandooris and kabobs. These breads play an important part in the meal, acting as a staple and as a means of scooping up food, often making forks and spoons unnecessary.

To test the heat of a tava, or your frying pan or griddle, before cooking Chapatis (below) and Parathas (page 60), Jagdessh says to sprinkle a good pinch of flour on it. When the tava is the correct temperature, the flour browns in 3 seconds. If it takes longer, the tava is too cool, and if the flour burns instantly, she says to let the tava cool slightly before beginning to cook the breads.

NOTE: The recipes for chapatis, pooris, and parathas call for ghee, a form of clarified butter, although clarified butter or melted unsalted butter can be substituted. Ghee is the fat used most often in Indian cooking. It has a high smoking point, which makes it ideal for sautéing and frying. The distinct, almost caramelized, flavor (a bit like unsweetened, condensed milk) is produced as the butter simmers and the water evaporates. It can be purchased in food shops specializing in Indian foods, or it's easy to prepare at home. To make ghee, melt 2 cups (4 sticks) of unsalted butter in a small saucepan over low heat. Simmer for about 15 minutes, or until the white milk solids on the bottom of the pan turn golden. Watch carefully for the color change. The simmering time will depend on the amount of water in the butter. Once the particles have turned golden, strain the mixture through a strainer lined with cheesecloth. Let the ghee cool, then pour it into a jar with a tight-fitting lid. Refrigerate it for up to six months or freeze it for up to a year.

CHAPATIS

INGREDIENTS

Makes eight chapatis.

- $2\frac{1}{3}$ cups sifted whole-wheat pastry flour
- 1 teaspoon kosher salt or flaked sea salt
- about $\frac{3}{4}$ cup water
- additional flour for shaping
- ghee (see above), clarified butter, or melted unsalted butter, for brushing

a tava, a 10-inch cast-iron frying pan, or a heavy griddle

These are flat, unleavened disks made with atta, a very fine whole-wheat flour available in Indian stores. As an alternative, Jagdessh suggests using the whole-wheat flour sold for making pastry, with the coarser bits of bran sifted out, and I find this works just as well. She makes ten to fifteen chapatis every night for dinner, cooking them on an ungreased tava, a concave iron pan, on top of the stove. My cast-iron frying pan makes a good substitute, as does a griddle. Jagdessh also uses a special rolling pin that is thicker in the middle, but a regular one works just fine. Eat chapatis warm.

Put the flour in a medium-size bowl. Dissolve the salt in the $\frac{3}{4}$ cup water. Add the water mixture to the flour and combine with your fingertips or a spoon, until the flakes of dough start to come together. If necessary, gradually work in additional water, about 1 tablespoon at a time, to make a very sticky dough.

Jagdessh's method at this point is to pour the water into her cupped hand, sprinkling it over the dry dough and working it in, discarding any excess water. After you've made this dough several times, you will be able to master her traditional technique.

Using unfloured knuckles, knead the dough in the bowl very thoroughly. When the dough feels firm and elastic, but still slightly sticky, cover the bowl with plastic wrap and let stand for 5 to 10 minutes. The dough should become firmer and no longer sticky.

Put a little flour in a shallow dish. Lightly flour a work surface. Using floured fingers, pull off eight walnut-size pieces of dough. Between your floured palms, roll each piece of dough into a ball. Flatten each ball into a disk with a lump in the middle by rotating the dough between the palm of one hand and the fingers of the other hand. Use your fingers to press and gently pull out the rim, turning the dough to make a circle. The disk will be about $2\frac{1}{2}$ to 3 inches in diameter.

Press the disk into the dish of flour to lightly coat it on both sides. Then roll it out with a rolling pin into a circle about 7 inches across and $\frac{1}{8}$ inch thick. (Jagdessh likes to stretch the dough more by flipping it from hand to hand.)

Heat the tava, frying pan, or griddle over moderately high heat until very hot, but do not add any oil or the kitchen will fill with smoke. When the pan is the proper temperature, a pinch of flour sprinkled into the pan will brown in 3 seconds. Cook a chapati in the pan for about 30 seconds, or until the color of the upper surface changes. Using your fingers or a thin-bladed metal spatula, flip the chapati over so the speckled, cooked surface is on top. Cook for about 30 seconds longer. Flip it over again and use a dry dish towel to press down the edges of the chapati as it rises and puffs up, so the bread cooks evenly. Flip the chapati again and repeat with the other side. Lift out of the pan, place on a clean dish towel, and lightly brush the top with ghee, clarified butter, or melted unsalted butter. As you cook them, keep the chapatis hot on a baking sheet in a 250F oven, loosely covered with foil. Serve hot.

JAGDESSH USES HER FINGERS TO MIX TOGETHER THE FLOUR AND $\frac{3}{4}$ CUP SALT WATER.

SHE SPRINKLES EXTRA WATER THROUGH HER CUPPED HANDS INTO THE DOUGH, IF IT IS DRY.

THE FLAKES OF DOUGH COME TOGETHER AS IT IS MIXED.

USING UNFLOURED KNUCKLES, SHE KNEADS THE DOUGH IN THE BOWL.

USING FLOURED FINGERS, JAGDESSH PULLS OFF WALNUT-SIZE PIECES OF DOUGH.

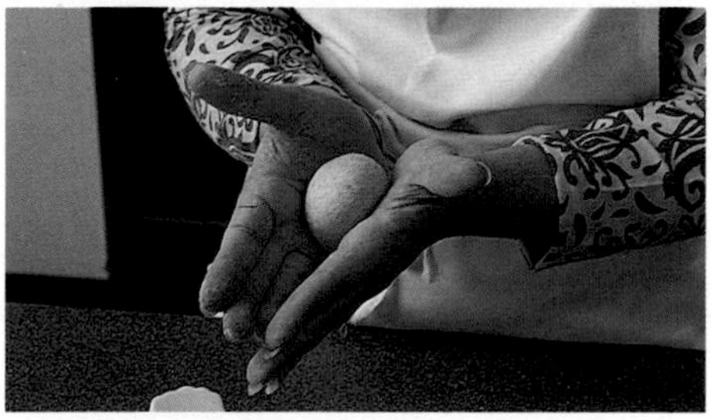

SHE SHAPES EACH PIECE OF DOUGH INTO A BALL BY ROLLING IT BETWEEN HER FLOURED PALMS.

OPPOSITE
No Indian meal is complete without a selection of flat breads to accompany the exotically spiced dishes. In Indian homes, the breads are often used for scooping up foods, removing the need for forks and spoons. When Indian food is served in Western homes or in restaurants, however, it is usually eaten with silverware. This meal includes naan (foreground), as well as chapatis (middle) and parathas (background).

TO SHAPE A CHAPATI, JAGDESSH ROTATES A BALL OF DOUGH BETWEEN HER PALM AND FINGERS.

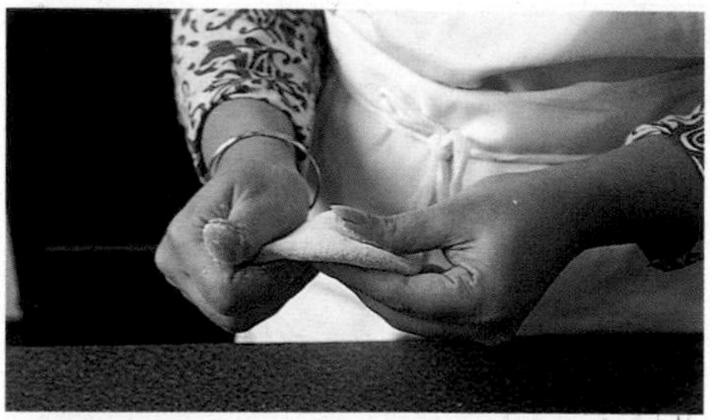

SHE THEN USES HER FINGERS TO PRESS AND GENTLY PULL OUT THE RIM, TURNING THE DOUGH TO MAKE A CIRCLE.

USING AN INDIAN-STYLE ROLLING PIN, SHE ROLLS THE FLOURED DOUGH INTO A 7-INCH CIRCLE.

SHE THEN FLIPS THE CIRCLE FROM HAND TO HAND SEVERAL TIMES TO STRETCH THE FRAGILE DOUGH.

SHE USES HER FINGERS TO FLIP THE CHAPATI OVER AFTER IT HAS COOKED FOR 30 SECONDS.

USING A FOLDED DISH TOWEL, JAGDESSH PRESSES DOWN ON THE PUFFED AREAS OF THE CHAPATI SO IT COOKS EVENLY.

POORIS

INGREDIENTS

Makes eight pooris.
1 recipe Chapati dough (page 56)
additional flour for shaping
vegetable oil for frying

one or two baking sheets, lined with paper towels for draining
a heavy, deep, 10-inch frying pan

These use the same dough as chapatis, but they are smaller and puffed up like pillows because they are cooked in hot fat, rather than in a dry pan.

Prepare the dough and shape and roll it as for Chapatis, making the circles only 5 inches in diameter. Heat about 1 inch of oil in the frying pan over moderately high heat until it reaches 375F. Add one poori to the oil. At first it will sink to the bottom of the pan, then it will float and begin to puff up. Turn it over using two slotted spoons or a large skimmer and a metal spoon. Spoon some oil over the top, then turn it over again. It will puff up more after turning. This whole cooking process will take about $1\frac{1}{2}$ minutes. The poori will puff up like an overstuffed pillow and be very lightly speckled with brown.

Using the two spoons, lift the poori from the oil and let it drain a second or so over the pan, then transfer to the baking sheets lined with paper towels. Repeat with the remaining pooris.

Serve each poori immediately after it is fried and drained.

PARATHAS

INGREDIENTS

Makes eight parathas.
1 recipe Chapati dough (page 56)
additional flour for shaping
ghee (page 56), clarified butter, or melted unsalted butter

a tava, a 10-inch cast-iron frying pan, or a heavy griddle

A cooked paratha contains crisp layers of rich dough.

Parathas are made in a similar way to chapatis, with the same dough, but they are flakier and richer. The chapati dough is brushed with ghee, folded several times, and cooked with more ghee on a tava, a frying pan, or a griddle to make a crisp, rich, flaky bread. Serve parathas as soon as possible after cooking.

Prepare and divide the dough as for Chapatis. Roll each piece of dough into a ball. Press the ball of dough in a small bowl of flour, turning it over so it is lightly dusted on both sides. Roll out the dough into a circle, about 5 inches across and $\frac{1}{8}$ inch thick.

Lightly brush some melted ghee, clarified butter, or melted unsalted butter over the circles of dough. Fold each into thirds like an envelope – top third down and bottom third up. Fold the ends in to make a square package of dough. Dip all sides of the dough in the flour. Roll out the package with a rolling pin, turning the dough to make a 7-inch square about $\frac{1}{8}$ inch thick. It is traditional to flip the square from hand to hand a couple of times to stretch the dough.

Heat a tava, frying pan, or griddle until very hot, but do not add any oil. When the tava, frying pan, or griddle is the proper temperature, a pinch of flour sprinkled into the pan will brown in 30 seconds. Cook the paratha in the hot pan for 30 seconds. Flip it over and cook the second side about 30 seconds. Turn the paratha over again and lightly brush the top with ghee, clarified butter, or melted unsalted butter. Turn the paratha over and brush the other side as before. The cooked paratha should be crisp, speckled with brown patches, and slightly puffy. As you cook them, keep the parathas warm on a platter or baking sheet in a single layer, uncovered, in a 250F oven.

TO DEVELOP THE FLAKY LAYERS, JAGDESSH FOLDS THE DOUGH LIKE AN ENVELOPE. SHE THEN FOLDS THE ENDS IN TO MAKE A SQUARE PACKAGE OF DOUGH.

SHE DIPS ALL SIDES OF THE DOUGH INTO FLOUR BEFORE SHE ROLLS IT OUT.

SHE FLIPS THE DOUGH BETWEEN HER HANDS SEVERAL TIMES TO STRETCH IT.

SHE SPREADS MELTED GHEE ON EACH SIDE OF THE PARATHA AS IT COOKS. YOU CAN ALSO USE MELTED CLARIFIED BUTTER OR BUTTER. IT IS THE EXTRA FAT THAT GIVES THE PARATHA ITS RICHNESS.

NAAN

INGREDIENTS

Makes eight naan.

$1\frac{3}{4}$ cups self-rising white flour

2 tablespoons plain yogurt, preferably with active cultures

1 teaspoon kosher salt or flaked sea salt

about $\frac{1}{2}$ cup lukewarm water (95F to 105F)

Naan is a Punjabi leavened bread made with white flour and yogurt, which ferments the dough and adds flavor. Jagdessh prefers to use the chemical leavening agents in self-rising flour, rather than yeast, to raise this bread.

These breads are traditionally baked in a clay oven sunk into the ground, called a tandoor. *Although restaurants often have a* tandoor, *few Indian homes – let alone houses in England or the U.S. – do, so Jagdessh cooks her naan under a very hot broiler. Other home cooks use heated baking sheets in an oven heated on the maximum setting, but Jagdessh says her method works best – and I can vouch that the results are excellent. Jagdessh also makes flavored naan. She rolls out the dough and brushes it lightly with melted ghee (page 56) as below. Then she presses cumin or sesame seeds or a little minced onion into the dough before broiling.*

Serve naan warm.

Combine the flour, yogurt, and salt in a large bowl. Add the lukewarm water, 1 tablespoon at a time, working it into the flour mixture with your fingers and bringing the flakes of dough together. Add just enough water to make a soft, slightly sticky dough.

Knead the dough roughly in the bowl for a couple of seconds, then cover with a damp dish towel and let stand in a warm spot so the dough ferments, about 1 hour. During the last 15 minutes of standing time, heat the broiler and broiler pan.

Flour your fingers and pull off a piece of dough about the size of a walnut. Between your palms, form the dough into a ball, then roll it out with a rolling pin on an unfloured work surface into an oval 8 to 9 inches long and about $\frac{1}{3}$ inch thick. Repeat with the remaining dough to make eight naan.

Put one naan on the hot broiler pan and broil, about 3 to 4 inches from the source of heat, until it puffs up and is speckled with brown spots. Naan cook very quickly, in about 30 seconds, so watch it constantly. Turn it over and cook the second side. Repeat with the remaining seven naan.

JAGDESSH ADDS WATER THROUGH HER FINGERS UNTIL THE DOUGH IS SOFT AND SLIGHTLY STICKY.

USING FLOURED FINGERS, SHE PULLS OFF WALNUT-SIZE PIECES OF DOUGH.

SHE ROLLS OUT EACH BALL OF DOUGH INTO AN OVAL, 8 TO 9 INCHES LONG.

SHE BROILS THE NAAN FOR ABOUT 30 SECONDS ON EACH SIDE UNTIL IT IS PUFFED AND SPECKLED WITH BROWN. IT IS THEN READY TO SERVE.

MIDDLE EASTERN BREADS

Claudia Roden, who has written the definitive book on Middle Eastern food, A New Book of Middle Eastern Food (Viking, 1986), says that for some in the Middle East, bread, more than any other food, is considered a direct gift from God. Middle Eastern and Indian flat breads must be first cousins, as there are so many similarities. The crackerlike lavash, although leavened with yeast, is cooked rapidly on a very hot, ungreased pan, as are chapatis. Pita bread, also made with yeast, is like naan – thin, soft, and flat – and it is cooked rapidly, in the oven, where it puffs up spectacularly. Like Indian breads, lavash and pitas are used for scooping up dips and sauces. Pitas, which have an inside "pocket," can also be stuffed with meat, kabobs, vegetables, or felafel.

PITA BREAD

INGREDIENTS

Makes twelve pitas.

- 1 cake compressed fresh yeast (0.6 ounce), or 1 envelope active dry yeast (2½ teaspoons) plus ½ teaspoon granulated sugar
- 1¼ cups lukewarm water (95F to 105F)
- 1 tablespoon olive oil
- 3½ to 4 cups white bread flour (preferably unbleached and stone-ground)
- 1¼ teaspoons kosher salt or flaked sea salt

a heavy baking sheet

Pita bread, the daily bread of the Middle East, should not be flabby or leathery, as are many commercial versions. If your pitas are tough, replace half of the bread flour with unbleached all-purpose flour to reduce the gluten content. This will make the flour mixture softer and the baked pitas more tender. Cool pitas for at least 10 minutes before eating, or cool them completely and store in plastic bags or freeze.

Crumble the fresh yeast into a large bowl. Mix in ¼ cup of the lukewarm water until smooth. If using dry yeast, mix the granules and the sugar with ¼ cup of the lukewarm water and let stand until foamy, 5 to 10 minutes (page 18). Stir the remaining 1 cup lukewarm water and the olive oil into the yeast mixture.

Add about 1 cup of the flour and the salt to the yeast mixture in the large bowl, beating with your hand to make a smooth batter. Add enough of the remaining flour, ½ cup at a time, to make a soft dough. As you begin to add the flour, first beat the batter with your hand or a wooden spoon; as the dough becomes firmer, vigorously knead in the flour with lightly floured hands working in the bowl. The dough should eventually become soft, but not sticky. Turn out the dough onto a lightly floured work surface. Cover it with a sheet of plastic wrap and let it rest for about 5 minutes.

Knead the dough with lightly floured hands until it becomes smooth, silky, shiny, and firm, but still elastic, 3 to 5 minutes, adding more flour as needed. (My Turkish friend Zeynep says it should feel like a baby's bottom.) Wash and dry the bowl and oil it. Put the dough in the bowl and turn the dough over so the top is oiled. Cover with a damp dish towel. Let the dough rise at room temperature until doubled in size, about 1½ hours.

Punch down the dough, and turn it out onto a lightly floured work surface. Weigh the dough and divide it into twelve equal pieces, or roll it into a fat rope and cut it into twelfths. Roll each piece between your palms into a rough ball. Form each one into a smooth ball (see Oatmeal Rolls, page 25). Place the balls on the work surface, cover with

A PITA BREAD BEGINS TO PUFF UP AFTER IT HAS BEEN IN THE OVEN FOR 1 MINUTE.

AFTER 2 MINUTES IT PUFFS EVEN MORE.

a dry dish towel or sheet of plastic wrap, and let rest for 10 minutes. This helps the dough to relax, making it easier to roll out.

Using a very lightly floured rolling pin, roll out each ball on a very lightly floured work surface into a round, about 6 inches across and ¼ inch thick. (If they are too thin they will become crisp, like crackers, when baked.) Rolling them out takes a bit of practice because the dough will spring back. Lay the dough rounds on floured dish towels or a floured baking sheet and let stand at room temperature until they puff up slightly, about 30 minutes. During the last 15 minutes of standing, heat the oven to 500F. Place the baking sheet on a shelf of the oven to heat up. (Nonstick ones work well, as do well-seasoned old baking sheets. If you have only newer ones, they may need to be very lightly greased.)

Wearing very thick oven mitts, transfer a round to the very hot baking sheet and lightly mist or sprinkle it with water to keep it pale. If you prefer, and they fit, you can bake more than one at a time. Bake for 2 minutes, without opening the door. After checking that it hasn't browned too much, bake for another minute or so (depending on how hot your oven gets) until the pita is puffed like a pillow, yet still pale. If the pita starts to brown before it is firm, lower the oven temperature slightly. Transfer the pitas to a wire rack and let stand until just warm. Then cover with a dry dish towel to keep the crust soft. Bake the remaining rounds in the same way.

LAVASH

This bread is rolled so thin it cooks rapidly to make a bubbly, crisp cracker. If it puffs up like pita or naan, roll the circles thinner (let rest for 10 minutes first). Serve the same day, with mezze (appetizers), such as baba ghanoush, stuffed grape leaves, hummus, taramasalata, and tabbouleh.

INGREDIENTS

Makes about fifteen.

- 2½ cups white bread flour (preferably unbleached and stone-ground)
- ¾ cup whole-wheat pastry flour (preferably stone-ground)
- 1 teaspoon kosher salt or flaked sea salt
- 1 cake compressed fresh yeast (0.6 ounce), or 1 envelope active dry yeast (2¼ teaspoons)
- plus ½ teaspoon granulated sugar
- about 1¼ cups lukewarm water (95F–105F)
- extra flour for dusting

griddle, or cast-iron or other heavy frying pan

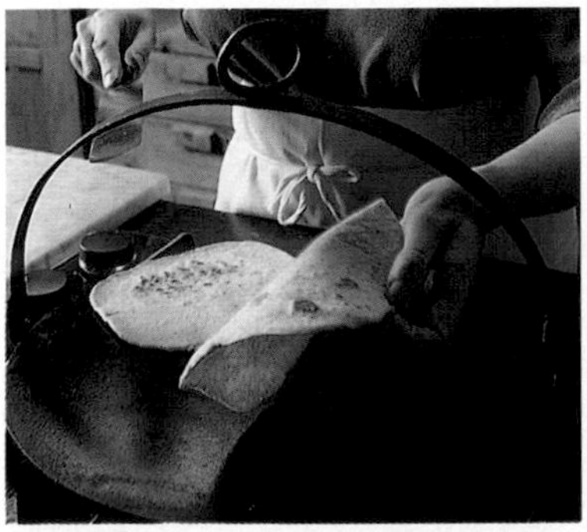

REMOVE EACH LAVASH FROM THE GRIDDLE WHEN THE TOPS OF THE BUBBLES ARE LIGHTLY BROWNED.

Stir together the flours and salt in a large bowl. Make a well in the centre of the flour mixture. Crumble the fresh yeast into another bowl and stir in ½ cup of the lukewarm water until smooth. If using dry yeast, mix the granules and the ½ teaspoon sugar with ½ cup of the lukewarm water and let stand until foamy, 5–10 minutes (page 18). Add the yeast mixture to the well in the flour. Stir in the flour from the bowl with your hand or a wooden spoon to make a soft, but not sticky dough. If the dough is dry and crumbly, add as much of the remaining water as needed, one tablespoon at a time.

Turn out the dough onto a lightly floured work surface and knead for about 5 minutes until smooth. Put the dough back into the bowl, cover with a damp dish towel and let rise at room temperature, away from drafts, until doubled in size – about 1 hour. Punch down the dough and turn out onto a floured work surface. Weigh the dough and divide into 15 equal walnut-size pieces, or roll it into a fat rope and divide into 15 pieces. Shape into smooth balls as for Pita Bread (left), cover with a dry dish towel or sheet of plastic wrap and let rise for 30 minutes.

Working with one ball at a time, roll out each as thinly as possible on a very lightly floured surface with a very lightly floured rolling pin to make an almost translucent round, about 5 inches across, using as little flour as possible. Stack the rolled-out dough between sheets of waxed paper, if you like. Heat the griddle or frying pan until very hot. Gently dust off any excess flour (the flour will scorch in the pan, causing black specks – you may need to wipe out the pan after cooking each). Cook the round for about 1 minute, then flip it over and briefly cook the other side (30 seconds at the most) – the bread should be lightly browned on top of the bubbles which have formed. Remove with a spatula to a wire rack to cool. Cook the remaining dough in the same way. If your griddle is large enough, you can cook two breads at once. Cool in single layers on wire racks.

BRANCH BREAD

INGREDIENTS

Makes twelve crispbreads.
$2\frac{1}{2}$ cups unbleached all-purpose flour
$\frac{3}{4}$ cup medium rye flour
$\frac{3}{4}$ cup whole-wheat bread flour (preferably stone-ground)
$1\frac{1}{2}$ teaspoons kosher salt or flaked sea salt
$1\frac{1}{2}$ teaspoons granulated sugar
$1\frac{1}{4}$ cups milk
2 tablespoons unsalted butter
water for brushing
additional kosher salt or flaked sea salt

two baking sheets, lightly greased

USING A SHARP KNIFE, CUT A SERIES OF CHEVRONS IN THE DOUGH.

I have my friend Stephen Pouncey to thank for this Icelandic recipe, which he gleaned and translated on a deer-stalking trip in Sweden. Branch bread is a crispbread – made without yeast, and designed to keep. If you are in a hurry, however, choose another recipe, as these take some time to roll and bake. When rolling out the dough, it should be as thin as a flower petal.

Branch bread is good to serve with soups, cheeses, pâtés and dips. It is also excellent for feeding to teething babies (without the salt topping). After cooling, store carefully in an airtight container because these are very fragile. They will keep for up to one month.

Mix together the flours, salt, and sugar in a large bowl. Make a well in the center.

Heat the milk in a small saucepan over moderately low heat until small bubbles appear around the edges. Remove the milk from the heat and stir in the butter. When the butter has melted, pour the hot liquid into the well in the flour mixture. Stir the flours into the liquid using a wooden spoon. As soon as the dough becomes cool enough to handle, work it into a smooth dough with your hands, pressing the dough together to eliminate any lumps, as if making shortbread, rather than kneading it.

Turn out the dough onto a lightly floured work surface and cover with the upturned bowl; the dough should be lukewarm (95F to 105F). Let the dough rest for 30 minutes. Heat the oven to 425F.

Divide the dough into twelve equal pieces. Roll out each piece as thinly as possible into a round. Each will take nearly 5 minutes to roll. Using a 9- to $9\frac{1}{2}$-inch dinner plate as a guide, trim the dough; discard the scraps. Transfer one round to each prepared baking sheet, lifting it carefully, or sliding the baking sheet underneath. Using a sharp knife, cut a series of chevrons in the dough to make a spruce tree design.

Brush the dough very lightly with water and sprinkle with the additional salt to taste. Bake two breads at a time until lightly browned, slightly puffy, and crisp, 8 to 10 minutes. Keep your eye on them, as they bake very quickly. Transfer the breads to wire racks to cool completely. Repeat with the remaining dough.

During the baking, the chevrons in branch bread open out to look like the branches of a spruce tree.

Quaintly old-fashioned, toasted crumpets remain a favorite afternoon teatime treat. Serve them hot with good-quality butter.

CRUMPETS OR "LES ÉPONGES"

Well-made crumpets – light, with large air holes, and very tasty – are absolutely scrumptious. The rubbery commercial ones I have found in England are travesties best avoided. In the States, English muffins resemble crumpets more than they do our English muffins, but crumpets have a moist, almost damp crumb. Crumpets are eaten whole, not split in two, either hot from the griddle or toasted, and spread with butter. Do not stint on the butter. Crumpets also freeze well, and you can toast them straight from the freezer. Les éponges is what a young French friend calls these crumpets, and the name has stuck.

Fellow food writer Elaine Hallgarten gave me a copy of The Modern Baker Confectioner and Caterer, *by Master Baker John Kirkland, published in 1907, and his advice and recipe remain invaluable. I have found the combination of flours in this recipe works well.*

INGREDIENTS

Makes about fifteen crumpets.

- 1½ cups white bread flour (preferably unbleached and stone-ground)
- 1½ cups unbleached all-purpose flour
- ¼ teaspoon cream of tartar
- 1 cake compressed fresh yeast (0.6 ounce), or 1 envelope active dry yeast (2¼ teaspoons) plus ½ teaspoon granulated sugar
- 2¼ cups lukewarm water (95F to 105F)
- 2 teaspoons kosher salt or flaked sea salt
- ½ teaspoon baking soda
- ½ cup lukewarm milk (95F to 105F)

- a heavy nonstick griddle or a heavy 10-inch nonstick or cast-iron frying pan
- four 3⅛- to 3½-inch crumpet rings, insides well greased with melted unsalted butter

Sift together the flours and cream of tartar into a large bowl. Crumble the fresh yeast into a medium-size bowl. Mix in the lukewarm water until smooth. If using dry yeast, mix the granules and the sugar with ¾ cup of the lukewarm water and let stand until foamy, 5 to 10 minutes (page 18). Stir in the remaining 1½ cups of lukewarm water.

Mix the yeast mixture into the flour to make a very thick, but smooth batter, beating vigorously with your hand or a wooden spoon for 2 minutes. Cover the bowl with plastic wrap and let stand in a warm spot until the batter is doubled in volume, about 1 hour.

Add the salt and beat the batter for about 1 minute. Then cover the bowl and let stand in a warm spot until the batter increases in volume by about one-half, 15 to 20 minutes.

Dissolve the baking soda in the lukewarm milk. Then gently stir it into the batter. The batter should not be too stiff or your crumpets will be "blind" – without holes – so it is best to test one before cooking the whole batch.

Heat an ungreased, very clean griddle or frying pan over moderately low heat for about 3 minutes until moderately hot; your palm will feel warm when held 1½ inches above the griddle for about 30 seconds. Put a well-buttered crumpet ring on the griddle and heat for 15 seconds. Spoon or pour $\frac{1}{3}$ cup of the batter into the ring. The amount of batter will depend on the size of your crumpet ring.

As soon as the batter is poured into the ring, it should begin to form bubbles. If bubbles do not form, add a little more lukewarm water, a tablespoon at a time, to the batter in the bowl and try again. If the batter is too thin and runs out under the ring, gently work in a little more all-purpose flour and try again. As soon as the top surface is set and covered with bubbles, 7 to 8 minutes, the crumpet is ready to flip over.

To flip the crumpet, remove the ring with a towel or tongs, then turn the crumpet carefully with a spatula. The top, cooked side should be chestnut brown. Cook the second, holey side of the crumpet for 2 to 3 minutes, or until pale golden. The crumpet should be about $\frac{3}{4}$ inch thick. Once the batter is the proper consistency, continue with the remaining batter, cooking the crumpets in batches, three or four at a time. Remove the crumpet from the griddle. Butter the crumpet rings well after each use.

BEAT THE BATTER VIGOROUSLY WITH YOUR HAND UNTIL IT IS THICK AND SMOOTH.

GENTLY STIR IN THE MILK MIXTURE.

SPOON OR POUR ABOUT $\frac{1}{3}$ CUP BATTER INTO EACH BUTTERED CRUMPET RING.

USING A DISH TOWEL, EASE OFF THE RING WHEN THE UPPER SURFACE IS HOLEY.

USING A SPATULA, FLIP THE UNMOLDED CRUMPET OVER AND COOK 2 TO 3 MINUTES LONGER. THE HOLEY SIDE SHOULD BE PALE GOLDEN.

A cozy afternoon tea with homemade muffins (front) and crumpets in front of a roaring fire is just the thing to brighten up a damp, cold British winter's day.

A plate of freshly made pikelets are kept warm next to the fire. Pikelets are the northern cousins of crumpets, traditionally made in Derbyshire, Yorkshire, and Lancashire. They are cooked on a griddle like crumpets, but without the restraining rings. As a result, they look like small, thin pancakes.

To make pikelets, use the ingredients for Crumpets (page 65), but increase the amount of milk to $1\frac{1}{4}$ cups. Make the batter the same way, then drop 2 tablespoons batter in pools directly onto a hot, ungreased griddle or cast-iron frying pan. Cook for about 3 minutes on each side. This should yield about 30 pikelets.

ENGLISH MUFFINS

Early in the 20th century, Master Baker John Kirkland (page 65) wrote that these muffins are different in almost every respect from crumpets: "Muffins are thick, extremely light fermented dough cakes, not holey or tough, three inches across and almost two inches thick." He recommended using flour with a moderately strong gluten level for best results, and I find that this mixture of flours works well.

The dough is very soft indeed, and that, along with the three risings, gives the muffins their lightness. They are nothing like the rubbery raisin and bran ones sold commercially, or the really disappointing "sourdough English muffins" I came across in New England supermarkets. To American tastes, these will not be what is usually expected in an English muffin; English muffins in the States are more like our crumpets. But please do try this recipe; it's not at all difficult and the results are truly delicious.

INGREDIENTS

Makes eight muffins.

- 2½ cups white bread flour (preferably unbleached and stone-ground)
- ¾ cup unbleached all-purpose flour
- 2 teaspoons kosher salt or flaked sea salt
- 1 cake compressed fresh yeast (0.6 ounce) or 1 envelope active dry yeast (2½ teaspoons)
- ½ teaspoon granulated sugar
- 1 cup lukewarm water (95F to 105F)
- ½ cup lukewarm milk (95F to 105F)
- cornmeal, rice flour, or corn flour for dusting

two or four baking sheets
a heavy griddle or a 10-inch, cast-iron frying pan

The "proper" way to eat English muffins is to open them slightly with a fork at the middle joint, toast them on both sides, and then tear them open with the fork and spread thickly with butter. Store them wrapped at room temperature or freeze them.

Mix the flours with the salt in a large bowl and warm the bowl of flour (page 15). This will help the yeast start working and give the muffins their light texture.

Crumble the fresh yeast into a small bowl. Mix in the sugar and ½ cup of the lukewarm water until smooth. If using dry yeast, mix the granules and the sugar with ½ cup of the lukewarm water and let stand until foamy, 5 to 10 minutes (page 18).

Make a well in the warmed flour. Add the yeast mixture, the remaining lukewarm water, and the milk and mix with your hand to make a very soft, slightly sticky dough. Turn out the dough onto a lightly floured work surface and knead with floured hands for 10 minutes until the dough is soft, elastic, smooth, and no longer sticky. Shape the dough into a ball.

Clean and dry the bowl and oil it. Return the dough to the bowl and turn the dough over so the top is oiled. Cover with a damp dish towel. Let rise in a warm spot, away from drafts, until doubled in size, about 1 hour.

Punch down the dough and turn it out onto a lightly floured surface. Knead it again for 5 minutes. Return the dough to the bowl and cover again. Let rest for 30 minutes.

Divide the dough into eight pieces. According to John Kirkland, "The usual method is to squeeze the dough through a ring made by the thumb and forefinger of one floured hand," and this is the method I use. Squeeze off the ball of dough and drop it on to a baking sheet well dusted with cornmeal, rice flour, or corn flour. Sprinkle the dough with more cornmeal, rice flour, or corn flour. Cover the tray of muffins with another baking tray, then a damp dish towel. Let rise in a warm spot for 30 minutes.

Heat a griddle or frying pan about 2 minutes over moderate heat until moderately hot. With a metal spatula, invert the muffins, three at a time, onto the hot griddle. Cook about 12 minutes or until the undersides are golden brown. Turn the muffins over and cook 10 to 12 minutes longer, or until the second side is browned and the sides of the muffins spring back when gently touched. Transfer the muffins to a warm serving platter and cover with a dry dish towel. Wipe out the griddle or pan with a cloth and continue cooking the remaining muffins.

USE YOUR HAND TO MIX A VERY SOFT, SLIGHTLY STICKY DOUGH.

DIVIDE THE DOUGH INTO BALLS BY SQUEEZING IT THROUGH YOUR THUMB AND FOREFINGER.

COVER THE DOUGH BALLS WITH A BAKING SHEET, THEN A TOWEL AND LET RISE.

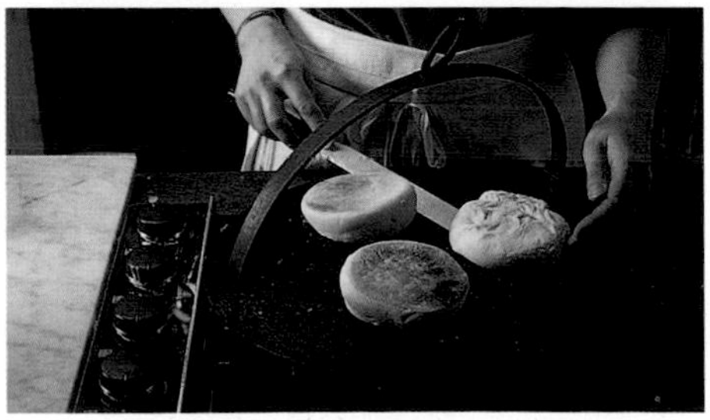

USING A SPATULA, FLIP OVER EACH MUFFIN SO BOTH SIDES ARE GOLDEN BROWN.

HOE CAKES

"Do not think of making this recipe unless you have good bacon fat," says Caroll Boltin, adamantly. "They will be tasteless." She has spent many years researching the American pioneers and their early settlements in New York State's Hudson Valley.

"This was a fast way to have bread in colonial times. It was cheap, easy, and quick, and everyone had bacon fat in the larder." The simple, gritty cornmeal batter was cooked over the open fire in a flat garden hoe – hence the name – and eaten immediately with soup or a vegetable stew.

This is Caroll's recipe, which she often makes at Philipsburg Manor, a historic restoration in North

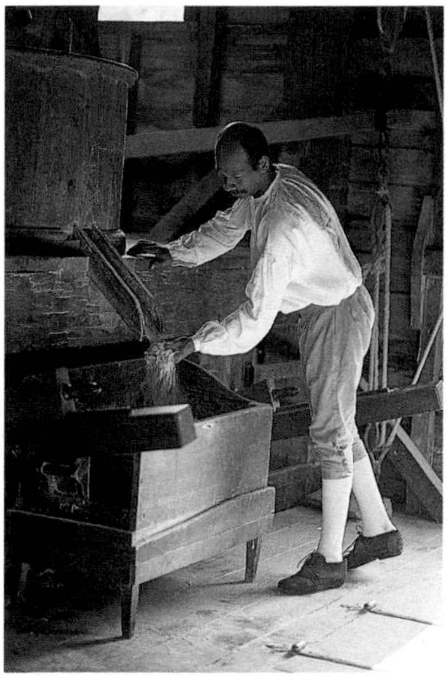

The water-powered mill at Philipsburg Manor (right), on the Pocantico River at North Tarrytown, New York, has been grinding and selling cornmeal since early in the 18th century. Here, miller Peter Curtis employs a traditional grinding method similar to those used by the Manor's earliest millers.

Tarrytown, New York, to illustrate what 17th-century life was like. To cook the cakes, wealthier settlers would have used a spider, a kettle with built-in legs that sat in the fireplace, but a heavy cast-iron frying pan on the stove top works just as well for the modern cook.

Be sure to eat these cakes while they're still hot; they do not keep well.

INGREDIENTS

Makes about two dozen small cakes.

- $1\frac{1}{3}$ cups yellow cornmeal (preferably stone-ground)
- $\frac{1}{2}$ teaspoon kosher salt or flaked sea salt
- about $2\frac{1}{2}$ cups boiling water
- bacon fat (see Note) or vegetable oil, for cooking

- a heavy 10-inch, cast-iron or nonstick frying pan
- a baking sheet lined with paper towels for draining

Mix together the cornmeal and salt in a small bowl, then stir in enough of the boiling water to make a sloppy batter that barely holds its shape, similar to a pancake batter. Let stand for 5 minutes.

Heat a frying pan on the stove over moderately high heat or over the glowing embers of a fire – there should be no flames – until hot, about 2 minutes.

Add plenty of bacon fat or vegetable oil to the hot pan so it is about $\frac{1}{4}$ inch deep. Heat the fat about 2 to 3 minutes until the surface is rippling and a small bit of the batter bubbles as soon as it is dropped into the fat. Drop the batter by generous tablespoons into the pan. Do not crowd the pan; the cakes should be cooked in batches. Cook the cakes until the undersides are golden and crisp, 1 to 2 minutes. Flip the cakes over with two slotted spatulas and cook the other side 1 to 2 minutes until browned and crisp. Transfer to the baking sheets lined with paper towels to drain. Adjust the heat as necessary to maintain the temperature of the fat, and continue to cook the remaining cakes.

NOTE: You'll need about $\frac{2}{3}$ cup of bacon fat to cook these in, about the amount rendered from 1 pound of bacon.

MADDYBENNY FADGE

INGREDIENTS

Makes eighteen fadge.

- 1 pound all-purpose potatoes, peeled, boiled, drained, and freshly mashed
- 2 tablespoons unsalted butter
- $\frac{1}{2}$ teaspoon kosher salt or flaked sea salt, or to taste
- about $\frac{3}{4}$ cup unbleached all-purpose flour
- bacon fat or vegetable oil, for frying
- a griddle or a heavy frying pan

This recipe comes from Rosemary White, of Maddybenny Farm, Portrush, Northern Ireland. I met her when she won the Great Irish Breakfast award for her farmhouse bed and breakfast a few years ago; the judge had said, "Her breakfast was magnificent, and the presentation faultless." To win the prize, Rosemary prepared her famous Ulster Fry – lean, crisp bacon, meaty sausages, mushrooms, apple rings, and eggs accompanied by fadge, the local potato cakes, and her Maddybenny Wheaten Bread (page 79). The secret of a good breakfast, Rosemary says, is freshness. "I never start to cook for my guests in the morning till I see the whites of their eyes." Serve fadge hot.

Put the hot mashed potatoes in a large bowl. Add the butter and salt. Knead in the flour, adding just enough to bind the potatoes, making a soft, but not sticky dough. Too much flour will make the dough tough. Cover and chill for several hours or overnight.

Roll out the dough with a lightly floured rolling pin on a lightly floured work surface to a $\frac{1}{2}$ inch thickness. Cut into triangles or squares. Heat a griddle or cast-iron frying pan over moderately high heat. Add a little bacon fat or oil to the griddle, just enough to prevent the fadge from sticking. Cook the fadge in batches until brown on one side, about 1 minute. Turn the fadge over and cook the second side until brown. Keep warm in a 250F oven while cooking the remainder. Add more fat to the griddle as needed.

NOTE: The exact amount of flour needed for this recipe and Manx Potato Cakes (below) depends on the consistency of the mashed potatoes. The dough should be soft, but not sticky. Do not mash the potatoes or make the dough in a food processor – the machine will make the results gluey and disgusting.

ROLL OUT THE DOUGH ON A LIGHTLY FLOURED WORK SURFACE, THEN CUT IT INTO TRIANGLES OR SQUARES.

RIGHT
A sizzling farmhouse breakfast of fadge, crisp bacon, mushrooms and a sunny-side-up egg.

MANX POTATO CAKES

INGREDIENTS

Makes about nine.

- 1 pound all-purpose potatoes, peeled, boiled, drained, and freshly mashed
- $\frac{1}{2}$ teaspoon kosher salt or flaked sea salt,
- plenty of freshly ground black pepper
- 2 tablespoons unsalted butter
- 1 large egg, lightly beaten
- $\frac{1}{4}$ cup shredded aged sharp Cheddar cheese
- about $\frac{3}{4}$ cup self-rising white flour (see Maddybenny Fadge, Note, above)
- bacon fat or vegetable oil, for frying
- a griddle or a heavy frying pan

My Manx grandmother (from the Isle of Man), who prided herself on keeping a good table and a larder, made these potato cakes for high tea to go with ham and poached eggs. These are richer than the Maddybenny Fadge (above). Eat immediately after cooking.

Prepare the dough as for Maddybenny Fadge (above), adding the black pepper, egg, and cheese to the potatoes with the salt and butter. There is no need to chill this dough.

Pull off nine egg-size pieces of dough and roll them between your palms, flouring your hands to prevent sticking, if necessary. Flatten the dough balls to make thin cakes, about 3 inches across and $\frac{1}{4}$ inch thick.

Heat a griddle or cast-iron frying pan over moderately high heat. Add a little bacon fat or oil to the griddle, just enough to prevent the cakes from sticking. Fry the cakes in batches until golden brown, crispy, and slightly puffed, about 3 minutes. Turn the potato cakes over with a metal spatula and cook the second side about 3 minutes longer, until crisp. Add more fat to the griddle as needed.

BLINIS

Blinis are light, crumbly, flavorful, yeast-leavened pancakes. Their intense, slightly bitter taste comes from the speckled gray-brown buckwheat flour. Traditionally, blinis should be eaten with sour cream or melted butter and Beluga or pressed caviar, but these days lumpfish roe, salmon caviar, chopped hard-boiled egg, and/or smoked fish are more usual – and easier on the budget. Eat these while still warm.

INGREDIENTS

Makes about fourteen blinis.

1 cake compressed fresh yeast (0.6 ounce) or 1 envelope active dry yeast (2½ teaspoons)
1 teaspoon granulated sugar
¾ cup lukewarm water (95F to 105F)
1 large egg, separated
1¼ cups buckwheat flour
1 teaspoon kosher salt or flaked sea salt
¾ cup lukewarm milk (95F to 105F)
1 tablespoon unsalted butter, for frying

a nonstick crêpe pan, a heavy frying pan, or a griddle

WHISK THE BATTER UNTIL IT IS VERY THICK.

WHISK IN THE LUKEWARM MILK. THE BATTER SHOULD BE THE CONSISTENCY OF HEAVY CREAM.

Crumble the fresh yeast into a large bowl. Mix in the sugar and ¼ cup of the lukewarm water until smooth. If using dry yeast, mix the granules and the sugar with ¼ cup of the lukewarm water and let stand until foamy, 5 to 10 minutes (page 18).

Whisk the remaining ½ cup lukewarm water and the egg yolk into the yeast mixture. Whisk in the flour and salt to make a very thick batter. Cover with a damp dish towel. Let rise in a warm place, away from drafts, until doubled in volume, 1½ to 2 hours.

Whisk in the lukewarm milk to make a batter the consistency of thick heavy cream. Cover again and let stand in a warm place until small bubbles appear on the surface, about 1 hour. Beat the egg white with a pinch of salt in a small bowl with an electric mixer until it forms stiff peaks, then gently fold it into the batter with a rubber spatula.

Heat a crêpe pan, frying pan, or griddle over moderate heat until moderately hot, 1½ to 2 minutes or until your palm held 1½ inches above the pan feels warm after 15 seconds. Swirl 1 teaspoon of the butter into the pan. When the butter has melted, spoon a scant ¼ cup of batter into the pan and gently spread the batter with the back of a spoon to make a 4-inch pancake. Cook until the edges of the blini have set and small bubbles form on the surface, 2 to 3 minutes. Turn the blini over with a spatula and cook the second side for about 2 minutes, or until dry and the top springs back when pressed lightly in the center with your fingertips. Keep warm in a 300F oven, uncovered, in a single layer, while cooking the remaining batter. Add more butter to the pan as needed.

COOK EACH BLINI UNTIL THE UPPER SURFACE HAS SET, 2 TO 3 MINUTES, THEN TURN THE BLINI OVER WITH A SPATULA AND COOK THE SECOND SIDE ABOUT 2 MINUTES. CONTINUE UNTIL ALL BLINIS ARE SET.

GRIDDLE OATCAKES

INGREDIENTS

Makes twelve oatcakes.

$1\frac{3}{4}$ cups steel-cut oats
$\frac{1}{2}$ teaspoon kosher salt or flaked sea salt
2 tablespoons bacon fat (see Note) or meat drippings, melted
$\frac{1}{4}$ to $\frac{1}{2}$ cup boiling water
all-purpose flour for rolling

two baking sheets
one or two heavy griddles or heavy 12-inch nonstick or cast-iron frying pans
two jelly-roll pans fitted with wire racks

Scottish griddle oatcakes are thin, crumbly, brittle-crisp biscuits made from ground steel-cut oats, salt, lard or good, flavorful meat drippings or bacon fat, and hot water. As there is no leavening, the lightness comes from the steam produced during cooking. The shortness and the taste depend on the fat used – bacon fat adds a good flavor.

Oatcake expert F. Marian McNeill declared, in The Scots Kitchen *(Edinburgh: Blackie, 1929), "Oatcakes are especially good with herring, sardines, cheese, buttermilk, or broth, or spread with butter and marmalade to complete the breakfast." That is surely true, but today you are more likely to see oatcakes in the Scottish Highlands served at tea time with butter, homemade raspberry jam, or a heather honey. In fancy restaurants Scottish soft cheeses are sometimes offered with oatcakes, although these are rarely homemade.*

Medium-ground steel-cut oats are commonly used in the Highlands for oatcakes. In the States, the steel-cut oats sold are usually the coarse-ground type. Even the oats labeled fine-ground are coarser than Scottish medium-ground oats, so I've found it necessary to grind the oats briefly in a food processor to obtain the proper texture. This takes just a minute or so, though.

Triangular curly-edged oatcakes are cooked on a griddle, while a circular variety is baked in the oven.

You need to be careful when making oatcakes because they are likely to become crumbly as you roll them out. If this happens, you can add a few drops of hot water, or gently warm the dough in a very low oven if it has stiffened. According to Master Baker John Kirkland (page 65), "The springing effects [the expansion of the dough when baked] in their turn are modified for good or evil according to the manner in which the dough has been manipulated. If properly handled, the dough will be short and plump. If badly treated, [it will be] thin and hard."

Put the oats in a food processor and grind until they turn mostly to a powder, with a few small bits of oats remaining in it, $1\frac{1}{2}$ to 2 minutes. (This will yield about $1\frac{1}{3}$ cups.) Mix together the oats and salt in a medium-size bowl. Stir in the melted bacon fat or drippings with a rubber spatula until the oats are well coated with the fat. Mix in $\frac{1}{4}$ cup of the boiling water, then add additional water as needed until the mixture binds together. Stir the mixture for 2 minutes until the water is absorbed. The dough should be firm, but not too sticky or crumbly.

With lightly floured hands, press the dough together and divide into two equal-size rough balls. Line each of the baking sheets with waxed paper. Place one of the balls of dough on the baking sheet. With a floured rolling pin, roll the dough into a round, about 10 inches across and $\frac{1}{8}$ inch thick, using your floured hands to press in and re-form the edges if they start to crack or crumble. Cut the round into six triangles with a sharp knife or pastry wheel. Repeat with the other half of the dough. Let the dough triangles dry, uncovered, for 20 minutes.

Heat the oven to 300F. Heat a griddle or frying pan over moderately low heat for about 3 minutes, until moderately hot; your palm will feel warm when held $1\frac{1}{2}$ inches above the griddle after about 30 seconds. To speed up the cooking process you can use two griddles or frying pans, or a griddle and a frying pan – whatever you have – if you like. Do not grease the griddle.

USING A SHARP KNIFE, CUT THE ROLLED-OUT DOUGH INTO SIX TRIANGLES.

COOK THE TRIANGLES UNTIL THE EDGES START TO CURL UPWARD.

Cook the triangles in batches, about three at a time, spaced apart, on the griddle, until they curl upward, 4 to 5 minutes. Turn them over with a metal spatula and cook the second side for about 4 to 5 minutes, until they become paler in color and look cooked. Transfer to the wire racks on the jelly-roll pans in single layers. When all the oatcakes are cooked, place the jelly-roll pans with the oatcakes in the oven to dry out for about 20 minutes. (Catherine Brown, an authority on Scottish cooking, says that to remove excess moisture, oatcakes used to be dried in a special toaster in front of the fire.) Remove the oatcakes from the oven and take the racks off the pans. Let them cool completely and then store them in airtight containers.

PUPUSAS

Anà Sylvia Landeverde, a young professional cook from El Salvador, showed Anthony Blake and me how to make her country's national dish of white cornmeal griddle cakes, which are flavored with cheese and topped with chili-pickled cabbage and carrots. They were delicious, and were scoffed down as they came off the griddle.

INGREDIENTS

Makes eight pupusas.

PICKLED TOPPING:
3 cups finely shredded cabbage
1 cup finely shredded carrots
freshly ground black pepper, to taste
1 teaspoon kosher salt or flaked sea salt
$\frac{1}{2}$ cup white-wine vinegar
1 tablespoon chopped fresh oregano leaves or 1 teaspoon dried, crushed
$\frac{1}{2}$ to 1 teaspoon chopped fresh hot chili pepper, cored and seeded, or to taste

GRIDDLE CAKES:
$1\frac{1}{2}$ cups white cornmeal (masa harina)
$\frac{1}{2}$ teaspoon kosher salt or flaked sea salt
$\frac{3}{4}$ cup cold water from the tap
3 tablespoons fresh lime juice
$\frac{3}{4}$ cup shredded aged sharp Cheddar cheese
vegetable oil for cooking

one or two heavy griddles or heavy 8- to 10-inch cast-iron frying pans

A ready-to-eat pupusa with the pickled vegetable topping.

Prepare the pickled topping at least 2 hours before you plan to eat. Mix together all the topping ingredients together, then cover and let stand at room temperature for 2 hours. Stir well before using.

To prepare the griddle cakes, mix together the cornmeal and salt, then the water and lime juice to make a stiff, clammy dough. Work it together lightly with your fingertips until you have a smooth ball. If the dough is crumbly, add one tablespoon water; if it is sticky, work in a little cornmeal. Cover the dough and let stand for 30 minutes.

Weigh the dough and divide into eight equal pieces. Between your palms, press each ball of dough into a fairly thick cake about $3\frac{1}{2}$ inches in diameter and about 1 inch thick. Place 1 tablespoon of the cheese in the center of each cake, pressing it in firmly. Pinch the edges of the dough together over the cheese, then roll it in your hands so the cheese is securely enclosed. Using your hands, flatten the ball to make a rough disk 4 to $4\frac{1}{2}$ inches across and about $\frac{1}{4}$ inch thick, patting it and turning it with your palms, trying to make sure the cheese doesn't break through the dough. Keep shaped pupusas covered with plastic wrap while you repeat the process with the remaining dough.

Heat the oven to 250F to keep the cooked pupusas warm on a platter, uncovered, while the others cook. (These take a few minutes to cook, so to speed up the process you can use two griddles or two frying pans, thus cooking four pupusas at once.)

Heat the griddle or pan over moderately high heat about 3 minutes, until moderately hot. Lightly brush the griddle with oil. Cook the griddled cakes, two at a time if they fit in your griddle or pan, turning them frequently, reducing the heat if necessary, until the cheese melts and they are speckled with brown and slightly puffy, about 5 minutes. Brush the griddle or pan with oil as needed. When they are all cooked, top with the pickled vegetables and serve immediately.

ANÀ PUTS THE SHREDDED CHEESE IN THE CENTER OF THE THICK DOUGH CAKE.

ANÀ TRANSFERS THE HOT PUPUSA TO A PLATE.

QUICK BREADS

The varied breads in this chapter are called quick breads because the batters are simply mixed and then baked. No lengthy kneading or rising periods are necessary, so you can have freshly baked bread in a short time. They are all made without yeast, relying instead on chemical leavening agents (baking soda and baking powder), which rapidly produce bubbles of gas when they come in contact with moisture and warmth.

To leaven a dough or batter, baking soda, an alkali, must be combined with a slightly acidic dry ingredient like cream of tartar, or with an acidic liquid like buttermilk, sour milk, or a milk and yogurt mixture. Baking soda is also used when doughs contain brown sugar, molasses, any form of citrus, sour cream, or dried fruit. Baking powder is a ready-mixed combination of alkali and acid leavening agents. The gases that baking powder and baking soda produce help the dough to rise, although with not quite the same effect as yeast. Once mixed, the dough or batter is quickly shaped or spooned into the pan. There is no need for prolonged kneading with these breads, as the gluten in the flour should not be developed; for this reason, softer flours – all-purpose or self-rising flour (all-purpose flour with baking powder and salt added) – are used instead of strong, high-gluten bread flours. The finished dough should be baked immediately, while the leaveners are still active.

OPPOSITE *A morning's baking.* ABOVE *A bemused lad at afternoon tea.*

Most of these breads cook fairly rapidly, and you will find they have a denser texture than yeast breads and they stale more quickly. Enriching the dough with butter or oil, eggs, or fruit helps to produce a longer-keeping loaf. These are sweet and savory breads to accompany meals, take along on picnics, have in the kitchen for ready snacks, or serve with a cup of tea to revive sagging spirits late in the afternoon. Fresh Soda Bread (page 88) is a real morning treat, and Blueberry Muffins Hertz (page 76) are always welcomed for breakfast, as a snack, or in packed lunches. I often include Bacon Loaf (page 80) when I am planning the menu for a party, as it is good to serve with a selection of cheese.

On chilly winter days, try the Herb Rolls (page 82) with steaming vegetable soups. The flavor of the fresh herbs and mild cream cheese makes this a great combination, which my family always enjoys.

NOTE: Adding extra baking powder or baking soda will not improve the texture. Rather, it will add a nasty chemical tang to the finished result, and the combination of bleached flour and too much of a leavening agent can often produce a chlorine aftertaste.

BLUEBERRY MUFFINS HERTZ

INGREDIENTS

Makes twelve muffins.
1 cup unbleached all-purpose flour
1 cup whole-wheat flour (preferably stone-ground)
$\frac{1}{3}$ cup granulated sugar
1 tablespoon baking powder
a large pinch of kosher salt or flaked sea salt
$1\frac{1}{4}$ cups milk
$\frac{1}{4}$ cup vegetable oil
1 large egg
2 teaspoons fresh lemon juice
$1\frac{1}{4}$ cups fresh or frozen blueberries, preferably tiny wild blueberries

a 12-cup muffin pan, well greased, or lined with paper or foil liners

OPPOSITE *A selection of sweet quick breads. Left to right (front): Tina's Breakfast Loaf; Date and Apple Loaf (page 81), and Smithy Loaf (page 79). On tray: Gingerbread (page 78) and Blueberry Muffins Hertz.*

American muffins bear no resemblance to English muffins; they are made with all-purpose flour and baking powder rather than from a yeast batter, and are baked in muffin pans instead of being cooked on a griddle. They look, and can taste, rather like cupcakes, or what we Brits call "fairy cakes," though they are less sweet, and have a moist, spongy crumb and a light texture. The best homemade muffins are a world away from the sawdust-dry, dense commercial variety, and wild blueberry muffins are the best of all.

My husband's mother, Annette Hertz, welcomed me into the family as only an all-American mother can. She enthusiastically introduced me to Maine's finest bounty – fresh seafood, rich ice cream, and the exquisite-tasting wild blueberries that she uses to make muffins for her grandchildren. This is her recipe, using a mixture of all-purpose and whole-wheat flours. (Annette uses a 50/50 flour blend that she buys from her supermarket.)

Maine wild blueberries are small, about the size of fresh currants, intensely flavored, and slightly tart, with more depth of taste than the fatter, cultivated ones. As fresh blueberries are only available for a few weeks, you can use frozen blueberries, straight from the freezer, out of season. The blueberries could also be replaced with fresh red currants, cranberries, huckleberries, pitted cherries, blackberries, diced apple, or dried fruits and nuts.

You can also experiment with spices – try cinnamon, nutmeg, pumpkin-pie spice, or add a bit of grated fresh lemon or orange rind. Or try one of the freshly ground spice mixtures on page 140. The oil can be replaced with an equal quantity of melted unsalted butter for a richer taste. Muffins should be eaten warm from the oven, or at least on the day of baking. They can also be frozen for one month.

Heat the oven to 400F. Mix together the flours, sugar, baking powder, and salt in a large bowl. Whisk together the milk, oil, egg, and lemon juice in a medium-size bowl. Stir the milk mixture into the dry ingredients until almost combined. Quickly but gently fold in the blueberries with a rubber spatula; the mixture should still look lumpy. Overmixing will make the muffins tough. Spoon the batter into the prepared muffin pan, filling each two-thirds full.

Bake the muffins for 20 to 25 minutes, or until they have a distinct cracked peak in the middle and are golden brown and firm to the touch. A wooden pick inserted in the center of a muffin should come out clean. If the muffins seem slightly wet or soft, bake a few minutes longer. Cool the muffins in the pan about 1 minute. Turn them out onto a wire rack to cool for a few minutes.

Blueberry Muffins Hertz are delicious served warm.

TINA'S BREAKFAST LOAF

INGREDIENTS

Makes one large cake.

TOPPING:

$\frac{1}{2}$ cup walnuts, coarsely chopped
$\frac{1}{4}$ cup firmly packed brown sugar
1 tablespoon ground cinnamon

CAKE:

8 tablespoons unsalted butter, softened
1 cup granulated sugar
1 teaspoon vanilla extract
$1\frac{1}{2}$ cups unbleached all-purpose flour
1 teaspoon baking powder
$\frac{1}{2}$ teaspoon baking soda
a pinch of kosher salt or flaked sea salt
1 cup sour cream
2 large eggs

a 9 × 5 × 3-inch loaf pan, greased, lined with waxed paper and greased

This recipe dates back to the late seventies, when I was working in Paris. It comes from Tina Ujlaki, now the food editor of Food & Wine *magazine in New York City, who used to make this simple and satisfying cake as an antidote to all the elaborate, rich French* pâtisserie *we consumed while we were there. This cake is a favorite of Tina's family. I enjoy serving it warm for breakfast with freshly brewed coffee.*

Heat the oven to 375F. Mix all the topping ingredients in a small bowl with your fingertips until blended.

To make the cake: Beat together the butter, granulated sugar, and vanilla with an electric mixer at high speed, or with a spoon, until the mixture is pale yellow and fluffy. Sift together the flour, baking powder, baking soda, and salt onto a sheet of waxed paper. Whisk together the sour cream and eggs in a small bowl. Add the flour mixture and the sour cream mixture to the butter and sugar, in batches, and mix on low speed, or stir just until the batter is thoroughly combined. The batter will be quite soft.

Spoon half the batter into the prepared pan. Sprinkle half of the topping over the batter. Spoon the remaining batter into the pan. Evenly sprinkle the remaining topping over the batter and press it lightly into the surface.

Bake the cake for 45 to 55 minutes, or until it is lightly browned and a wooden pick inserted in the center comes out clean. Cool the cake in the pan on a wire rack for about 30 minutes.

Carefully turn the cake out of the pan, remove the waxed paper from the bottom, and put upright on a serving platter. Then cut into slices and serve warm.

GINGERBREAD

INGREDIENTS

Makes one large loaf.

- $1\frac{1}{2}$ cups self-rising flour
- $\frac{1}{2}$ teaspoon baking soda
- 1 tablespoon ground ginger
- 1 teaspoon ground cinnamon
- $\frac{3}{4}$ teaspoon ground nutmeg
- $\frac{1}{2}$ teaspoon ground cloves
- 8 tablespoons (1 stick) cold unsalted butter, diced
- $\frac{3}{4}$ cup firmly packed dark brown sugar
- 1 cup milk
- $\frac{1}{2}$ cup dark unsulfured molasses
- $\frac{1}{2}$ cup golden syrup (see Notes), or $\frac{1}{4}$ cup honey and $\frac{1}{4}$ cup light corn syrup
- 1 large egg, beaten

a $10 \times 5 \times 2\frac{1}{2}$-inch loaf pan (see Notes), greased, bottom lined with waxed paper and greased

In my time as a pastry chef I have made many gingerbreads, but this is the most wonderful, sticky, spicy gingerbread I've ever tasted. It is dark, moist, well-spiced, not particularly sweet, and the flavor is unhampered by fruit or nuts. For the best flavor, let the gingerbread age a couple of days before eating.

Heat the oven to 350F. Sift the flour, baking soda, and spices into a large bowl. Rub in the butter with your fingertips until the mixture looks like fine crumbs. Stir the sugar and milk in a medium-size saucepan and bring just to a simmer. Remove from the heat and stir in the molasses and golden syrup (or the honey and corn syrup). Let stand until lukewarm. Then whisk in the egg.

Pour the milk mixture into the flour mixture and whisk until smooth. Pour the batter into the prepared pan. Bake for 50 to 60 minutes, or until a skewer inserted off center comes out clean. (As the gingerbread bakes it will bubble up and rise, then fall, leaving a large, moist depression.) Let cool completely in the pan. Turn the cake out of the pan and remove the paper. Wrap the cake in waxed paper and then in foil.

NOTES: A $10 \times 5 \times 2\frac{1}{2}$-inch loaf pan isn't commonly found in American kitchens or cookware shops, but this gingerbread works beautifully in a 9-inch springform pan.

Golden syrup is found in jars or cans in most gourmet shops or better supermarkets.

WHISK THE BATTER UNTIL IT IS SMOOTH. IT SHOULD BE FAIRLY THIN.

BAKE UNTIL A SKEWER INSERTED OFF CENTER COMES OUT CLEAN.

Homemade gingerbread is an old-fashioned treat that still has great appeal. The flavor will be at its best if you bake this a couple of days before serving.

SMITHY LOAF

INGREDIENTS

Makes one loaf.
1 cup boiling water
2 cups dark raisins
8 tablespoons (1 stick) unsalted butter
¾ cup firmly packed dark brown sugar
2 teaspoons pumpkin-pie spice or freshly ground spice mixture (page 140)
1 teaspoon baking soda
a pinch of kosher salt or flaked sea salt
1¾ cups unbleached all-purpose flour
1 teaspoon baking powder
2 large eggs, slightly beaten

an 8½ × 4½ × 2¾-inch loaf pan, greased, bottom lined with waxed paper and greased

I'm not sure where this recipe came from originally, but it was given to me by Malcolm Appleby, who is a distinguished silversmith – hence the loaf's name. Malcolm lives in Scotland, in what was once a railway station. This recipe reminds me of the teas he serves on his station platform in sight of his herb garden and the "bulb" garden (made from colored lights). Malcolm has the most marvelous sense of humor, and I always smile when I make this good loaf. Eat this bread the day after it's made, sliced and buttered.

Heat the oven to 350F. Bring the 1 cup of water to a boil in a large saucepan. Add the raisins, butter, sugar, pumpkin-pie spice, baking soda, and salt. Lower the heat and simmer gently for 5 minutes, stirring occasionally to combine the ingredients, until the raisins have plumped and the butter is melted. Let the mixture cool slightly. Stir in the flour and baking powder until well combined, then stir in the beaten eggs. Scrape the batter into the prepared pan.

Bake the loaf for 50 to 60 minutes, or until a wooden pick inserted in the center comes out clean. Completely cool the loaf in the pan on a wire rack. Then turn it out and cover with plastic wrap or foil.

STIR IN THE FLOUR AND BAKING POWDER UNTIL WELL COMBINED.

SCRAPE THE BATTER INTO THE PREPARED LOAF PAN.

Maddybenny *Wheaten* Bread

MADDYBENNY *WHEATEN* BREAD

INGREDIENTS

Makes four medium-size loaves.
4¾ cups whole-wheat flour (preferably stone-ground)
1 tablespoon baking soda
1 tablespoon granulated sugar
2 teaspoons kosher salt or flaked sea salt
2¾ to 3 cups buttermilk

a 13 × 9 × 2-inch baking pan, greased

Another of Rosemary White's delicious and easy recipes from Northern Ireland (see her recipe for fadge on page 70). Here, four loaves are baked in one pan and then broken apart after baking. Any spare loaves can be frozen, well wrapped, for up to one month.

Heat the oven to 425F. Stir together the flour, baking soda, sugar, and salt in a large bowl. Make a well in the center. Add 2¾ cups of the buttermilk. Using a rubber spatula, mix the flour into the buttermilk to form a soft, but not sticky dough. (Depending on the flour, you may add up to ¼ cup extra buttermilk, 1 tablespoon at a time.)

As soon as the dough comes together, turn it out onto a lightly floured work surface. With lightly floured hands, knead the dough gently for a few seconds, just until the dough looks even and has no floury patches. It still should look quite lumpy. Place the dough in the prepared pan and, with lightly floured hands, press it gently into the corners. Cut a deep cross on top with a sharp knife to score four equal rectangular sections. Bake the bread for 35 to 45 minutes, or until it has a firm, brown crust.

Turn out the bread onto a wire rack. Cover it with a clean dish towel, tucking the ends of the towel under the bread loosely. Let it cool to warm, if you wish, or cool it completely. Cut or break into four loaves.

A selection of savory quick breads. Left to right: Beer Bread (opposite), Herb Rolls (page 82), Bacon Loaf, and Maddybenny Wheaten Bread (page 79).

BACON LOAF

INGREDIENTS

Makes one large loaf.

4 ounces thick-sliced bacon, diced into ¼-inch pieces (about 1 cup diced)
2½ cups unbleached all-purpose flour
2 teaspoons baking powder
¼ teaspoon freshly ground black pepper, or to taste
a large pinch of kosher salt or flaked sea salt
6 tablespoons cold unsalted butter, diced
4 ounces thickly sliced lean ham, diced into ¼-inch pieces (about 1 cup diced)
3 large eggs, beaten
⅓ cup buttermilk

a 10 × 5 × 2½-inch loaf pan or a 9 × 5 × 3-inch loaf pan, greased

This richly flavored loaf smells so tantalizing in the oven, it's difficult to wait until it is cool enough to slice. Although the recipe comes from an American relative in Boston, I like to make it with thickly sliced smoked English bacon and a thick slice of good ham. In the States, if you can't get English bacon, use thick-sliced double-smoked bacon, available from a good butcher or gourmet foods store. This loaf is best on the day it is made.

Heat the oven to 350F. Put the bacon into a cold frying pan and fry over moderately high heat for 5 minutes, stirring frequently, until crisp. Remove from the heat.

Sift together the flour, baking powder, pepper, and salt into a large bowl. Rub in the butter until the mixture looks like fine crumbs. Make a well in the center.

Stir the bacon and the bacon fat into the flour mixture. Add the ham, eggs, and buttermilk and stir to form a stiff batter. Spoon the batter into the prepared pan and smooth the surface. Bake the loaf for 45 to 55 minutes, or until it is lightly browned and a wooden pick inserted into the center comes out clean. Let cool in the pan on a wire rack for 10 minutes. Turn out the loaf onto the rack. Eat warm or let cool completely.

STIR IN THE CRISP BACON, HAM, EGGS, AND BUTTERMILK TO MAKE A STIFF BATTER.

SPOON THE STIFF BATTER INTO THE PREPARED LOAF PAN.

DATE AND APPLE LOAF

INGREDIENTS

Makes one loaf.

- 8 tablespoons (1 stick) unsalted butter, softened
- $\frac{1}{2}$ cup plus 2 tablespoons firmly packed dark brown sugar
- 2 large eggs
- $\frac{3}{4}$ cup self-rising flour
- $\frac{3}{4}$ cup stone-ground whole-wheat flour or whole-wheat pastry flour
- 1 cup walnuts, coarsely chopped
- $\frac{3}{4}$ cup diced pitted dates
- $\frac{3}{4}$ cup peeled, grated tart apple
- about 2 tablespoons milk

an $8\frac{1}{2} \times 4\frac{1}{2} \times 2\frac{3}{4}$-inch loaf pan, greased, bottom lined with waxed paper and greased

Use a well-flavored, tart apple for this slightly sweet loaf. In England I like this best made with Bramley cooking apples. In the States I suggest using Rhode Island greenings, Jonathans, Ida Reds, or a good, firm Granny Smith apple. The quantity of milk needed will depend on the flour you choose. This bread is tasty sliced and spread with butter or cheese.

Heat the oven to 350F.

Beat together the butter and sugar in a large bowl with an electric mixer at high speed, or with a spoon, until light and fluffy. Beat in the eggs one at a time. With mixer on low speed, stir in the flours, walnuts, dates, and apple. Stir in enough milk to make a batter that clings to a wooden spoon, but falls when the spoon is tapped. Spoon the batter into the prepared pan.

Bake the loaf for 1 to $1\frac{1}{4}$ hours, or until a wooden pick inserted in the center comes out clean. Cool the loaf in the pan on a wire rack for 10 minutes. Then turn out the loaf onto a wire rack, remove the waxed paper from the bottom, and cool completely.

Make Date and Apple Loaf (above) in the fall when apples are at their best.

BEER BREAD

INGREDIENTS

Makes one loaf.

- $3\frac{1}{4}$ cups white whole-wheat flour (page 21), regular whole-wheat flour, or whole-wheat pastry flour, preferably stone-ground
- 3 tablespoons firmly packed light brown sugar
- 1 tablespoon baking powder
- $\frac{1}{2}$ teaspoon kosher salt or flaked sea salt
- $\frac{3}{4}$ cup Guinness stout
- $\frac{3}{4}$ cup water

an $8\frac{1}{2} \times 4\frac{1}{2} \times 2\frac{3}{4}$-inch loaf pan, well greased

A very quick loaf, this takes just over an hour from start to finish. Eat it with a good aged cheese, such as Cheddar, or with a soup. I prefer to use very coarse Irish wheaten flour, which I am able to buy in Ireland (it isn't available anywhere else), but white whole-wheat flour, regular whole-wheat flour, or whole-wheat pastry flour will work fine too. Your choice depends on how coarse or fine-textured you like your bread.

This bread is a British favorite, but it may not be to everyone's taste. If your family or friends are not fond of beer, you should probably choose another recipe. Eat this loaf the day you make it, or toast it later. It can also be frozen for one month.

Heat the oven to 350F. Mix together the flour, sugar, baking powder, and salt in a large bowl. Stir in the beer and water to make a fairly stiff dough. Knead the dough gently three or four times on a lightly floured work surface.

Gently shape the dough into an oblong the length of the pan. Place the dough in the pan and press it into the corners. Bake for 40 to 50 minutes, or until golden and a pick inserted in the center comes out clean. Turn out onto a wire rack and cool.

HERB ROLLS

INGREDIENTS

Makes twelve rolls.

- 3 cups self-rising flour
- ½ teaspoon kosher salt or flaked sea salt
- ¼ teaspoon freshly ground black pepper
- 1 cup cottage cheese
- about ½ cup milk
- 1 large egg
- 2 tablespoons olive oil
- 2 tablespoons chopped fresh parsley
- 4 teaspoons snipped fresh chives
- 4 teaspoons coarsely chopped fresh thyme leaves (stemmed)
- additional milk for brushing

a baking sheet, greased

Fresh herbs are vital for this recipe – dried herbs simply won't do. The rolls look rough and craggy, which is part of their charm. The flavor goes well with winter vegetable soups, as well as with salads. Eat these warm with butter. The rolls can be kept in a plastic bag for a day, and they freeze well for up to one month.

Heat the oven to 350F. Sift together the flour, salt, and pepper into a large bowl.

Put the cottage cheese, ½ cup of the milk, the egg, olive oil, and the herbs into a food processor. Process until smooth. If you don't have a food processor, finely mince the herbs; put the cottage cheese, milk, egg, and olive oil into a medium-size bowl, and whisk until well blended and as smooth as possible.

Stir the cheese mixture into the flour with a rubber spatula, adding additional milk if necessary, a tablespoon at a time, to make a soft, but not sticky dough.

Turn the dough out onto a lightly floured work surface and lightly knead four to six times until it is fairly smooth. Divide the dough into twelve equal pieces. Gently shape each piece into a rough ball. Arrange them spaced apart on the prepared baking sheet. Brush the rolls with milk. Bake for about 25 minutes, or until they turn golden brown and sound hollow when tapped underneath. Transfer to a wire rack to cool slightly.

Lovage, tansy, bee balm, and summer savory are among the more unusual aromatic herbs and plants, dating from the 17th century, flourishing in the kitchen garden of Philipsburg Manor (page 69). The combination of chives, parsley, and thyme in the ingredients for Herb Rolls (above) makes the most of readily available herbs, but it is only a suggestion. Use any mix of herbs you like, as long as they are fresh. Oregano or marjoram would be lovely instead of thyme, and you could use basil leaves in place of the parsley.

When Europeans arrived in New England in the 17th century, corn was growing in abundance, and they soon adapted many Native American recipes for cooking and baking the indigenous crop. Ever since, cornmeal has been a staple in American kitchens and corn bread, in numerous regional guises, is popular all across the country.

My selection of cornmeal recipes (right) includes Corn Dabs (below), a colonial recipe baked in corn-stick pans, and in individual antique rectangular molds with crisp bacon pieces added, and Corn Bread (page 84).

For the best cornmeal, search out small local mills who stone-grind the corn. Buy it in small quantities and, for freshness, keep it in the refrigerator or freezer.

Freshly baked corn bread is on the menu at Windham Hill Inn, in West Townshend, Vermont.

CORN DABS

This recipe is an authentic heirloom from colonial America, and may be a surprise to modern tastes. Although the corn dabs look like corn sticks, they are much denser and coarser, and they will not rise because they do not use any leavening.

"Leavening agents did not arrive until 1820," explains food historian Caroll Boltin (page 69). "White flour was scarce, so the cornmeal used alone would give a gritty texture." However, the dabs remain moist and creamy on the inside, thanks to the addition of sour cream – an example of the Dutch settlers' influence in New York State's Hudson Valley.

These plain and simple dabs were eaten with rich oyster or clam stews and fish soups – a good combination. They are a nice change from today's more usual, sweeter baked cornmeal muffins and breads. Eat them while they're still warm.

INGREDIENTS

Makes seven to ten dabs, depending on the pan.

- ¾ cup boiling water
- 1 cup yellow cornmeal
- ¼ cup sour cream
- 1 large egg, lightly beaten
- 1 tablespoon melted bacon fat or lightly salted butter (see Note)
- ¼ teaspoon salt
- plenty of melted bacon fat or lightly salted butter for greasing

a cast-iron corn-stick pan, greased

Heat the oven to 425F.

Pour the boiling water over the cornmeal in a large bowl. Mix well with a fork. Then add the sour cream. Mix thoroughly and let stand for 10 minutes to soften the cornmeal. Put the corn-stick pan on a baking sheet and place in the oven to heat up for 10 to 15 minutes, until pan is just smoking.

Stir the egg, bacon fat or butter, and salt into the batter. Stir in the crumbled bacon too, if you wish. Pour the batter into a large glass measuring cup for easier handling.

Open the oven door and pull the rack with the corn-stick pan on it toward you. Generously brush the melted bacon fat or butter into the hot corn-stick pan. Return it to the oven for a couple of minutes to heat the fat. Pour the batter into the molds to almost full – the batter should sizzle when it hits the very hot fat. Bake the dabs for 20 to 25 minutes, or until crusty and golden, just slightly puffed, and the edges pull away from the pan; a wooden pick inserted in the center should come out clean. Turn out the dabs immediately.

NOTE: Three strips of bacon will render enough fat for the recipe and for greasing the pan; you can also crumble the cooked bacon and add it to the batter for more flavor in the dabs.

CORN BREAD

INGREDIENTS

Makes nine squares.

- 1 cup unbleached all-purpose flour
- 1 cup yellow cornmeal (preferably stone-ground)
- ¼ cup granulated sugar
- 4 teaspoons baking powder
- ½ teaspoon kosher salt or flaked sea salt
- 1 cup milk
- 2 large eggs, lightly beaten
- 2 tablespoons unsalted butter, melted
- 1 teaspoon caraway seeds

an 8-inch-square cake pan, preferably nonstick, greased

This is Caroll Boltin's favorite recipe for corn bread. "The caraway seeds are an authentic colonial addition," says Caroll, who has researched American settlers (see page 69). "It reflects the Dutch influence on cooking here in the Hudson Valley of New York State."

Heat the oven to 375F.

Stir together the flour, cornmeal, sugar, baking powder, and salt in a large bowl. Add the milk, eggs, and melted butter and stir well to make a smooth batter. Stir in the caraway seeds. Scrape the batter into the prepared pan.

Bake the bread for 20 to 25 minutes, or until the corn bread is golden, firm to the touch, and has shrunk from the corners of the pan, and a wooden pick inserted in the center comes out clean. Cool the corn bread on a wire rack for 10 minutes, then turn it out onto a platter. Serve warm, cut into squares.

NOTE: If you prefer to make corn muffins, bake the batter in a twelve-cup muffin pan, greased or lined with paper or foil liners.

CAROLL BEATS *CARAWAY* SEEDS INTO THE CORN BREAD BATTER.

SHE SCRAPES THE BATTER INTO THE PREPARED CAKE PAN. THE CORN BREAD IS THEN READY TO BE BAKED.

PHOEBE LETT'S TREACLE BREAD

INGREDIENTS

Makes two loaves.

- $4\frac{3}{4}$ cups whole-wheat flour (preferably stone-ground)
- $1\frac{1}{2}$ cups unbleached all-purpose flour
- 1 tablespoon firmly packed dark brown sugar
- 2 teaspoons kosher salt or flaked sea salt
- 2 teaspoons baking soda
- $1\frac{1}{2}$ teaspoons ground ginger
- 4 tablespoons cold unsalted butter, diced
- about 3 cups buttermilk
- $\frac{1}{3}$ cup dark unsulfured molasses
- 1 large egg
- 1 tablespoon sesame seeds for sprinkling (optional)

two $8\frac{1}{2} \times 4\frac{1}{2} \times 2\frac{3}{4}$-inch loaf pans or two 8-inch-round cake pans, greased, bottoms lined with waxed paper and greased

I love making this simple and well-flavored Irish loaf – it smells wonderful, and has become a picnic favorite. This recipe is a specialty of Phoebe Lett, who lives in Enniscorthy, County Wexford, in Ireland. Phoebe and her husband Bill are tremendous hosts; after spending five minutes with them you feel you've known them a lifetime.

A restaurant in Wexford serves an excellent first course – triangles of this warm treacle bread with Cashel Blue cheese (an Irish blue cheese) melted on top, surrounded by a good salad with a nicely tart dressing. Or simply eat this bread sliced, with butter and cheese.

Since treacle isn't widely available in the U.S., I've adapted this recipe to use dark unsulfured molasses, but you can use treacle instead.

Heat the oven to 400F.

Stir together the flours, sugar, salt, baking soda, and ginger in a large bowl. Rub in the butter with your fingertips, or cut in with a pastry blender, until the mixture looks like fine crumbs.

Whisk together 3 cups of the buttermilk, molasses, and egg in a medium-size bowl. Quickly stir the buttermilk mixture into the dry ingredients using a wooden spoon. The dough should be heavy and slightly sticky; if there are dry crumbs, add a little more buttermilk, one tablespoon at a time.

Flour your hands and gently knead the dough in the mixing bowl until it comes together – a few seconds only. It will still look rough and lumpy. Divide the dough in half and shape each half into an oval (or a round, if using round pans). Put one piece into each pan and press the dough into the corners. Sprinkle the tops with the sesame seeds, if you wish, and press them firmly into the loaves so they don't fall off when the loaves are turned out.

Bake the loaves for 10 minutes, then reduce the oven temperature to 375F and bake for another 35 to 40 minutes. (Cover the loaves loosely with a sheet of foil if they brown too quickly.) When they are done, the loaves will have a crunchy crust and be well-risen; a wooden pick inserted in the center will come out clean.

Turn the loaves out, remove the waxed paper from the bottoms, and cool completely on wire racks. Wrap and keep at room temperature for a day before slicing. The extra loaf can be frozen up to one month.

THE DOUGH SHOULD REMAIN ROUGH AND LUMPY AFTER IT HAS BEEN GENTLY KNEADED. DIVIDE IT IN HALF, SHAPE INTO OVALS AND PLACE IN THE PANS.

Treacle bread is best simply served with butter, as here, or with cheese. Sesame seeds add extra texture.

TOP
John Doyle (right) discusses the day's events on the farm with his nephew, while Mary's bread bakes in the cast-iron pot. Extra ashes have been placed on top of the pot so the bread bakes evenly.
ABOVE
After about 40 minutes, Mary removes the perfectly baked bread.

BASIC BROWN BREAD

Phoebe Lett (page 85) insisted we visit Mary Curtis, whom she calls "a true country woman – her bread is supreme." Mary and her husband farm at Bree in County Wexford, Ireland. In 1989 she won the Farmers Journal Farm Woman of the Year award in an impressive competition that involved cooking an entire meal in front of an audience, making an evening gown (not in public), and changing the wheel on a farm vehicle against the clock. With four grown-up children who still come home each weekend, the Curtises "go through a lot of bread," and Mary bakes three loaves at a time to make the best use of her forty-year-old, oil-fired Rayburn oven.

"No two days will I make the same bread – I'll add sesame, poppy or caraway seeds, or thyme and sage to go with soups," she says. Mary grows her own vegetables and herbs, and uses the full-fat unpasteurized milk from her own cows to make buttermilk. When it comes to flour she prefers Odlums cream flour ("cream" meaning unbleached) and Abbey stone-ground wholemeal (whole-wheat) flour, which she calls "good and coarse."

To bake a batch of brown bread in the traditional way – in a cast-iron pot suspended over the red embers of an open fire – Mary walked across a couple of fields, over a stile, and under a barbed-wire fence to visit her next-door neighbors, Pat and John Doyle, farming brothers well into their eighties. The open-fire method was regularly used in rural areas of Ireland for baking until the 1950s and, as Mary has discovered, it bakes wonderful, slightly smoky bread; the closed pot traps the steam inside to produce a softer than usual crust.

The Doyles prepared the fire a good hour before the bread was put in to bake, so the flames had died down and the embers glowed red. Then they suspended a massive, solid iron pot on a chain from a swing arm and heated it until moderately hot.

"To test the pot, sprinkle a little flour inside. It should change color slowly," she says. "If it turns black instantly, swing the pot away from the fire for a few minutes." Mary placed her shaped brown loaf into the pot, covered the pot with its heavy lid, then heaped hot ashes on top of the lid so the loaf would cook evenly.

After 40 minutes spent chatting about old times on the farm, she checked on the bread's progress – it looked wonderful. The cooked loaf was wrapped in a cloth to soften the crust, left to cool, then eagerly devoured.

Here is Mary's recipe for brown bread, adapted for more modern kitchens. This loaf is best eaten within twenty-four hours.

INGREDIENTS

Makes one medium-size loaf.

$2\frac{1}{2}$ cups whole-wheat flour (preferably stone-ground)
$\frac{3}{4}$ cup unbleached all-purpose flour
$\frac{1}{4}$ cup unprocessed wheat bran
$\frac{1}{4}$ cup toasted wheat germ
1 teaspoon baking soda
1 teaspoon kosher salt or flaked sea salt
2 tablespoons cold unsalted margarine or butter
$1\frac{1}{4}$ to $1\frac{3}{4}$ cups buttermilk

a heavy baking sheet, well floured

Heat the oven to 425F. Mix together the flours, bran, wheat germ, baking soda, and salt in a large bowl. Rub in the margarine or butter using your fingertips, lifting the mixture high above the bowl to aerate the dough, until it looks like fine crumbs.

Stir in enough of the buttermilk to make a stiff dough; it will look a bit rough. Turn the dough out onto a well-floured work surface and quickly knead it with the heel of your hand, pushing the dough from the middle out and then pulling it back. Use your other hand to rotate the dough as you knead it. As soon as the dough looks smooth, shape it into a flat disk. Place the loaf on the prepared baking sheet. Cut a cross in the top of the loaf. Bake the bread for 35 to 45 minutes, or until the loaf is crusty, browned, and sounds hollow when tapped underneath. Transfer to a wire rack and cool completely.

NOTE: Mary Curtis gave me an old recipe for buttermilk from the days when every farm made its own buttermilk and butter. You need to start a buttermilk "plant," which will ferment milk. Stir together 2 cakes compressed fresh yeast (0.6 ounce each) and 3 tablespoons plus 2 teaspoons granulated sugar in a large bowl until smooth. Heat 5 cups of milk until lukewarm (95F to 105F). Gradually stir the milk into the yeast mixture. Cover the bowl with a dish towel and let stand for a couple of days at room temperature. The mixture should smell and taste like buttermilk. Line a strainer with a double thickness of cheesecloth and strain the mixture. Refrigerate the buttermilk, and it is ready to use. (It will keep for one day, covered.) The residue in the cheesecloth can be used to make the next batch of buttermilk. Rinse the residue in the cheesecloth with lukewarm water, then put it into a clean container, preferably one scalded in boiling water. Add a generous teaspoon of sugar, mix, add the milk, and proceed as before.

USING HER FINGERTIPS, MARY RUBS IN THE MARGARINE.

ALL THE INGREDIENTS ARE STIRRED TO MAKE A STIFF DOUGH.

USING THE HEEL OF HER HAND, MARY KNEADS THE DOUGH.

SHE PATS THE LOAVES INTO FLAT DISKS.

PROUD MARY'S LOAVES ARE READY FOR THE OVEN.

SHE TESTS A LOAF BY TAPPING IT ON THE BOTTOM.

SODA BREAD

INGREDIENTS

Makes four large soda bread triangles.

$3\frac{1}{4}$ cups self-rising flour
1 teaspoon granulated sugar
$\frac{1}{2}$ teaspoon kosher salt or flaked sea salt
2 tablespoons cold unsalted butter, diced
about $1\frac{1}{2}$ cups buttermilk

a 12-inch, heavy, cast-iron or nonstick frying pan with a lid or baking sheet to cover

This is Mary Curtis's recipe for soda bread, the traditional bread of Ireland, which is quickly made from self-rising flour and buttermilk and cooked on top of the stove in a heavy cast-iron frying pan. "It's a quick way to have fresh bread, and it's good and puffy and fluffy," says Mary. Make sure the pan is large enough to turn the bread with ease – otherwise cook it in two batches or use two frying pans. Eat this bread while it's still warm.

Heat the pan over moderately low heat while you make the dough. Sift together the flour, sugar, and salt into a large bowl. Rub in the butter with your fingertips or cut in with a pastry blender, lifting the mixture a few inches above the bowl and letting it fall to aerate the dough, until the mixture looks like fine crumbs. Stir in enough buttermilk to just moisten the dry ingredients and to make a soft, light, and fluffy dough; don't overwork the dough. Quickly turn it out onto a floured surface and knead four to five times until the dough comes together and forms a rough, fairly lumpy ball. Pat out to a disk about 8 to 9 inches in diameter and about 1 inch thick. Cut the disk in quarters.

Lightly brush the pan with oil. Put the bread into the heated pan, cover, and cook over moderately low heat for 15 to 20 minutes, turning the quarters over two or three times so they cook evenly. The finished bread should be golden brown and well puffed. Remove the bread from the pan, transfer to a wire rack, and cover with a dry dish towel until ready to serve.

MARY RUBS IN THE BUTTER, LIFTING THE FLOUR MIXTURE ABOVE THE BOWL.

USING FLOURED FINGERS, SHE PATS THE DOUGH INTO A FLAT DISK.

USING A SHARP KNIFE, SHE CUTS THE DOUGH INTO QUARTERS.

THE DOUGH QUARTERS ARE COVERED WHILE THEY COOK.

AFTER 5 MINUTES COOKING, MARY FLIPS OVER THE QUARTERS TO ENSURE EVEN COOKING.

SHE PLACES THE COOKED BREAD ONTO A WIRE RACK.

OPPOSITE
Soda bread from a local bakery, along with cheese, farmhouse butter, and a fruit tart, made a simple, impromptu picnic when Anthony and I were in Co. Cork, Ireland.

Farmhouse
Country Butter

COFFEE

FRIED DOUGHS

"Where can you find a really good doughnut these days?" lamented an elderly friend as she recalled her favorite childhood treat. A good doughnut is light, flavorful, and made from kneaded dough, perhaps filled with plenty of proper fruit jam, cooked in lard or a good vegetable oil, then coated in crunchy white sugar. Such doughnuts may no longer be easy to find commercially, but they are not at all difficult to make.

I'm quite conservative about what I eat for breakfast and was about to help myself to a bowl of granola at the Windham Hill Inn in West Townshend, Vermont, when innkeeper Linda Busteed appeared with a plate of freshly cooked doughnuts. My in-laws jumped for joy. "Positively the finest you'll ever taste," they said, being long-term fans of Windham Hill's cooking. They were right (see Megan's Potato Doughnuts, page 96), but they didn't guess the secret of their lightness (mashed potatoes).

OPPOSITE Freshly made doughnuts, New Orleans style. ABOVE Doughnuts frying.

Doughnuts and fried doughs originated as the last scraps of a big batch of bread dough. The pieces would be sweetened and cut, or filled with fruit or jam, and then fried – either as a treat for the children, or as a necessity for a quickly cooked breakfast, as Lois Keller explains (page 99). For Ina McNeil (page 100), fry breads are an essential part of the early fall powwows (large gatherings of Native Americans). Although she travels all over the U.S. to cook sweet and savory fry breads in huge quantities for these events, she still makes them regularly for her family. Lois Keller's German Whole-Wheat Grebble (page 99) is similar to Ina's baking-powder fry bread (though handled in a very different way), but Lois' dough is formed into twisted strips.

Doughnuts and fried doughs can be rich, such as the brioche-like Fancy Ring Doughnuts (page 95) or the Dutch Oliebollen (page 98), or quick and simple, like The Fry-Bread Queen's Fry Bread. But either way, homemade doughnuts are a treat indeed.

TIPS FOR FRYING DOUGHS:

– Use good quality, fresh vegetable oil (lard or solid white vegetable shortening can also be used), cool the oil, and strain it after each use through a coffee filter or strainer lined with white paper towels. If necessary, skim the oil with a skimmer or a long-handled, fine strainer between batches of doughnuts to remove any charred crumbs, which will ruin both the taste and appearance of your doughnuts.

– To avoid accidents, don't fill the pan more than one-third full with oil – it will bubble up when you add the doughnuts. Keep the lid close by to cover the fat, should it ever catch fire, and never leave the pan unattended.

– For the best results, the oil should have reached the correct temperature – 360F on a frying or candy thermometer. Many electric fryers have a built-in thermostat. To test the temperature if you don't have a thermometer, drop a cube of bread in the oil. It should

brown in 40 seconds at that heat. If the oil is too cool, the doughnut will sink to the bottom, absorb the oil, and become greasy. If the oil is too hot, the outsides will be hard and overcooked while the centers are still raw.
– Fry the doughnuts (which should be at room temperature) a few pieces at a time – don't crowd the pan.
– Turn the doughnuts over frequently with a skimmer or slotted spoon so they cook and brown evenly. Adjust the heat under the oil and test its temperature between batches; reheat it, if necessary.
– Remove the doughnuts with a fry basket or a slotted spoon, a skimmer, or a pair of long-handled tongs, then drain on plenty of paper towels. Eat as soon as possible – they don't keep and can't be frozen.

JAM DOUGHNUTS

INGREDIENTS

Makes about fourteen doughnuts.

- 3 to 3½ cups white bread flour (preferably unbleached and stone-ground)
- 1 teaspoon kosher salt or flaked sea salt
- 1 cake compressed fresh yeast (0.6 ounce) or 1 envelope active dry yeast (2½ teaspoons)
- ¼ cup granulated sugar
- 1 cup lukewarm milk (95F to 105F)
- 2 large eggs at room temperature, lightly beaten
- 2 tablespoons melted unsalted butter, at room temperature
- about ¼ cup raspberry jam
- vegetable oil for deep-fat frying
- granulated sugar for sprinkling

- a 2½-inch round biscuit or cookie cutter
- 2 baking sheets, lightly floured
- a deep-fat fryer or 6-quart Dutch oven

I like homemade raspberry or strawberry jam in the center of my doughnut, but a nice tart apricot conserve, chunky, dark marmalade, or even a little mincemeat left from Christmas can be substituted. This dough is flavorful and very light. The secret to making these doughnuts is to seal the cut circles of dough thoroughly so the filling doesn't leak out during cooking. Eat the same day for best texture and taste.

Mix together 3 cups of the flour and the salt in a large bowl. Make a well in the center of the flour. Crumble the fresh yeast into the well. Add the sugar and 2 tablespoons of the lukewarm milk. Mix until the liquid is smooth. Add the remaining milk to the well. If using dry yeast, mix the granules with 2 tablespoons of the lukewarm milk and 2

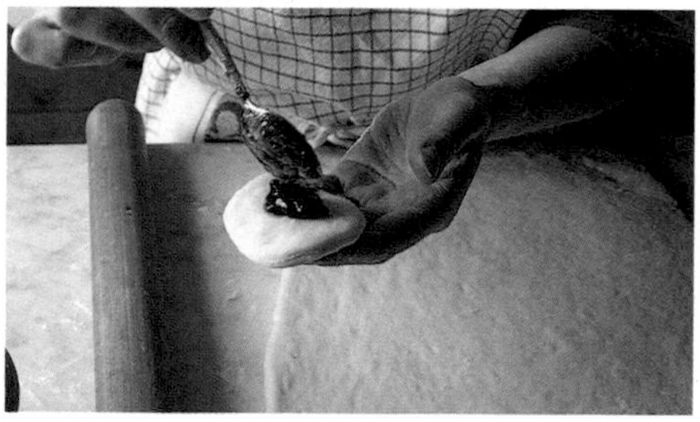

SPOON ABOUT 1 TEASPOON OF JAM IN THE CENTER OF ONE DOUGH ROUND.

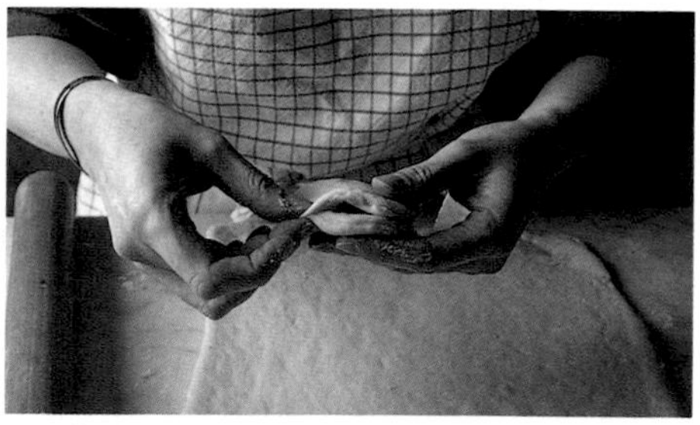

COVER WITH A SECOND DOUGH ROUND AND PRESS AND PINCH THE EDGES TOGETHER TO SEAL THOROUGHLY.

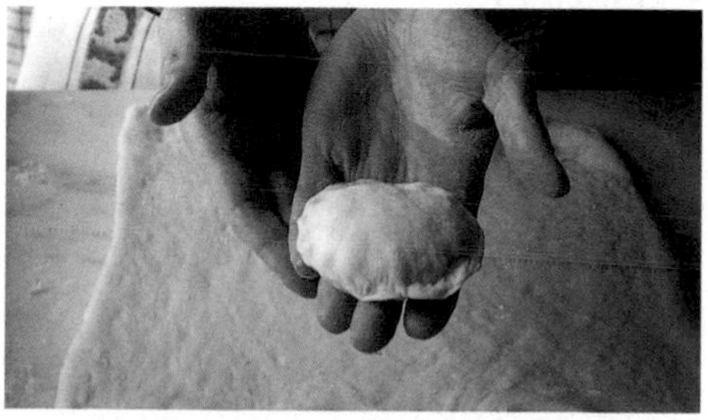

THE FILLED DOUGHNUT SHOULD BE SEALED ALL AROUND SO JAM DOESN'T LEAK OUT DURING FRYING.

LIFT THE DOUGHNUTS OUT OF THE HOT OIL WHEN THEY ARE WELL BROWNED AND PUFFED.

Made with flavorful and very light dough, these jam-filled doughnuts will be popular with children and adults. For extra sweetness, you can gently roll the doughnuts in granulated sugar, coating both sides, instead of just sprinkling the tops.

tablespoons sugar in a small bowl and let stand until foamy, 5 to 10 minutes (page 18). Add the yeast mixture to the well in the flour along with the remaining milk and sugar.

Add the eggs and butter to the well. Mix these liquid ingredients together. Work in the flour to make a soft, but not sticky dough. If there are crumbs of dry dough, add a little extra milk, 1 tablespoon at a time. If the dough sticks to your fingers, work in extra flour, 1 tablespoon at a time.

Turn out the dough onto a lightly floured surface and knead until smooth and elastic, about 10 minutes, adding a little more flour as needed to prevent sticking. Clean and dry the bowl and oil it lightly. Put the ball of dough back into the bowl and turn it over. Cover and let rise, until doubled in size, about 2 hours.

Punch down the risen dough. Turn out onto a lightly floured surface and knead for a few seconds. With a lightly floured rolling pin, gradually roll out the dough into a 12-inch circle about $\frac{1}{2}$ inch thick. When rolling out the dough, let it rest periodically to relax the dough.

Cut out rounds with the floured biscuit or cookie cutter. Re-roll the scraps and cut; you should have about 28 rounds.

Spoon about 1 teaspoon of jam in the center of one round. Brush the edges with a little water. Cover with a second round and press and pinch the edges together to seal thoroughly. Repeat with the remaining dough. Place on lightly floured baking sheets, spacing them apart, and cover lightly with plastic wrap. Let rise at warm room temperature, away from drafts, until almost doubled in size, about 30 minutes.

Meanwhile, pour the oil into the deep-fat fryer or Dutch oven to a depth of about 3 inches. Slowly heat until the oil registers 360F on a frying thermometer (see page 91). Lower three doughnuts into the hot oil with a slotted spoon. Fry the doughnuts, turning them frequently, until well browned and puffed, about 4 minutes. Lift out the doughnuts and drain on paper towels. Fry the remaining doughnuts in batches. While still warm, sprinkle the doughnuts with granulated sugar. Let cool.

ONTARIO APPLE DOUGHNUTS

On a trip to Canada a few years ago, I had the chance to visit the vast apple orchards in Ontario's Norfolk County. I wanted to visit Mrs. Judson's apple doughnut shop, and indeed drove by it many times, but tight schedules frustrated me. Eventually a kindly apple grower provided a breakfast of Mrs. Judson's just-fried apple doughnuts. They were simply delicious, and I've tried to reproduce the recipe. They are excellent for dessert served hot with a sauce made from puréed fresh, canned, or cooked dried apricots.

INGREDIENTS

Makes about fourteen triangular doughnuts.

1 recipe Jam Doughnuts dough (page 92)
1 large Granny Smith apple
1 tablespoon water
granulated sugar to taste
optional filling ingredients: ground cinnamon, grated lemon or orange rind, raisins, chopped walnuts or pecans
vegetable oil for deep-fat frying
ground cinnamon mixed with granulated sugar for sprinkling

2 baking sheets, lightly floured
a deep-fat fryer or 6-quart Dutch oven

Prepare the Jam Doughnut dough through the first rising. While the dough is rising, peel, core, and thickly slice the apple. Place in a small saucepan with the water, cover, and cook very slowly, stirring occasionally, until the apple is very soft. Add granulated sugar to taste, and small amounts of any of the optional filling ingredients.

Punch down the dough, transfer to a lightly floured work surface, and knead for a few seconds. Gradually roll out the dough with a rolling pin to a large rectangle, about $\frac{1}{2}$ inch thick, letting the dough rest periodically. With a floured knife, cut the dough into 3-inch squares. Re-roll the scraps and cut into squares. Place 1 teaspoon of the apple filling into the center of each square. Brush the edges lightly with water. Fold each square in half diagonally over the filling to form a triangle. Seal by pressing and pinching the edges together. Place the triangles, spaced apart, on lightly floured baking sheets. Cover with plastic wrap and let rise at warm room temperature, away from drafts, until almost doubled in size, 20 to 30 minutes.

Meanwhile, pour the oil into the deep-fat fryer or Dutch oven to a depth of about 3 inches. Slowly heat over moderate heat until the oil registers 360F on a frying thermometer (see page 91).

Place three dough triangles in the fry basket and lower into the hot oil, or slip them, one at a time, into the oil with a slotted spoon. Do not crowd the pan. Fry the doughnuts, turning them often so they brown evenly, until nicely puffed and golden, about 4 minutes. Lift out the doughnuts with the fry basket or slotted spoon and place on paper towels to drain. While still warm, sprinkle the doughnuts with cinnamon-sugar. Fry the remaining doughnuts in batches. Eat the same day.

For a delicious dessert, serve these apple doughnuts while they are still warm with apricot purée and crème fraîche.

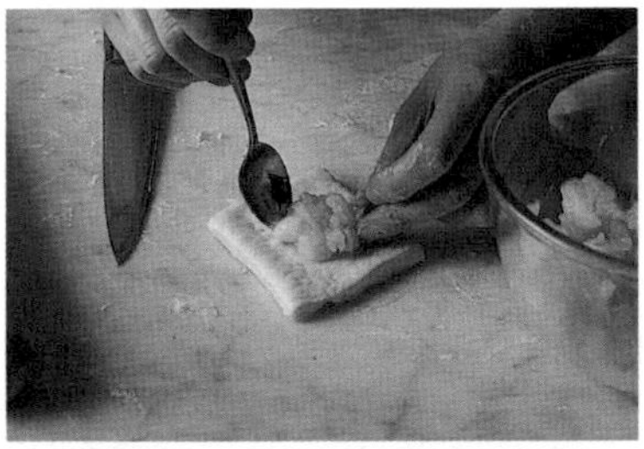

PLACE ONE TEASPOON OF THE APPLE FILLING IN THE CENTER OF EACH DOUGH SQUARE.

FOLD EACH SQUARE OVER THE FILLING TO FORM A TRIANGLE.

WORK THE BUTTER INTO THE DOUGH, SQUEEZING THE TWO TOGETHER UNTIL THOROUGHLY COMBINED.

RIGHT Fancy Ring Doughnut

FANCY RING DOUGHNUTS

INGREDIENTS

Makes about eighteen doughnuts.

- 4 cups white bread flour (preferably unbleached and stone-ground)
- 1 teaspoon kosher salt or flaked sea salt
- 1 cake compressed fresh yeast (0.6 ounce), or 1 envelope active dry yeast (2½ teaspoons) plus ½ teaspoon granulated sugar
- ¾ cup milk, at room temperature
- ⅓ cup granulated sugar
- 4 large eggs at room temperature, lightly beaten
- 8 tablespoons (1 stick) unsalted butter, cut up, at room temperature
- vegetable oil for deep-fat frying
- confectioners' sugar for sprinkling

- a 2¾- to 3-inch doughnut cutter, or a 3-inch round biscuit or cookie cutter plus a ½-inch round cutter
- 2 baking sheets, lightly floured
- a deep-fat fryer or 6-quart Dutch oven

The dough here is very rich – it's a type of brioche – and it makes the lightest, finest-textured doughnuts. After chilling and shaping the dough, gently bring it back to warm room temperature before frying to avoid a heavy, soggy result. Eat these the day they are made.

Stir together the flour and salt in a large bowl. Crumble the fresh yeast into a small bowl. Stir in 2 tablespoons of the milk until smooth. If using dry yeast, mix the granules with 2 tablespoons of the milk and the ½ teaspoon of sugar in a small bowl and let stand until foamy, 5 to 10 minutes (page 18).

Mix the sugar into the flour mixture. Make a well in the center of the flour and pour in the yeast mixture, the remaining milk, and the beaten eggs. Using your hand, combine all the ingredients in the well, then gradually work in the flour from the bowl to make a smooth batter. Beat the batter with your hand, pulling and stretching the dough, until smooth and elastic, about 10 minutes. The dough will be very sticky at this stage. Cover the bowl with a damp dish towel and let stand at room temperature, away from drafts, until doubled in size, about 1½ hours.

Punch down the dough with floured knuckles. Keeping the mixture in the bowl, work the butter into the dough, squeezing the two together until thoroughly combined. The dough should look smooth and glossy, with no streaks, and should be somewhat sticky.

Cover the bowl with a damp dish towel and refrigerate for at least 4 hours or until doubled in size (the dough can be left in the refrigerator overnight at this point).

Punch down the dough – it should be quite firm. Turn out the dough onto a floured work surface. Roll out the dough with a floured rolling pin to a circle about 1 inch thick. Using the floured doughnut cutter or the larger floured biscuit or cookie cutter, stamp out circles. If using the biscuit or cookie cutter, use the smaller cutter to stamp out a round in the center of each. Re-roll the scraps and centers and cut: you should have about 18 rings. Place the rings, spaced apart, on floured baking sheets, cover with dry dish towels, and let rise, away from drafts, until they have doubled in size and warmed to room temperature, 30 minutes to 1 hour.

Meanwhile, pour the oil into the deep-fat fryer or Dutch oven to a depth of about 3 inches. Slowly heat until the oil registers 360F on a frying thermometer. Lower about three rings of dough into the hot oil. Fry the doughnuts, stirring from time to time and turning the rings, for about 3 minutes, or until golden brown. Lift the doughnuts out with the fry basket or slotted spoon and drain on paper towels. Cook the remaining doughnuts in batches. Sprinkle the doughnuts, while still warm, with the confectioners' sugar. Let cool.

MEGAN'S POTATO DOUGHNUTS

INGREDIENTS

Makes about eighteen doughnuts.

- 1 cup freshly mashed potatoes, made from 8 ounces peeled all-purpose potatoes
- 3 to 4 cups unbleached all-purpose flour
- $\frac{3}{4}$ cup granulated sugar
- 1 tablespoon baking powder
- 1 teaspoon kosher salt or flaked sea salt
- $\frac{1}{2}$ teaspoon ground ginger
- $\frac{1}{4}$ teaspoon grated fresh nutmeg
- 3 tablespoons unsalted butter, diced, at room temperature
- 2 large eggs, lightly beaten
- 1 cup milk
- a few drops vanilla extract
- vegetable oil for deep-fat frying
- confectioners' sugar for sifting

- a $2\frac{3}{4}$- to 3-inch doughnut cutter, or a 3-inch round biscuit or cookie cutter, plus a $\frac{1}{2}$-inch round cutter
- a deep-fat fryer or 6-quart Dutch oven

These are the best doughnuts I've ever tasted. Last summer my in-laws introduced me to the beautiful Windham Hill Inn, in West Townshend, Vermont, during their annual visit to the Marlboro music festival. These were so wonderful I asked innkeeper Linda Busteed for the secret. "Potatoes and spice, and Megan," she replied giving the credit to her assistant, Megan McCooey. Eat these the day you make them.

Put the potatoes into a large bowl. They should be free of lumps and at room temperature. Add 3 cups of the flour, the sugar, baking powder, salt, and spices. Add the rest of the ingredients and mix thoroughly until the liquid ingredients are just blended in and the pieces of butter are incorporated. The dough will be sticky. If it is too loose, add a little more of the remaining flour, about 1 tablespoon at a time, until it holds together.

Turn out the dough onto a floured work surface. Knead for about 1 minute, or until just smooth. Roll out the dough with a floured rolling pin to a 9-inch circle about $\frac{1}{3}$ inch thick. Cut out rounds using the floured doughnut cutter or the larger floured biscuit or cookie cutter. If using the biscuit or cookie cutter, stamp out the center of each round – to make a ring – using the floured smaller cutter. Re-roll the trimmings and cut out more rings. If you wish, the center rounds can also be fried.

Pour the oil into the deep-fat fryer or Dutch oven to a depth of about 3 inches. Slowly heat over moderate heat until the oil registers 360F on a frying thermometer (see page 91). Place about three rings of dough in a fry basket and lower the basket into the hot oil, or slip the rings, one at a time, into the hot oil with a slotted spoon. Don't overcrowd the pan. Fry the rings, turning frequently so they brown evenly, for about 5 minutes, or until puffy and golden brown. Lift the rings out with the fry basket or slotted spoon and place on paper towels to drain. Sift confectioners' sugar over the doughnuts, and let cool. Fry the remaining doughnuts in batches.

Innkeeper and cook Linda Busteed rises early each morning to prepare freshly baked goods for her guests. These light potato doughnuts are served at least once a week. Here she is cutting out a batch in her sunny kitchen.

Serve these spicy doughnuts and the fried centers with freshly brewed coffee.

Gnocci fritti are best served warm sprinkled with freshly grated Parmesan cheese.

GNOCCI FRITTI

INGREDIENTS

Makes about fifty-seven gnocci fritti.

4 cups white bread flour (preferably unbleached and stone-ground)
1 teaspoon kosher salt or flaked sea salt
1 cake compressed fresh yeast (0.6 ounce), or 1 envelope active dry yeast ($2\frac{1}{2}$ teaspoons) plus $\frac{1}{2}$ teaspoon granulated sugar
$\frac{3}{4}$ cup warm milk plus $\frac{1}{2}$ cup warm water, mixed (105F to 115F)
1 tablespoon olive oil
vegetable oil for deep-fat frying
freshly grated Parmesan cheese (about $\frac{1}{2}$ cup), kosher salt, or flaked sea salt for sprinkling

a deep-fat fryer or 6-quart Dutch oven

This is a savory fried dough from Italy. The dough is cut into squares, which puff up to resemble pillows as they cook. Gnocci fritti are eaten warm, dusted with Parmesan cheese, accompanied by thin slices of good prosciutto. This recipe will serve eight or ten as a first course. These take some time to fry, about 30 minutes, so you may want to invite guests into the kitchen to eat them freshly cooked.

Mix together the flour and salt in a large bowl. Make a well in the center of the flour. Crumble the fresh yeast into a small bowl. Stir in 2 tablespoons of the warm liquid until smooth. Then stir in the rest of the liquid and the olive oil. If using dry yeast, mix the granules with 2 tablespoons of the warm liquid and the sugar and let stand until foamy, 5 to 10 minutes (page 18). Stir in the rest of the warm liquid and the olive oil.

Add the yeast mixture to the well in the flour. Mix in the flour from the bowl to make a fairly firm dough. If necessary, add a little more warm water, 1 tablespoon at a time, if the dough seems dry and won't come together.

Turn out the dough onto a lightly floured work surface and knead for 5 minutes. The dough should be glossy and elastic. Cover the ball of dough with the upturned bowl and let stand at room temperature for 30 minutes. The dough will rise slightly and become quite pliable. Punch down the dough with floured knuckles. With a lightly floured rolling pin, roll out the dough on a lightly floured work surface, to a 14-inch square about $\frac{1}{4}$ inch thick.

With a floured, large, sharp knife, cut the dough into 2-inch squares. Re-roll and cut the scraps, or fry the odd-shaped pieces. Cover the dough squares with dry dish towels so they don't form a hard crust.

Pour the oil into the deep-fat fryer or Dutch oven to a depth of about 3 inches. Slowly heat over moderate heat until the oil registers about 360F on a frying thermometer (see page 91). In the time this takes, the dough will have risen slightly. Place about four squares of dough in the fry basket and lower the basket into the hot oil, or slip them, one at a time, into the hot oil with a slotted spoon. Don't overcrowd the pan. Fry the dough squares, turning them frequently, until they are puffed and evenly golden brown, about 3 minutes. Lift out the squares with the fry basket or slotted spoon and place on paper towels to drain. Keep warm on a baking sheet in a 250F oven. Fry the remaining squares in batches. Arrange the warm squares on a serving dish. Sprinkle with Parmesan cheese or salt and serve immediately with prosciutto.

Enjoy oliebollens Dutch style as a snack. The dough is very rich, so they also make a delicious dessert if served with a scoop of vanilla ice cream.

OLIEBOLLEN

INGREDIENTS

Makes about fourteen doughnuts.

- 2 cups white bread flour (preferably unbleached and stone-ground)
- ½ teaspoon kosher salt or flaked sea salt
- 1 cake compressed fresh yeast (0.6 ounce) or 1 envelope active dry yeast (2¼ teaspoons)
- 2 teaspoons granulated sugar
- 1 cup lukewarm milk (95F to 105F)
- the grated rind and juice of half a large lemon, or a whole small lemon (about 1 teaspoon rind and 4½ teaspoons juice)
- scant ½ cup currants
- scant ½ cup raisins
- 1 medium-size Golden Delicious apple (a 6- to 7-ounce apple)
- vegetable oil for deep-fat frying
- granulated sugar for rolling (about ⅓ cup)

a deep-fat fryer or 6-quart Dutch oven

These Dutch doughnuts are very light and moist, and are flavored with plenty of dried fruit, chopped apple, and lemon. The cooked puffy doughnuts are rolled in sugar while still hot.

Mix the flour and salt in a large bowl. Make a well in the center of the flour. Crumble the fresh yeast into a small bowl. Stir in the sugar and half the lukewarm milk until smooth. If using dry yeast, mix the granules with the sugar and half the lukewarm milk and let stand until foamy, 5 to 10 minutes (page 18). Pour the yeast mixture into the well. Mix in a little of the flour in the bowl to make a thin batter. Cover the bowl with a dry dish towel or plastic wrap and let stand until spongy, about 20 minutes (page 16).

Add the remaining milk and the lemon rind and juice to the well and mix thoroughly with the yeast mixture. Gradually work in the remaining flour in the bowl with your hands to make a very soft, quite sticky dough.

Knead the dough very thoroughly in the bowl by pulling the dough up with your fingers and pushing it down with the heel of your hand for 10 minutes. It should stiffen somewhat, yet still be a bit sticky, and come away in one piece from the side of the bowl.

Sprinkle the currants and raisins over the dough. Quickly peel, core, and dice the apple into ¼-inch pieces (you should have about 1 cup). Sprinkle over the dough. Work the dried fruit and apple into the dough by gently squeezing the mixture through your fingers until the fruits are evenly distributed, but not crushed. Cover the bowl with a damp dish towel. Let rise at room temperature, away from drafts, until doubled in size, about 1 to 1½ hours. Meanwhile, pour the oil into the deep-fat fryer or Dutch oven to a depth of about 3 inches. Slowly heat the oil over moderate heat until it registers 360F on a frying thermometer (see page 91). Using an ice cream scoop, scoop up the dough and form into a rough ball shape. Fry the doughnuts, gently turning them from time to time, until golden brown, well puffed, and cooked through, about 3 to 4 minutes. Do not overcrowd the pan. Keep the remaining dough covered while these fry. Lift the doughnuts out with the fry basket or a slotted spoon and place on paper towels to drain. While still warm, roll the doughnuts in sugar to coat and let cool. Fry the remaining dough in batches. For best texture and flavor, eat the doughnuts the day they are made.

WHOLE-WHEAT GREBBLE

INGREDIENTS

Makes about twenty-two doughnuts.

- $1\frac{1}{3}$ cakes compressed fresh yeast (0.8 ounce) or $1\frac{1}{2}$ envelopes active dry yeast ($3\frac{3}{4}$ teaspoons)
- $\frac{1}{2}$ cup warm water (105F to 115F)
- $\frac{1}{4}$ cup firmly packed light brown sugar or mild honey
- about $4\frac{1}{4}$ cups whole-wheat bread flour (preferably stoneground)
- $\frac{1}{2}$ teaspoon baking soda
- $1\frac{1}{2}$ cups cottage cheese
- 2 large eggs
- 2 tablespoons melted unsalted butter
- 2 teaspoons kosher salt or flaked sea salt
- vegetable oil for deep-fat frying
- confectioners' sugar for serving

a deep-fat fryer or 6-quart Dutch oven

This German recipe has been passed down to Lois Keller through her husband Jerry's family. Its origins lie in the ingenuity of farmers' wives, she explained. "They used to mix up their bread dough at night, wrap the warmed bowl in blankets – don't forget, this was before central heating and winter nights were very cold – and leave the dough to rise overnight. In the morning, they could fry the dough quickly in lard to make a good, fresh breakfast." The Keller family lives near Ellis in west-central Kansas on a 5,000 acre farm of mixed crops – wheat, corn, and beans – and "nodding donkeys" (oil wells). Lois is an amazing woman. She works in the fields all day drilling oil or driving the combine, then cooks a massive meal for everyone. After dinner, she is still hard at work. "Some people knit in the evening, but I hand-clean some of our wheat." Lois grinds the wheat in a machine that resembles a huge coffee grinder, making it as coarse or as fine as she likes. It takes 3 or 4 minutes to grind $1\frac{1}{2}$ pounds of wheat kernels, which is enough for a loaf of bread. This dough can also be shaped and made into light, slightly sweet rolls (for shaping and baking instructions, see Oatmeal Rolls, page 25).

Crumble the yeast into a small bowl. Stir in the warm water and the sugar or honey until smooth. If using dry yeast, sprinkle the granules over the warm water. Stir in the sugar or honey and let stand until foamy, 5 to 10 minutes (page 18).

Mix together half the flour with the baking soda, making a well in the center. Blend the cottage cheese, eggs, butter, and salt until smooth. Pour this mixture into the well. Add the yeast mixture to the food processor or blender and process briefly. Tip this into the well and mix together, working in the rest of the flour until the dough comes together and is soft, but not sticky.

Turn it out onto a floured surface. Flour your hands and knead the dough for 10 minutes until it is firm, smooth, and elastic, only adding extra flour to prevent it from sticking. Put the ball of dough back into the washed, dried, and oiled bowl and turn it over. Cover with a damp dish towel and let stand at warm room temperature, away from drafts, until doubled in size, about 1 hour.

Pour the oil into the deep-fat fryer or Dutch oven to a depth of about 3 inches. Slowly heat over moderate heat until the oil registers 360F on a frying thermometer (page 91).

Divide the dough into twenty-two equal pieces. Using a floured rolling pin, roll each piece into an oval about $\frac{1}{4}$ inch thick. Cut a slit lengthwise down the center of each dough oval, cutting through the dough and almost to the edges. Shape the ovals by twisting the ends of each in opposite directions. Place about three dough twists in a fry basket and lower the basket into the hot oil. Fry the grebbles, turning constantly, for about 2 minutes, or until puffed, golden brown, and crispy. Lift out the grebbles with the fry basket and drain on paper towels. Eat immediately dusted with confectioners' sugar.

BELOW RIGHT Grebbles can be sprinkled with confectioners' sugar just before serving.

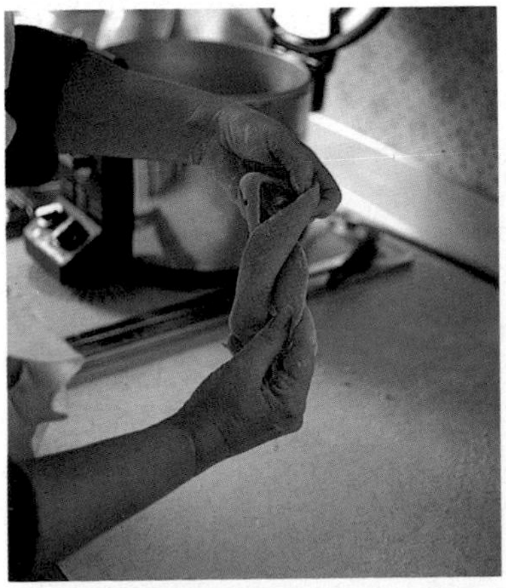

LOIS TWISTS EACH END OF THE OVAL IN THE OPPOSITE DIRECTION.

THE FRY-BREAD QUEEN'S FRY BREAD

INGREDIENTS

Makes about twenty large diamonds.

- 4 cups unbleached all-purpose flour
- 1 cup nonfat dry milk powder
- $\frac{1}{2}$ cup granulated sugar
- 3 tablespoons baking powder
- scant tablespoon kosher salt or flaked sea salt
- $1\frac{1}{4}$ to $1\frac{1}{2}$ cups cold water from the tap
- vegetable oil for deep-fat frying

a deep-fat fryer or 6-quart Dutch oven

Ina McNeil is the great-granddaughter of Chief Sitting Bull of Little Bighorn fame. She is also known as the "fry-bread queen" because of her cooking at huge powwows and feasts.

On the Sioux reservation where Ina was born, along the North/South Dakota border, women compete to make the best fry bread for powwows. The meetings are large, and making enough fry bread can involve using up to 35 pounds of flour. "This recipe is very quick," Ina says. "My mother says that the mood you are in will determine how your fry bread will turn out. So be happy and people will enjoy your bread and be happy, too."

Ina grew up watching her mother and grandmother make fry bread, so she learned to cook by sight and touch, rather than by using exact measurements. The secret of a good fry bread, she says, is not to overwork the dough when you knead it. Make sure it feels elastic and springy.

Mix the flour, powdered milk, sugar, baking powder, and salt in a large bowl. Make a well in the center of the flour. Add $1\frac{1}{4}$ cups water to the well. Gradually mix in the flour in the bowl with your hand to make a soft biscuit-like dough. It should not be dry or stiff. If the dough seems sticky, add flour, 1 tablespoon at a time. If too dry, add water, 1 tablespoon at a time.

Pour oil into the deep-fat fryer or Dutch oven to a depth of about 3 inches. Slowly heat over moderate heat until the oil registers 360F on a frying thermometer (see page 91).

Turn out the dough onto a lightly floured work surface. Roll with a lightly floured rolling pin or pat out the dough to a large rectangle, about $\frac{1}{4}$ inch thick. With a floured, sharp knife, cut the dough into 4- to 5-inch triangles or diamond shapes. Re-roll the scraps and cut. Cut a slit along the center of each piece with a small knife, cutting through the dough and almost to the edges, to help the middle cook at the same rate as the edges. Shake or brush off the excess flour.

Place a couple of triangles of dough in the fry basket and lower the basket into the hot oil, or drop the dough one piece at a time into the oil with a slotted spoon, without crowding the pan.

Fry the pieces of bread, turning them so they cook evenly, until they puff and are browned, about 2 minutes. Lift the pieces out with the fry basket or slotted spoon and place on paper towels to drain. Eat while still warm.

INA DROPS A DOUGH TRIANGLE INTO THE HOT OIL TO FRY.

BEFORE STARTING TO FRY, INA TESTS THE OIL'S TEMPERATURE BY DROPPING IN A SMALL PIECE OF DOUGH. "IT SHOULD PUFF UP AND RISE TO THE SURFACE IMMEDIATELY," SHE SAYS.

Right DRAIN FRY BREAD ON PAPER TOWELS AS SOON AS IT IS REMOVED FROM THE HOT OIL.

Right INA SHAPES A PIECE OF ROLLED-OUT DOUGH BY THROWING IT FROM HAND TO HAND TO FLATTEN IT INTO A ROUND THE SIZE OF A SIDE PLATE.

Far Right INA FRIES THE YEAST FRY BREAD ONE PIECE AT A TIME. AS SHE DRAINS A HOT, JUST-FRIED BREAD ON PAPER TOWELS, SHE PREPARES TO FRY ANOTHER.

YEAST FRY BREAD WITH RAISINS

Ina McNeil (opposite) adds raisins to this yeast dough and fries it as a favorite snack for her grandchildren.

When I visited Ina with Anthony Blake she made this fry bread (without raisins and confectioners' sugar). We ate it like a taco, filled with chili-spiced meat, bean sauce, lettuce, tomatoes, grated cheese, and salsa. How we feasted! As Ina explained, "You are not invited to a native American's home unless they can feed you."

INGREDIENTS

Makes about twenty breads.

- 1 cake compressed fresh yeast (0.6 ounce) or 1 envelope active dry yeast ($2\frac{1}{2}$ teaspoons)
- 2 tablespoons granulated sugar
- 2 cups lukewarm water (95F–105F)
- 1 large egg, beaten
- 2 tablespoons vegetable oil
- 2 teaspoons kosher salt or flaked sea salt
- scant $\frac{1}{4}$ cup raisins
- 5 to $5\frac{1}{4}$ cups white bread flour (preferably unbleached and stone-ground)
- extra flour, for dusting
- vegetable oil, for deep-fat frying
- confectioners' sugar, for sprinkling

deep-fat fryer or 6-quart Dutch oven

Crumble the fresh yeast into a large bowl. Whisk in the sugar and lukewarm water until smooth. Let stand 15 minutes, until foamy. If using dry yeast, mix the granules with the sugar and water and let stand until foamy, 5–10 minutes (page 18).

Whisk the egg, oil, and salt into the yeast mixture. Stir in the raisins. Stir in half the flour to make a sloppy batter. Work in enough of the remaining flour to make a soft, sticky dough.

Turn out the dough onto a lightly floured surface. Knead for 5 minutes, until smooth and elastic, using the heel of your hand to stretch out the dough. Shape it into a ball. Wash, dry, and oil the bowl. Put the dough in the bowl, and turn it over so the top is oiled. Cover with a dish towel and let rise at room temperature, away from drafts, until doubled in size, about 1 hour.

Punch down the dough in the bowl, then shape it into a ball again. Cover and let rise again at room temperature, away from drafts, until doubled in size, about 1 hour.

Pour enough oil into the deep-fat fryer or Dutch oven to reach to a depth of about 3 inches. Slowly heat over moderate heat until the oil registers 360F on a frying thermometer (page 91).

Punch down the dough. With floured hands, pinch off an egg-size piece of dough. Flatten into a disk, then toss it from hand to hand, pulling it out into a round the size of a bread plate. (Ina shapes and fries the dough one piece at a time.) Place the dough into a fry basket and lower the basket into the oil, or slip the round into the oil with a slotted spoon. Fry the round about 1 minute on each side, turning it over with a slotted spoon. It should puff up instantly. Remove from the oil and drain on paper towels. Sprinkle with confectioners' sugar and eat immediately.

RISERVA
1979
San Cosma
ANTI CLASSICO

SAVORY BREADS

For far too long even good restaurants served bland and boring bread. If you were lucky, the melba toast might be nicely browned and crisp. Bread was necessary, but not important enough to merit a special baker or source. Now top chef-owners vie to offer the biggest choice of savory breads, presenting customers with ever-expanding breadbaskets and even loaded carts to confuse indecisive diners.

The selection of savory breads you can make is virtually endless, requiring only a good basic dough and some imagination. Kneading fruity, slightly peppery extra-virgin olive oil into a plain white dough and letting it rise slowly produces a flavorful, mellow loaf with a light, open texture and a thin, tearable crust (see Pugliese, page 104). Working olives – black, green, or those stuffed with anchovies, almonds, or pimientos – into a dough makes a bread that is particularly good to eat with Mediterranean dishes, or to use for sandwiches. A fabulous tomato bread can be made with sun-dried tomatoes, or sun-dried tomato purée. However, avoid using ordinary tomato paste, which tends to make a pretty loaf, but one that lacks flavor or is too sweet. Adding smoked tomatoes to bread is the latest fashion – very esoteric.

You can make powerfully flavored savory loaves simply by spreading a basic dough with sliced yellow or red onions that have been sautéed until soft in olive oil and seasoned with plenty of fresh thyme. Then you roll up the dough like a jelly-roll, enclosing the onions as a filling. Another idea is to twist pieces of dough around whole roasted garlic cloves to make savory rolls. Pesto sauce made from fresh basil in season, cilantro, crisp cracklings left from a pork roast, or cracked black peppercorns can also be used as flavorings for wonderful savory breads. Serve a thick slice with a bowl of soup for a satisfying, nourishing meal.

OPPOSITE Italian Pugliese
ABOVE Outdoor Italian bread oven

In this chapter, I use enriched brioche dough – often thought of as only a breakfast bread – to make a flavorful cheese loaf (see Brioche de Gannat, page 111) and as a rich and spectacular bread casing for a whole Brie (see Alyson Cook's Brie en Brioche, page 113). This may be served warm with a salad for a main course, or as part of a buffet spread.

Pissaladière (page 113), Flamiche aux Maroilles (page 116), Tarte Flambée (page 114), and Focaccia (page 108) are made from flattened doughs that act as plates, or trays, for a topping or filling. The crust can be thin, crisp, and crunchy, or soft, deep, and chewy. Scattered on top of or pushed into the dough are herbs, salt, and cheese, or an elaborately rich mixture, such as ratatouille.

Any of these doughs will lend itself to endless experimentation, though I am not a fan of too-trendy combinations, like tandoori pizza or Caribbean pizza, topped with pineapple and ham.

PUGLIESE

INGREDIENTS

Makes one very large loaf.

- $10\frac{1}{2}$ cups white bread flour (preferably unbleached and stone-ground)
- 2 tablespoons kosher salt or flaked sea salt
- 2 cakes compressed fresh yeast (0.6 ounce each) or 2 envelopes active dry yeast ($2\frac{1}{2}$ teaspoons each)
- 1 teaspoon granulated sugar
- $3\frac{1}{2}$ to 4 cups lukewarm water (95F to 105F)
- $\frac{1}{2}$ cup extra-virgin olive oil

a large, heavy baking sheet, floured

A Tuscan hillside covered with olive trees. It is the fruity taste of golden-green extra-virgin and virgin olive oils from this part of Italy that flavors many Italian breads. If you buy a good-quality oil, you will be rewarded with authentic-tasting breads. It is not worth using a cheaper substitute.

This soft-crumbed, yet chewy, white olive-oil bread with a pale, thin crust is based on one I tasted in Puglia, Italy. Store this bread, wrapped, at room temperature for two to three days.

Mix together the flour and salt in a large mixing bowl. Make a well in the center of the flour. Crumble the fresh yeast into a small bowl. Stir in the sugar and 3 tablespoons of the lukewarm water until smooth. Let stand for 5 to 10 minutes, or until it starts to become foamy. If using dry yeast, mix the granules and the sugar with 3 tablespoons of the lukewarm water and let stand until foamy, 5 to 10 minutes (page 18).

Pour the yeast mixture into the well in the flour, adding 3 cups of the remaining lukewarm water. Roughly mix in the flour from the bowl with your hand or a wooden spoon. Then mix in the olive oil and continue mixing until the dough comes together. If the dough remains dry and crumbly, gradually add the remaining water, about $\frac{1}{4}$ cup at a time, as necessary; the dough should be soft, but not sticky, and should hold its shape. Turn out the dough onto a lightly floured work surface. Knead for 10 minutes until it becomes very smooth and elastic.

Shape the dough into a ball. Wash, dry, and oil the bowl. Return the dough to the bowl, and turn the dough over so the top is oiled. Cover with a damp dish towel and let rise at cool to normal room temperature, away from drafts, until the dough has doubled in size, 1 to 3 hours (this will depend on the temperature of the room and the dough). Gently turn out the dough onto the prepared baking sheet, without punching it down. Gently pull out the sides of the dough, then tuck them underneath to make a neat, pillow-like round loaf. Do this several times, but do not knead the dough, punch it down, or turn it over.

Cover the dough with a damp dish towel and let rise, away from drafts, until almost doubled in size, 1 to $1\frac{1}{2}$ hours. During the last 15 minutes of rising, heat the oven to 450F. Lightly dust the loaf with flour. Bake the bread for 20 minutes.Then lower the oven temperature to 375F and bake for 25 to 35 minutes longer, or until the loaf is nicely browned and sounds hollow when tapped underneath. Transfer the loaf to a wire rack and cool completely.

VARIATIONS: PUGLIESE WITH TOMATOES AND BASIL Chop the contents of one 8-ounce jar well-drained sun-dried tomatoes packed in olive oil. Chop enough fresh basil to yield $\frac{1}{2}$ cup. Knead the tomatoes and basil into the dough when it is smooth and elastic, just before the first rising. Proceed with the recipe as above.

PUGLIESE WITH OLIVES Roughly chop 6 to 9 ounces pitted black or green olives, or stuffed green olives; the more you use, the more pronounced the flavor will be. Knead the olives into the dough when it is smooth and elastic, just before the first rising. Proceed with the recipe as above.

TUCK THE SIDES UNDERNEATH TO MAKE A TIDY, PILLOW-LIKE ROUND.

SOFT-CRUMBED PUGLIESE IS DELICIOUS EATEN FRESH SOON AFTER BAKING.

Fresh basil, juicy, sun-ripened tomatoes, and mozzarella cheese are the natural partners for freshly baked ciabatta.

CIABATTA

INGREDIENTS

Makes two medium-size loaves

- $4\frac{3}{4}$ cups white bread flour (preferably unbleached and stoneground)
- 2 cakes compressed fresh yeast (0.6 ounce each)
- $1\frac{3}{4}$ cups cold water from the tap
- $\frac{1}{2}$ cup extra-virgin olive oil
- 1 tablespoon kosher salt or flaked sea salt

two baking sheets, heavily floured

TIP A PORTION OF DOUGH ONTO EACH PREPARED BAKING SHEET TO FORM ROUGH-LOOKING RECTANGULAR LOAVES, ABOUT 1 INCH THICK. YOU MAY HAVE TO USE A SPATULA TO NUDGE THE DOUGH INTO SHAPE.

This new Italian loaf, all the rage in London, comes from the area around Lake Como in the north, and it is supposed to resemble a slipper. In any case, it is free-form – simply poured out of the bowl in which it has risen onto the baking sheet in a rough and ready rectangular loaf. It has large holes, and a soft, but chewy, floury crust. I find that many commercial loaves taste of stale olive oil or lack the pungency of good extra-virgin oil.

Finding a good recipe for this bread was difficult, and I made about thirty before I was happy with the results. Taking advice from chef Pierre Koffmann, I adapted his baguette recipe (page 32), adding a good quantity of olive oil to the dough, and altering the final consistency. As with the baguettes, it is not easy to achieve a perfect result the first time, even though the final loaf should taste very good. I have not had good results with easy-blend yeast or dried yeast granules, so I have only included instructions for using fresh yeast.

Put $3\frac{1}{4}$ cups of the flour into a large bowl. Make a well in the center of the flour. Crumble the fresh yeast into a small bowl. Stir in $\frac{1}{2}$ cup of the water until smooth. Pour the yeast mixture into the well in the flour. Then add the remaining water to the well and mix. Mix the flour from the bowl into the yeast mixture in the well with your hand or a wooden spoon to make a very sticky batterlike dough. Using your hand, beat the mixture for 5 minutes until very elastic. Cover the bowl with a damp dish towel and let rise at room temperature, away from drafts, for 4 hours until it rises and collapses. The dough will rise up enormously, so check that it does not stick to the dish towel.

Punch down the dough. Add the oil and salt to the dough and mix briefly with your hand. Then gradually work the rest of the flour in the bowl into the dough with your hand to make a soft, quite sticky dough. When all the dough is smooth and the flour has been thoroughly combined, cover the bowl with a damp dish towel and let rise at room temperature, away from drafts, until doubled in size, about 1 hour.

Using a very sharp knife, divide the dough in half, disturbing the dough as little as possible. Do not punch it down or try to knead or shape the dough at all. Tip a portion of dough onto each prepared baking sheet, nudging it with a spatula, to form two rough-looking rectangular loaves, about 1 inch thick. Sprinkle the loaves with flour and let rise, uncovered, at room temperature, away from drafts, until doubled in size, 45 minutes to 1 hour. During the last 15 minutes of rising, heat the oven to 425F.

Bake the loaves for about 35 minutes, or until they are browned and sound hollow when tapped underneath. Transfer the loaves to wire racks until lukewarm, and then serve. Or, eat within 24 hours, gently warmed. Freeze for up to one week only.

GRISSINI

INGREDIENTS

Makes about forty-six grissini.

- $2\frac{1}{3}$ to $2\frac{2}{3}$ cups whole-wheat bread flour (preferably stone-ground)
- $\frac{1}{2}$ cup white bread flour (preferably unbleached and stone-ground)
- 2 teaspoons kosher salt or flaked sea salt, or more to taste
- 1 cake compressed fresh yeast (0.6 ounce), or 1 envelope active dry yeast ($2\frac{1}{2}$ teaspoons) plus $\frac{1}{2}$ teaspoon granulated sugar
- 1 cup lukewarm water (95F to 105F)
- $\frac{1}{4}$ cup olive oil

two large baking sheets, lightly greased

Napoleon was so fond of what he called les petits bâtons de Turin *that he had them sent daily by post to his court. These thin, crunchy breadsticks are made from a simple yeast dough enriched with a little olive oil or lard. In England, I prefer making grissini with 85 percent brown flour, a whole-wheat flour that has had some of the wheat germ removed; it produces a texture somewhere between white and whole-wheat flour. This flour is not available in the States, so I've used a combination of flours. You can vary the proportions to your taste. Children particularly like the Parmesan variation. Another idea is to sprinkle the dough with sesame seeds, poppy seeds, or sea salt before baking.*

Once you get the hang of making grissini, the thin strips of dough can be rapidly rolled, pulled, and stretched by hand to form sticks. The distinctly nonuniform look of the finished result is very appealing. These go well with soups, salads, and antipasti, as well as dips, and are a wonderful replacement for the often-dreadful party nibbles. Store them in an airtight tin.

Mix together the $2\frac{1}{3}$ cups whole-wheat flour, the white flour, and salt in a large bowl and make a well in the center. Crumble the fresh yeast into a small bowl and stir in half the water until smooth. If using dry yeast, mix the granules and the sugar with half the water and let stand until foamy, 5 to 10 minutes (see page 18).

Add the yeast mixture to the well in the flour and mix in enough of the flour in the bowl to make a thick batter. Let stand for 20 minutes to sponge (page 16). Add the remaining water and the oil and mix to form a fairly firm dough. If the dough is sticky, work in small amounts of the remaining whole-wheat flour.

Turn out the dough onto a lightly floured work surface and knead for 10 minutes, or until it is smooth and elastic.

Return the dough to the washed and greased bowl and turn the dough over so the top is oiled. Cover with a damp dish towel and let rise at room temperature, away from drafts, until just doubled in size, about 1 hour. It is better to slightly underproof this

ROLL OUT THE DOUGH ON A LIGHTLY FLOURED WORK SURFACE TO A RECTANGLE ABOUT $\frac{1}{4}$ INCH THICK.

CUT THE RECTANGLE IN HALF LENGTHWISE, THEN SLICE EACH RECTANGLE CROSSWISE INTO STRIPS $\frac{1}{2}$ INCH WIDE.

USING YOUR HANDS, ROLL OUT AND STRETCH EACH STRIP UNTIL IT IS ABOUT 10 INCHES LONG. PLACE ON THE LIGHTLY GREASED BAKING SHEETS.

HALFWAY THROUGH THE BAKING TIME, TURN THE GRISSINI OVER SO THEY BROWN EVENLY.

dough than to overproof it. During the last 15 minutes of rising, heat the oven to 450F.

Punch down the risen dough. Roll it out on a lightly floured work surface with a lightly floured rolling pin to a large rectangle about ¼ inch thick.

Using a sharp knife, cut the rectangle in half lengthwise to make two long, narrow rectangles. Slice each rectangle crosswise into strips ½ inch wide. Using your hands, roll and stretch each strip until it is about 10 inches long. Place on the prepared baking sheets. Work as quickly as possible, as the grissini should be baked as soon as they are shaped. Do not give the dough a second rising.

Bake the grissini for 12 to 20 minutes, depending on how crispy you like them. Turn them over halfway through baking so they brown evenly. Transfer the grissini to wire racks to cool completely.

VARIATIONS: PARMESAN GRISSINI Add ⅔ cup grated Parmesan cheese to the flour with the salt. Then proceed with the recipe.

TOMATO GRISSINI Add 2 tablespoons drained and chopped oil-packed sun-dried tomatoes to the kneaded dough before letting it rise.

Serve grissini for nibbling with pre-dinner drinks or as part of a first course. Ideal accompaniments include fruity black olives and rich unsalted butter.

FOCACCIA

INGREDIENTS

Makes one large rectangular bread.

- 1 cake compressed fresh yeast (0.6 ounce), or 1 envelope active dry yeast ($2\frac{1}{2}$ teaspoons) plus $\frac{1}{2}$ teaspoon granulated sugar
- 1 cup cold water from the tap
- 3 tablespoons extra-virgin olive oil
- about $3\frac{1}{2}$ cups white bread flour (preferably unbleached and stone-ground)
- 2 teaspoons kosher salt or flaked sea salt
- 3 to 4 tablespoons extra-virgin olive oil, for sprinkling
- 2 teaspoons coarse sea salt, or 1 teaspoon kosher salt, or to taste, for sprinkling

a large, shallow roasting plan, about 10 × 14 inches, greased

DIMPLE THE DOUGH BY PRESSING YOUR FINGERTIPS INTO IT FIRMLY SO IT IS MARKED WITH INDENTATIONS ABOUT $\frac{1}{2}$-INCH DEEP.

This version of focaccia, flavored with olive oil and salt, comes from Genoa, Italy. Although it is made in a roasting pan, you can shape the dough into one or two rounds and bake them on jelly-roll pans. The crumb is open, light, and moist, and the crust thin and full of flavor – never soggy and rubbery, or too crisp and dry. The thickness and flavorings are determined by the baker or the region.

Enjoy this bread on picnics, with salads and cold meats, or as a snack.

Crumble the fresh yeast into a large bowl. Stir in $\frac{1}{2}$ cup of the water until smooth. Then stir in the remaining $\frac{1}{2}$ cup water and the 3 tablespoons oil. If using dry yeast, heat $\frac{1}{2}$ cup of the water to lukewarm (95F to 105F). Mix the yeast granules and the $\frac{1}{2}$ teaspoon sugar with the lukewarm water and let stand until foamy, 5 to 10 minutes (page 18). Stir in the remaining $\frac{1}{2}$ cup water and the 3 tablespoons oil.

With your hand or a wooden spoon, beat half the flour and the 2 teaspoons salt into the yeast mixture. Work in enough of the remaining flour to make a very soft, but not sticky dough. Turn out the dough onto a floured work surface and knead for 10 minutes until very smooth and silky. Wash, dry, and oil the bowl. Return the dough to the bowl, and turn the dough so the top is oiled. Cover and let rise at room temperature, away from drafts, until doubled in size, about 2 hours.

Punch down the dough. Turn out the dough onto a lightly floured work surface and roll it out with a lightly floured rolling pin to a rectangle the same size as your roasting pan. Lift the dough into the pan and pat it into the corners. Cover with a damp dish towel and let rise at room temperature, away from drafts, until not quite doubled in size, 45 to 60 minutes. Dimple the dough by pressing your fingertips into it firmly so it is marked with indentations about $\frac{1}{2}$ inch deep. Cover and let rise at room temperature until doubled in size, 1 to $1\frac{1}{2}$ hours. During the last 15 minutes, heat the oven to 425F.

Drizzle the 3 to 4 tablespoons oil over the dough so the dimples are filled, then sprinkle with the 2 teaspoons coarse salt. Put the focaccia in the oven, then spray the oven sides and bottom with water (avoiding the light bulb). This helps produce a good, moist bread. Bake for 5 minutes, then spray the oven sides and bottom again. Bake about 20 minutes longer until the focaccia is golden brown. Lift the focaccia onto a wire rack and eat while still warm.

A simple loaf of focaccia can turn into a feast when served as an antipasto with Italian salami, a bowl of homemade Italian vinegar-and-olive-oil dressing, and extra kosher salt to sprinkle over the bread. To serve Italian style, dip hunks of the bread in the dressing or into fruity olive oil. A carafe of crisp, dry Italian wine is all that is needed to complete the feast. The focaccia dough also makes a good base for a deep-crust pizza, but if you use it for pizza, do not dimple the dough or give it the third rising.

A selection of olive-oil flavored breads is an essential part of most Italian family feasts.

VARIATIONS: CHOPPED OLIVE FOCACCIA Work 3 ounces chopped pitted black oil-cured or calamata olives into the dough toward the end of the kneading time. Proceed as opposite, dimpling the dough and letting it rise. Drizzle with the oil, but omit the salt topping. Bake as opposite.

ROSEMARY FOCACCIA Add 1 tablespoon chopped fresh rosemary leaves to the dough with the last handful of flour. Then proceed with the kneading and rising. After you have dimpled the dough and it has risen, press small sprigs of fresh rosemary into the dough every 2 to 3 inches. Drizzle with the oil, but omit the salt topping, and bake as opposite. This smells heavenly as it bakes.

ROSEMARY-GARLIC FOCACCIA Prepare the dough as opposite, then dimple. Slice several garlic cloves into slivers. Press the garlic slivers into the dough. Cover and let rise as opposite. Press a few small sprigs of fresh rosemary into the dough. Drizzle with the oil, sprinkle with the salt topping, and bake as opposite.

RED-ONION FOCACCIA Prepare the dough as opposite, then dimple it and let it rise as directed opposite. Slice 2 small red onions into thin rings. Scatter the onion rings over the risen dough, then drizzle with the oil and sprinkle with the salt topping. Bake as opposite.

CHEDDAR CHEESE AND ONION LOAF

Made to eat warm or toasted with soups and salads, this bread is not for the faint-hearted. For a really full flavor, use a nutty, well-aged Cheddar cheese and strong onions; they will mellow and blend with the other ingredients during baking. It is important to roll up the dough tightly (page 26) to avoid gaps in the baked loaf.

INGREDIENTS

Makes one large loaf.

- 4¾ cups white bread flour (preferably unbleached and stone-ground)
- 1 tablespoon kosher salt or flaked sea salt
- 1 teaspoon dry mustard
- 1 cake compressed fresh yeast (0.6 ounce), or 1 envelope active dry yeast (2½ teaspoons) plus ½ teaspoon granulated sugar
- 1½ cups cold water from the tap
- 4 ounces aged Cheddar cheese, shredded (1⅓ cups)
- 3 ounces aged Cheddar cheese, cubed (⅔ cup)
- 1 medium-size onion, finely chopped (1 cup)
- 2 tablespoons vegetable oil
- milk, for glazing
- 1 small onion, sliced into ¼-inch-thick rings, for topping the loaf (½ cup)

a 9 × 5 × 3-inch loaf pan, greased

Mix together the flour, salt, and mustard in a large bowl. Make a well in the center of the flour. Crumble the fresh yeast into a small bowl. Stir in ¾ cup of the water until smooth. If using dry yeast, heat ¼ cup of the water to lukewarm (95F to 105F). Mix the yeast granules and the ½ teaspoon sugar with the lukewarm water and let stand until foamy, 5 to 10 minutes (page 18). Stir in ½ cup of the water.

Pour the yeast mixture into the well in the flour. Mix enough of the flour from the bowl into the yeast mixture with your hand or a wooden spoon to make a thin, smooth batter. Sprinkle the batter with a little flour to prevent a skin forming. Cover the bowl with a dish towel and let the batter stand until spongy and foamy, about 20 minutes.

Add the remaining ¾ cup water to the foamy batter and mix together. Gradually work in the flour from the bowl with your hand to make a soft, but not sticky dough. Turn out the dough onto a floured work surface and knead for 10 minutes, until smooth and elastic. Wash, dry, and oil the bowl. Return the dough to the bowl, and turn the dough over so the top is oiled. Cover with a damp dish towel and let rise at cool to normal room temperature, away from drafts, until doubled in size, about 2 hours.

Meanwhile, combine about 1 cup of the shredded cheese with all the cubed cheese; the variety of textures makes the filling more interesting. Sauté the chopped onion in the oil over low heat until it is soft and begins to turn golden, 10 to 12 minutes. Let cool.

Punch down the dough and turn it out onto a floured work surface. Roll out the dough with a floured rolling pin into a 10 × 15-inch rectangle. Sprinkle the cheese mixture over the dough, leaving a ½-inch border at all edges. Top with the sautéed onion. Roll up

Full, robust flavors characterize Roquefort and Walnut Loaf (left) and Cheddar Cheese and Onion Loaf. If you prefer, add a slightly nutty taste and more texture to either loaf by using $3\frac{1}{4}$ cups whole-wheat bread flour and $1\frac{1}{2}$ cups unbleached white bread flour, rather than all white flour as in the recipe. You can also substitute pecans for the walnuts.

tightly from a short side like a jelly-roll to make a loaf 10 inches long. Place the loaf, seam side down, into the prepared pan, tucking under the ends so it fits. Cover and let rise at room temperature, away from drafts, until doubled in size, about 1 to 2 hours. During the last 15 minutes of rising, heat the oven to 400F. Brush the loaf with a little milk, then sprinkle with the remaining $\frac{1}{3}$ cup shredded cheese. Bake the loaf for 20 minutes. While the loaf is baking, blanch the onion rings in a pan of boiling water for 1 minute, then drain. Brush the loaf again with milk. Arrange the blanched onion rings on top of the loaf and bake 25 to 30 minutes longer until the loaf sounds hollow when unmolded and tapped underneath. Turn out the loaf onto a wire rack to cool completely.

ROQUEFORT *AND WALNUT* LOAF

A good spinach salad, with young, tender leaves, fried bacon lardons (thick, matchstick-size strips of bacon), and a hot piquant dressing made by deglazing the bacon pan with vinegar, is the ideal accompaniment to this bread. Any well-made blue cheese – by which I mean one that tastes more of creamy, ripe, buttery blue cheese than of salt – can be substituted for the ewes' milk Roquefort. When buying cheese, always ask for a taste.

INGREDIENTS

Makes one large loaf.

1 recipe Cheddar Cheese and Onion Loaf dough (page 109)
5 ounces Roquefort cheese
4 ounces walnuts, coarsely chopped
milk, for glazing

a 9 × 5 × 3-inch loaf pan, greased

Prepare the dough as for the Cheddar Cheese and Onion Loaf. Cover and let rise, away from drafts, until doubled in size, about 2 hours.

Turn out the dough onto a floured work surface. Roll out the dough with a floured rolling pin into a 10 × 15-inch rectangle. Crumble the Roquefort cheese over the dough, leaving a $\frac{1}{2}$-inch border all around. Top with the walnuts.

Then roll up the dough from a short side like a jelly roll. Place the loaf, seam side down, in the prepared loaf pan, tucking under the ends. Cover and let rise at room temperature until doubled in size, 1 to 2 hours. During the last 15 minutes of rising, heat the oven to 400F. Brush the loaf with a little milk. Bake the loaf for 40 to 50 minutes, or until the loaf sounds hollow when unmolded and tapped underneath. Turn out the loaf onto a wire rack to cool completely.

BRIOCHE DE GANNAT

INGREDIENTS

Makes one large loaf.

- 2 to $2\frac{1}{4}$ cups white bread flour (preferably unbleached and stone-ground)
- 1 teaspoon kosher salt or flaked sea salt
- freshly ground black pepper, to taste
- 1 cake compressed fresh yeast (0.6 ounce), or 1 envelope active dry yeast ($2\frac{1}{2}$ teaspoons) plus $\frac{1}{2}$ teaspoon granulated sugar
- $\frac{1}{2}$ cup lukewarm milk (95F to 105F)
- 2 large eggs, at room temperature
- $\frac{1}{4}$ cup ($\frac{1}{2}$ stick) unsalted butter, melted
- 4 ounces Cantal or Gruyère cheese, shredded
- 1 large egg beaten with $\frac{1}{2}$ teaspoon kosher salt or flaked sea salt, to glaze

an $8\frac{1}{2} \times 4\frac{1}{2} \times 2\frac{3}{4}$-inch loaf tin, greased

This cheese brioche comes from the small town of Gannat in the Auvergne region of France, where flavorful Cantal cheese is made. The brioche dough in this recipe is not as complicated or as rich in eggs and butter as the dough for Michel Roux's Brioche (page 181); the richness here comes from the cheese. This brioche is light in texture, and I think it is best eaten on the day it is baked. Otherwise, this loaf tastes good toasted. I serve it with cheese and salads, or slice it and melt cheese on top. I've adapted this recipe from French Regional Cooking, *by Anne Willan (Morrow, 1979).*

Mix together 2 cups of the flour, the salt, and pepper from several turns of the peppermill in a large bowl. Make a well in the center of the flour.

Crumble the fresh yeast into a small bowl. Whisk in the lukewarm milk until smooth. If using dry yeast, mix the granules and the $\frac{1}{2}$ teaspoon sugar with the lukewarm milk and let stand until foamy, 5 to 10 minutes (page 18). Whisk the eggs and butter into the yeast mixture until well blended.

Pour the yeast mixture into the well in the flour. Gradually work the flour from the bowl into the liquid with your hand or a wooden spoon to make a soft, but not sticky dough, adding a little more flour as needed, 1 tablespoon at a time, to prevent the dough sticking to your fingers.

Turn out the dough onto a lightly floured work surface and knead for 10 minutes until smooth and elastic. Wash, dry, and oil the bowl.

Return the dough to the bowl, and turn the dough over so the top is oiled. Cover with a damp dish towel and let rise at cool to normal room temperature, away from drafts, until doubled in size, $1\frac{1}{2}$ to 2 hours.

Punch down the risen dough. Turn out the dough onto a lightly floured work surface and gently knead in the shredded cheese, reserving 2 tablespoons for sprinkling on top of the loaf just before baking. Shape the dough into a loaf to fit the loaf pan (page 24). Put the dough, seam side down, into the prepared pan, pinching and tucking under the ends so it fits. Then cover with a damp dish towel and let rise at room temperature, away from drafts, until it rises to the top of the pan, 1 to $1\frac{1}{2}$ hours. During the last 15 minutes of rising, heat the oven to 400F.

Gently brush the dough with the egg glaze, taking care not to "glue" the dough to the rim of the pan. Then sprinkle with the reserved 2 tablespoons of cheese. Bake the bread for 35 to 45 minutes, or until the loaf is golden brown and sounds hollow when unmolded and tapped underneath. Turn out the brioche onto a wire rack to cool completely.

THE GLAZED LOAF IS TOPPED WITH THE RESERVED CHEESE.

THE BRIOCHE DOUGH BAKES INTO A SOFT, DELICATE CRUMB.

PROVENÇAL VEGETABLE TARTS

INGREDIENTS

Makes two tarts; each serves six.

BREAD CRUST:

- $2\frac{3}{4}$ cups white bread flour (preferably unbleached and stone-ground)
- 2 teaspoons kosher salt or flaked sea salt
- 1 cake compressed fresh yeast (0.6 ounce), or 1 envelope active dry yeast ($2\frac{1}{2}$ teaspoons) plus $\frac{1}{2}$ teaspoon granulated sugar
- $\frac{3}{4}$ cup lukewarm milk (95F to 105F)
- 2 large eggs, at room temperature, lightly beaten
- $\frac{1}{4}$ cup ($\frac{1}{2}$ stick) unsalted butter, softened
- 2 tablespoons mixed chopped fresh herbs, such as parsley, basil, thyme, rosemary, and oregano

RATATOUILLE FILLING:

- 2 tablespoons extra-virgin olive oil
- 1 small onion, chopped ($\frac{3}{4}$ cup)
- 3 cloves garlic, chopped
- 1 large red bell pepper, seeded and diced ($1\frac{1}{2}$ cups)
- 5 medium-size tomatoes, peeled, seeded, and diced (3 cups)
- 1 medium-size eggplant (about 12 ounces), cut into thick matchstick strips ($\frac{1}{4} \times 2$ inches; $4\frac{1}{2}$ cups)
- 2 medium-size zucchini, cut into thick matchstick strips ($\frac{1}{4} \times 2$ inches; 3 cups)
- 1 to 2 teaspoons chopped fresh thyme leaves
- kosher salt or flaked sea salt and freshly ground black pepper, to taste
- 2 ounces Gruyère cheese, shredded
- 2 large eggs
- $\frac{1}{2}$ cup heavy cream

two 8- to 9-inch deep quiche pans or springform pans, lightly oiled

I adore ratatouille, whether served hot with roast lamb or cold as a salad. It also makes a substantial filling for these crisp, rich, herby, bread-crust tarts, which I serve warm with a big green salad for a summer lunch.

To make the bread crust: Mix together the flour and salt in a medium-size bowl. Make a well in the center of the flour. Crumble the fresh yeast into a small bowl. Whisk in the lukewarm milk until smooth. If using dry yeast, mix the granules and the $\frac{1}{2}$ teaspoon sugar with $\frac{1}{4}$ cup of the lukewarm milk and let stand until foamy, 5 to 10 minutes (page 18). Add the remaining milk. Whisk the eggs into the yeast mixture until well blended.

Pour the yeast mixture into the well in the flour. Work in the flour from the bowl, beating to make a smooth, soft, and slightly sticky dough. Knead the dough by pulling it up with your fingers and pushing it down in the bowl with the heel of your hand until very smooth and elastic, about 5 minutes. Beat in the butter and herbs until the dough is smooth, with no streaks of butter or herbs. Shape into a ball. Wash, dry, and oil the bowl. Return the dough to the bowl, and turn the dough over so the top is oiled. Cover and let rise at cool to normal room temperature until doubled in size, about 2 hours.

Meanwhile, make the filling. Heat the oil in a large, deep skillet. Add the onion and garlic and cook until tender, but not browned, 7 to 10 minutes. Add the red pepper and cook, stirring frequently, for 5 minutes. Stir in the tomatoes, eggplant, zucchini, thyme, and salt and pepper to taste. Cook, stirring occasionally, about 10 minutes, or until the vegetables are tender, but not mushy. Adjust the seasoning, and let cool.

Punch down the dough. Turn out the dough onto a floured work surface and divide into two equal portions. Roll out each portion with a floured rolling pin into an 11-inch round. Put one round into one of the pans, lining the base and sides by pressing the dough with your knuckles and fingers; the dough should be even with the top of the quiche pan, and it will extend up the side of a springform pan about 1 inch. Cover the dough with half of the cheese. Then fill with half the ratatouille. Line and fill the second pan with the remaining dough, cheese, and ratatouille.

Beat the eggs with the cream and a little salt and pepper to taste. Pour this mixture over the ratatouille in each pan, dividing equally, and using a fork to ease the vegetables apart; do not puncture the dough. Let stand, uncovered, away from drafts, until the dough starts to rise, about 15 minutes. Meanwhile, heat the oven to 400F. Bake the tarts for 30 to 35 minutes, or until they are golden brown and the fillings are set. Serve warm.

The ratatouille filling in this tart captures the sun-drenched flavors of the South of France. Juicy-ripe tomatoes, red bell peppers, eggplant, and zucchini, along with plenty of garlic, olive oil, and thyme combine to evoke images of summer along the Mediterranean. This tart is best served warm, so if you bake it in advance, reheat it in a 350F oven for 15–20 minutes.

RIGHT
The bottom round of dough should be six inches larger than the cheese.

FAR RIGHT
After Alyson wraps the cheese with the dough, she brushes it with the egg glaze.

Serve this the day it is baked, ideally with a selection of salads. The brioche dough, however, can be made and the recipe assembled the night before you plan to serve this loaf, then covered with plastic wrap and chilled overnight. Remove from the refrigerator, unwrap, and cover with a dry dish towel. Let the brioche rise at normal to warm room temperature until the dough puffs up, as directed. (This can take up to four hours.) Then bake it as described in the recipe.

ALYSON COOK'S BRIE EN BRIOCHE

INGREDIENTS

Makes one loaf.

- one and a half 0.6 ounce cakes compressed fresh yeast, or 1 tablespoon $\frac{3}{4}$ teaspoon ($1\frac{1}{2}$ envelopes) active dry yeast plus 1 teaspoon granulated sugar
- $\frac{1}{3}$ cup lukewarm milk (95–105F)
- 1 tablespoon kosher salt or flaked sea salt
- $5\frac{1}{4}$ cups white bread flour (preferably unbleached and stone-ground)
- 7 extra-large eggs, at room temperature, lightly beaten
- $1\frac{1}{2}$ cups (3 sticks) unsalted butter, softened
- 1 tablespoon granulated sugar
- one 2-pound whole Brie or Camembert cheese, 8 to 9 inches in diameter, slightly underripe
- 1 jar (about 12 ounces) spiced apricot chutney or mango chutney
- 1 extra-large egg beaten with $\frac{1}{4}$ teaspoon kosher salt or flaked sea salt, to glaze
- flour, for sprinkling
- 2 large, heavy baking sheets, one lined with a double thickness of parchment paper

I will be honest. The main point of the trip Anthony Blake and I took to California was to see my best friend Alyson, who comes from Somerset, England. We met many years ago at The Cordon Bleu, in London. She now owns a classy catering business in Los Angeles and is cooking for Hollywood legends who like to dine at home in style. This is one of Alyson's most-frequently requested dishes. It is ideal for parties.

Make the brioche dough as for Michel Roux's Brioche (page 181), using the proportions listed here. Add the yeast mixture to the flour, then beat in the eggs and knead the dough; finally, work in the butter and sugar mixture. Chill the dough after the first rising until it is firm, but not hard, 3 to 5 hours. Turn out the dough onto a lightly floured work surface. Cut off one-third of the dough and cover with a damp dish towel.

Measure the cheese, then roll out the large piece of dough with a lightly floured rolling pin into a round, about 6 inches larger than the cheese, and about $\frac{1}{2}$ inch thick. Spread the chutney evenly over the top of the cheese. Gently place the cheese upside-down in the center of the dough circle. Trim the edges of the dough, if necessary, to neaten it. Roll out the reserved dough into a circle $\frac{1}{2}$ inch larger than the cheese, and about $\frac{1}{2}$ inch thick.

Lightly brush the top of the cheese with the egg glaze. Bring the dough up around the sides of the cheese, in toward the center, leaving some of the cheese exposed in the middle, and pressing gently so the dough adheres to the cheese. Brush the top of the dough with the egg glaze. Place the other dough round on top of the cheese and gently pat the dough to seal it.

Lightly flour your hands and turn the wrapped cheese upside-down onto the prepared baking sheet. If necessary, gently mold the sides into an even shape with your hands.

Lightly score the top in a diamond or checkered pattern with the tip of a sharp knife. Cover loosely with plastic wrap and let stand at room temperature, away from drafts, until the dough puffs up, 30 to 45 minutes. During the last 15 minutes of rising time, heat the oven to 375F. Slide another baking sheet under the first to insulate the bottom so the brioche doesn't scorch.

Bake the brioche for 30 minutes. Lower the oven temperature to 350F. Brush with the egg glaze and bake 20 to 30 minutes longer, or until the brioche is puffed and golden brown. (Alyson says this gives a better finish than glazing before baking.) Let cool on the baking sheet. Then, using two large spatulas and, preferably, a helper, transfer to a cutting board or a large serving platter.

TARTE FLAMBÉE

INGREDIENTS

Makes two thin tarts; each serves two to three.

TART CRUST:

- $3\frac{1}{4}$ cups white bread flour (preferably unbleached and stone-ground)
- $1\frac{1}{2}$ teaspoons kosher salt or flaked sea salt
- 1 cake compressed fresh yeast (0.6 ounce), or 1 envelope active dry yeast ($2\frac{1}{2}$ teaspoons) plus $\frac{1}{2}$ teaspoon granulated sugar
- 1 cup cold water from the tap
- 1 teaspoon vegetable oil or unsalted butter, melted

TOPPING:

- 2 medium-size onions, very thinly sliced (2 cups)
- 8 ounces thick-sliced lean bacon
- 1 cup crème fraîche, or $\frac{1}{2}$ cup each sour cream and heavy cream
- freshly ground black pepper, to taste

two baking sheets or jelly-roll pans, lightly greased

Matchsticks of bacon, called lardons, and crème fraîche are combined with very thinly sliced onions to make the traditional topping for this rich, crisp Alsatian tart. Take care to slice the onions as thinly as possible, or they will still taste raw after the short baking time. I suggest you use the thin slicing blade of a food processor, or a mandolin.

Tarte flambée, with a wafer-thin, crunchy crust and a rich, but simple, shallow topping of crème fraîche, thinly sliced onions, and bacon slivers, can be found in almost every café-bar and restaurant in the Alsace region of France. It makes a good, inexpensive snack or ample first course.

In Riquewihr, Anthony Blake and I found the A la Fontaine restaurant, where bakers cooked these tarts to order in an outside oven situated right in the midst of the diners. The oven, built in typical Alsace style, is long, thin, and fired by logs underneath. The wood fire gives the tarts a smoky taste and a crisp crust – and it cooks the dough rapidly. The baker transferred each baked tart from the oven to the logs underneath to "flambé" it for a few seconds before serving.

Thanks to Patricia Well's invaluable book, The Food Lover's Guide to France *(Workman, 1987), we also visited the Ferme Auberge, in Weiterswiller. You can eat tarte flambée to your heart's content at this working farm and inn, where owner Simone Bloch bakes the tarts in her 45-year-old oven. Shaped like a metal coffin, 1 foot deep and 8 feet long, the oven stands on a brick platform in her small kitchen. I watched as she rapidly assembled tarts measuring 12 × 18 inches. She also adds cheese or mushrooms on request. The day we were there, tarte flambée was the only item on the menu, and nobody complained as more and more tarts kept appearing at the tables. Folding up the tarts in local fashion and eating with our fingers, Anthony and I managed three between us.*

To make the crust: Mix together the flour and salt in a large bowl. Make a well in the center of the flour. Crumble the fresh yeast into a small bowl. Stir in the water until smooth.

If using dry yeast, heat $\frac{1}{2}$ cup of the water to lukewarm (95F to 105F). Mix the granules and the $\frac{1}{2}$ teaspoon sugar with the $\frac{1}{2}$ cup lukewarm water and let stand until foamy, 5 to 10 minutes (page 18). Mix in the remaining $\frac{1}{2}$ cup of water.

Pour the yeast mixture into the well in the flour. Stir in the oil or melted butter. Mix enough of the flour from the bowl into the yeast mixture with your fingers or a wooden spoon to make a thin, smooth batter. Sprinkle the batter with a little flour to prevent a skin forming. Cover the bowl with a dish towel and let the batter stand until spongy and foamy, about 20 minutes.

Work the rest of the flour from the bowl into the batter with your hands or a wooden spoon to make a firm, not sticky dough. Turn out the dough onto a lightly floured work surface and knead for 10 minutes until smooth and elastic. Wash, dry, and oil the bowl. Return the dough to the bowl, and turn the dough over so the top is oiled. Cover with a damp dish towel and let rise at room temperature, away from drafts, until doubled in size, $1\frac{1}{2}$ to 2 hours. During the last 15 minutes of rising, heat the oven to 450F and prepare the topping.

Cut the bacon into thick matchstick shapes, called lardons, discarding any rind. If using sour cream and heavy cream, mix them together.

Punch down the risen dough. Turn it out onto a lightly floured work surface and divide into two equal portions. Roll out half the dough with a lightly floured rolling pin to a very thin rectangle the same size as your baking sheet or jelly-roll pan.

Roll the dough up on the rolling pin and unroll onto the prepared baking sheet or jelly-roll pan to cover it completely. Do not worry if the dough stretches and flops over the edges, because they will be folded in before baking. Repeat with the second piece of dough on the second prepared baking sheet or pan.

Spread one sheet of dough with $\frac{1}{2}$ cup of the crème fraîche or the cream mixture. Sprinkle with half of the sautéed onions and half of the bacon; season with plenty of pepper, to taste. Fold over the edges to make a $\frac{1}{2}$-inch border. Repeat the process with the second sheet of dough.

Bake the tarts for about 20 minutes, or until the tarts are golden and the bases crisp. Eat immediately.

PISSALADIÈRE

This is another recipe from my friend Alyson Cook (page 113). She says she likes to use a brioche dough for pissaladières because it is moister and richer than a plain white dough. She varies the topping, sprinkling capers over the traditional anchovies and tomatoes, or spreading lightly sautéed sliced onions on the dough before adding the tomato topping. Sometimes she replaces the oregano with fresh basil and then garnishes with fresh basil leaves. The black olives can be replaced with garlic slices.

INGREDIENTS

Makes one large pissaladière; serves six.

BREAD CRUST:

- 2 cups white bread flour (preferably unbleached and stone-ground)
- 1½ teaspoons kosher salt or flaked sea salt
- 1 cake compressed fresh yeast (0.6 ounce), or 1 envelope active dry yeast (2½ teaspoons) plus ½ teaspoon granulated sugar
- ½ cup lukewarm milk (95F to 105F)
- 2 large eggs, at room temperature, lightly beaten
- 7 tablespoons unsalted butter, softened

FILLING:

- 2½ tins (1¾ to 2 ounces each) flat anchovies packed in olive oil, drained
- ¼ cup milk
- 1 can (about 14½ ounces) plum tomatoes, drained
- 2 tablespoons tomato paste
- 2 tablespoons extra-virgin olive oil
- 2 cloves garlic, or to taste
- 1 tablespoon packed fresh oregano leaves
- kosher salt or flaked sea salt and freshly ground black pepper, to taste
- granulated sugar, to taste
- lemon juice, to taste
- about 3 ounces small pitted black olives

a 12 × 8 × 1-inch jelly-roll pan or a 13 × 9-inch baking pan, greased

To make the crust: Mix together the flour and salt in a large bowl. Make a well in the center of the flour. Crumble the fresh yeast into a small bowl. Stir in the lukewarm milk until smooth. If using dry yeast, mix the granules and the ½ teaspoon sugar with the lukewarm milk and let stand until foamy, 5 to 10 minutes (page 18).

Pour the yeast mixture into the well in the flour. Add the beaten eggs, mixing with your fingers or a small whisk to combine the ingredients. Gradually work in the flour from the bowl with your hands or a wooden spoon to make a very soft and quite sticky dough. Knead the dough by pulling it up with your hand and letting it fall back down, working in a circular motion. Work in the softened butter, using your hand like a whisk or rake, with fingers splayed, until it is well incorporated. Cover with a damp dish towel and let rise at room temperature, away from drafts, until doubled in size, 1½ to 2 hours.

Punch down the risen dough with your knuckles. Cover with plastic wrap and chill until firm, but not hard, 4 to 5 hours.

Meanwhile, prepare the topping: Soak the anchovies in the milk for 15 to 20 minutes to remove some of the excess salt. Drain the anchovies and discard the milk. Purée the plum tomatoes in a blender or food processor with the tomato paste, olive oil, garlic cloves, and oregano leaves. Or, you may chop the plum tomatoes, garlic cloves, and oregano leaves by hand and stir in the tomato paste and olive oil. Season to taste with salt and pepper, sugar, and lemon juice. Heat the oven to 400F.

Turn out the dough onto a lightly floured work surface and roll out with a lightly floured rolling pin into a 12 × 8-inch rectangle, or a rectangle to fill the baking pan you are using. Roll up the dough on the rolling pin and transfer to the prepared baking pan. Press it onto the bottom of the pan and into the corners, squeezing out any bubbles of air trapped between the pan and dough. Spoon the tomato mixture over the dough and spread evenly, leaving a ½-inch border at all edges.

Arrange the drained anchovies in a criss-cross pattern over the top. Put an olive in the center of each diamond.

Bake the pissaladière for 20 to 25 minutes, or until the crust is golden brown and crisp. Remove from the oven and brush the rim of the crust with olive oil. Drizzle a little olive oil over the topping as well. Then cool to warm, cut into squares, and serve.

PRESS THE DOUGH INTO THE BOTTOM AND CORNERS OF THE PAN.

ANCHOVIES AND BLACK OLIVES ARE THE TRADITIONAL TOPPING FOR THIS PIZZA-LIKE, FLAT TART.

Leek Tart (left) and Flamiche aux Maroilles are both made with a rich brioche dough crust, which makes an interesting change from more familiar piecrust.

FLAMICHE AUX MAROILLES

This is a savory cheese tart with a brioche crust. The ideal cheese for this is Maroilles, a strong, pungent, soft cheese with a brown rind that has been washed in beer as the cheese ripens. It is named after the town of Maroilles, in northern France, where it is made. However, Maroilles is next to impossible to find in the States, as it is almost never exported beyond the Continent. Edward Edleman, of the Ideal Cheese Shop, in New York City, suggested the following substitutes, in order of preference: Chaumes, Alsatian Muenster, Pont l'Evêque, Saint-Nectaire, Danish Esrom, or Appenzeller. Cooked leeks or onions may be used as substitutes for the cheese filling (see the subsequent recipe), but I prefer the version made with cheese. Serve flamiche warm from the oven, with a green salad.

INGREDIENTS

Makes one large tart; serves six to eight.

1 recipe Pissaladière dough (page 115)

FILLING:

8 ounces Maroilles cheese (see introduction), rinds removed and the cheese thinly sliced

½ cup crème fraîche or heavy cream

1 large egg

1 large egg yolk

¼ teaspoon freshly grated nutmeg

freshly ground black pepper and kosher salt or flaked sea salt, to taste

a deep 9- to 9½-inch quiche pan or deep-dish pie plate, buttered

Prepare the dough as for the Pissaladière. Cover with a damp dish towel and let rise at room temperature, away from drafts, until doubled in size, 1½ to 2 hours. Cover with plastic wrap and chill until firm, but not hard, 4 to 5 hours.

Turn out the dough onto a lightly floured work surface. Roll with a lightly floured rolling pin into a 12-inch round. Wrap the dough around the rolling pin and lift it over the prepared quiche pan or pie plate. Gradually unroll the dough so it is draped over the pan, then press it gently with your fingers onto the bottom and up the sides to evenly line the pan; do not stretch the dough. Press any overhanging dough down so it is flush with the top of the pan to make a neat crust.

Arrange the cheese in an even layer over the bottom of the dough. In a medium-size bowl, beat together the crème fraîche or cream with the egg and egg yolk, nutmeg, and plenty of black pepper and a little salt to taste, just until combined. Pour this mixture over the cheese. Let the tart rise at warm room temperature (75F), away from drafts, until it is puffy and the rim is almost doubled in size, 30 to 45 minutes. During the last 15 minutes of rising, heat the oven to 400F.

Bake the tart for 40 to 50 minutes, or until the filling is set and the crust is golden brown and crisp.

LEEK TART

INGREDIENTS

Makes one large tart; serves six to eight.

1 recipe Pissaladière dough (page 115)

FILLING:

2 pounds leeks, roots and tough green ends trimmed

4 tablespoons (½ stick) unsalted butter

kosher salt or flaked sea salt and freshly ground black pepper, to taste

½ cup crème fraîche or heavy cream

1 large egg

1 large egg yolk

a 9- to 9½-inch deep quiche pan or deep pie plate, buttered

Prepare the dough as for Pissaladière (page 115). Cover with a damp dish towel and let rise at room temperature, away from drafts, until doubled in size, 1½ to 2 hours. Punch down the dough. Cover with plastic wrap and chill until firm, but not hard, 4 to 5 hours.

Meanwhile, prepare the filling. Halve lengthwise and thoroughly rinse the leeks of sand and grit. Drain them well, then thinly slice. Melt the butter in a large, heavy-bottomed frying pan with a lid. Add the leeks and salt and pepper to taste, and stir. Cover with a disk of buttered parchment paper and the pan's lid and cook slowly until the leeks are very tender, but not browned, about 25 minutes. Let cool. Heat the oven to 400F. Turn out the dough onto a lightly floured work surface. Roll with a lightly floured rolling pin into a 12-inch round. Line the quiche pan or pie plate as for Flamiche aux Maroilles. Beat together the crème fraîche or cream, egg, and egg yolk in a medium-size bowl until just combined. Season lightly with salt and pepper. Spoon the leeks into the dough crust, then pour over the cream mixture. Bake the tart for 40 to 50 minutes, or until the filling is set and the crust is golden brown and crisp. Serve warm.

ETHIOPIAN SPICE BREAD

INGREDIENTS

Makes one large loaf.

6 tablespoons (¾ stick) unsalted butter

½ cup finely chopped onion

1 clove garlic, finely chopped

1 tablespoon plus 1½ teaspoons ground coriander

1 tablespoon plus 1½ teaspoons sweet paprika

1 tablespoon ground fenugreek

½ teaspoon freshly ground black pepper

½ teaspoon ground cinnamon

¼ teaspoon ground red pepper

large pinch freshly grated nutmeg

large pinch ground cloves

about 4½ cups white bread flour

2 teaspoons kosher salt or flaked sea salt

1 cake compressed fresh yeast (0.6 ounce) or 1 envelope active dry yeast (2½ teaspoons)

1½ cups cold water from the tap

3 tablespoons packed dark brown sugar

1 tablespoon unsalted butter, melted

a baking sheet, lightly greased

I found this recipe in The Independent, *a British newspaper, and have made it regularly ever since. It was attributed to Dr. Fiona Pharoah, and my thanks go to her and Kumud, who gave it to her. I have altered the recipe amounts and method slightly, but the basic recipe is the same. The texture is light, the color inside is golden, and the flavor is mild, yet intriguing, developing to its best after 24 hours. Everyone likes this!*

Melt the butter in a small saucepan. Add the onion, garlic, and spices and cook over low heat, stirring constantly, for 2 minutes until the spices are fragrant and lose their raw taste. Remove from the heat and let cool slightly.

Meanwhile, mix together the flour and salt in a large bowl. Make a well in the center of the flour. Crumble the fresh yeast into a small bowl. Stir in the cold water until smooth, then stir in the sugar. If using dry yeast, heat ½ cup of the cold water to lukewarm (95F to 105F). Mix the granules and 1 teaspoon of the sugar with ½ cup lukewarm water and let stand until foamy, 5 to 10 minutes (page 18). Add the remaining sugar and water.

Pour the yeast mixture into the well in the flour, followed by the spice and onion mixture. Mix enough flour from the bowl into the yeast mixture to make a medium-thick batter. Sprinkle the batter with a little flour to prevent a skin forming. Cover the bowl and let stand until the batter becomes spongy and foamy, about 20 minutes.

Work the rest of the flour from the bowl into the batter to make a fairly firm dough. Turn out the dough onto a lightly floured work surface and knead for 10 minutes until smooth and elastic, adding a little extra flour if the dough is sticky.

Return the dough to the bowl. Cover and let rise at room temperature, away from drafts, until doubled in size, about 2 hours. Punch down the dough. Break off a large walnut-size piece of dough and reserve. Turn out the dough onto a floured work surface and shape into a free-form loaf as for The Basic Loaf (page 17). Put the loaf on the prepared baking sheet. With a sharp knife, lightly score a cross on top of the loaf. Place the small nut of dough in the center of the cross. Cover and let rise at room temperature, away from drafts, until doubled in size, about 1 hour. During the last 15 minutes of rising, heat the oven to 375F. Bake for 40 to 50 minutes, or until the loaf is browned and sounds hollow when tapped underneath. If the small "nut" on top of the loaf is browning too quickly, cover loosely with foil. Transfer to a wire rack. Brush with the melted butter and let cool.

BAGELS

INGREDIENTS

Makes twenty small bagels.

- 3 to 3¼ cups white bread flour (preferably unbleached and stone-ground)
- 1½ teaspoons kosher salt or flaked sea salt
- 1 cake compressed fresh yeast (0.6 ounce) or 1 envelope active dry yeast (2½ teaspoons)
- ½ cup each milk and water, mixed, at room temperature (75F)
- 1 teaspoon granulated sugar
- 2 tablespoons melted unsalted butter or vegetable oil
- 1 large egg, separated
- sesame seeds or poppy seeds, for sprinkling

- three baking sheets, greased
- a steamer pot with a lid, or a large deep skillet, a wire rack, and aluminum foil

The popularity of the bagel – literally, "a roll with a hole" – has spread from Jewish communities to the wide world. A bagel was just a bagel to me until I realized I had married into a family of American East Coast bagel mavens. Yet they particularly love those made by a man called Noah in, of all places, Berkeley, California. "Noah's bagels have Yiddish in their souls," I was told. "There's nothing like them in Brooklyn."

Noah Alper bakes 250,000 bagels a week in the college town of Berkeley, and I met with him in his College Avenue shop. He defined the archetypical bagel for me. "It's important that it's big, crusty on the outside, chewy inside, tasty, and with plenty of seeds. Of course you don't have to be Jewish to know what a good bagel tastes like." I've adapted his recipe to make bagels that are smaller than what is usually encountered, because that is what I prefer.

Bagels were first made centuries ago in Poland. Badly made, a bagel will be rubbery, heavy, and soggy. The best ones, like Noah's, are finished by hand. The added toppings can be poppy seeds, sesame seeds, onions, caraway seeds, salt, or, as a California curiosity, sunflower seeds.

Eat bagels sliced and plain, toasted and buttered, spread with a schmear (a liberal coating) of cream cheese, or with cream cheese and lox or smoked salmon, onions, and pickles. These bagels are best eaten as soon as possible after baking, or cool, wrap in freezer bags, and freeze for up to one month. Remove from the bags and reheat straight from the freezer on the oven racks in a 350F oven for about 10 minutes before serving.

Mix together 3 cups of the flour and the salt in a large bowl. Make a well in the center of the flour. Crumble the fresh yeast into a small bowl. Whisk in the milk mixture until smooth. Stir in the sugar. If using dry yeast, heat ½ cup of the milk mixture to lukewarm (95F to 105F). Mix the yeast granules and the sugar with the lukewarm liquid and let stand until foamy, 5 to 10 minutes (page 18). Stir in the remaining ½ cup of liquid.

Pour the yeast mixture into the well in the flour, followed by the melted butter or vegetable oil. Lightly beat the egg white until frothy, then add to the well and mix with a small whisk until thoroughly combined. Gradually work in the flour from the bowl with your hand or a wooden spoon to make a soft and pliable dough. Turn out the dough onto a lightly floured work surface. Cover with the upturned bowl and let stand for 5 minutes. Then knead for 10 minutes until the dough is smooth and elastic, adding the remaining flour as needed, 1 tablespoon at a time, to prevent sticking. Wash, dry, and oil the bowl.

Return the dough to the bowl, and turn the dough over so the top is oiled. Cover with a

Noah Alper's bagel shop in Berkeley, California. Noah's method of bagel making – he steams his bagels before baking them, instead of poaching them – has caused something of a controversy among the bagel lovers of the Bay Area. Among his faithful followers, "super onion," with onion in the dough and sprinkled on top, is his best-seller.

A sumptuous brunch of fresh bagels with smoked salmon, cream cheese with snipped fresh chives, and just-brewed coffee.

dish towel and let rise, away from drafts, until doubled in size, $1\frac{1}{2}$ to 2 hours.

Punch down the dough. Weigh the dough and divide it into twenty equal portions, or roll it into a 20-inch rope and cut into twenty 1-inch pieces. Using your hands, and only flouring them and the work surface if it is necessary to prevent the dough from sticking, roll each piece into a sausage about 6 inches long. Taper the ends, then join them securely together using a little cold water to make a neat ring. Arrange the bagels, well apart, on the prepared baking sheets. Cover with dry dish towels and let rise at room temperature, away from drafts, until almost doubled in size, about 45 minutes. During the last 15 minutes of rising, heat the oven to 400F.

Bring some water to a boil in the bottom of a steamer pot or half fill a large, deep skillet with water and bring it to a boil. Reduce the heat so the water is simmering. Grease the steamer rack or a wire rack. (The rack must be greased after each batch, so keep a pastry brush and a bit of vegetable oil close at hand.) Place the steamer rack or wire rack over the simmering water. Arrange three or four bagels at a time, spaced apart, on the steamer rack or wire rack and cover with the steamer lid or a dome-shaped piece of aluminum foil; keep the remaining bagels covered. Steam for 1 minute.

Transfer the bagels to a baking sheet. If you prefer, the bagels can be poached, three at a time, for 30 seconds each.

Beat the egg yolk with 2 teaspoons cold water. Brush the steamed or poached bagels with the egg glaze. Leave plain, or sprinkle with sesame or poppy seeds. Bake the bagels for 20 to 25 minutes, or until they are golden brown and puffed up. Transfer to wire racks to cool.

FRUIT AND NUT BREADS

When I was four years old, I was so proud of my new green gingham uniform dress I refused to take it off at the end of my first day at school, despite a large sticky patch on the back of the skirt. During the school break we had been given a glass of milk and a buttered currant bun with a sticky, shiny glaze. My new little friends told me the only way to eat the bun – which I had never seen the likes of – was to sit on it, then cram the squashed mass into my mouth in one go. I did not think of the consequences, but ate the bun as instructed. What fun – what a good bun! It came from the Victoria Bakery in Barnet High Street, in north London, a bakery renowned for its fruit and nut breads, spicy buns, and hot cross buns. This unfortunate introduction to sweet fruit breads did not deter my enthusiasm for them. I have been collecting the best recipes for years.

For centuries, breads made from soft, rich doughs were held in high esteem, and took the place of the cakes we eat today. They were flavored with raisins, currants, or other dried fruits, such as apricots, prunes, peaches, and pears, and sometimes with spice and nuts. The large breads were leavened with the yeast that was a by-product from brewing ale until chemical leavening agents became generally available. Today, it is almost as if we have come full cycle, and once again sweet fruited breads are in fashion; however, some consider them a luxurious treat due to the high calorie content from the sugar (both refined and from the dried fruit) and the fat they contain.

OPPOSITE and ABOVE
Sandra's Saffron Buns

In this chapter, I want to pass on my enthusiasm and introduce you to traditional and modern varieties of fruit and nut breads. The famous Chelsea Buns of London (page 129), Bara Brith (page 127) from Wales, and the similar Barm Brack (page 126) from Ireland are among the breads generations of home bakers have served at teatime, instead of a cake. More modern fruit and nut breads include Viola's Caramel Cinnamon Rolls (page 125) from America, the attractive Peach Couronne (page 132), and the light Hazelnut, Apricot, and Honey Loaf (page 131). If all these seem too sweet, try the Walnut Bread (page 134), which is excellent with a good farmhouse cheese.

These breads are easy to make and do not require much skill, so they're ideal for introducing children to bread-making. You will find that homemade fruit and nut breads, including the ever-popular sticky buns, are light, moist, and full of flavor. They really are worth making, because many of the commercial varieties have become dense, flavorless, and far too sweet.

SANDRA'S SAFFRON BUNS

INGREDIENTS

Makes fourteen buns.

- 1 teaspoon saffron strands
- 2 tablespoons lukewarm water (95F to 105F)
- $3\frac{1}{4}$ cups white bread flour (preferably unbleached and stone-ground)
- $\frac{1}{2}$ teaspoon kosher salt or flaked sea salt
- 6 tablespoons granulated sugar
- $1\frac{1}{3}$ cups mixed dried fruit, rinsed (use a combination of currants and dark and golden raisins)
- $\frac{1}{4}$ cup (1 ounce) diced candied citrus peel (preferably orange and lemon peel)
- $\frac{3}{4}$ cup ($1\frac{1}{2}$ sticks) cold unsalted butter, diced
- 2 cakes compressed fresh yeast (0.6 ounce each) or 2 envelopes active dry yeast ($2\frac{1}{2}$ teaspoons each)
- $\frac{3}{4}$ cup lukewarm milk (95F to 105F)
- 2 tablespoons unsalted melted butter, for brushing
- 2 tablespoons coarse granulated sugar, coarse "raw" brown sugar, or demerara sugar, for sprinkling

two baking sheets, well greased

Quite by chance, Anthony Blake and I booked a fortnight's bed and breakfast stay at the house of one of Cornwall's finest bakers, named Sandra. She was apparently tireless, and relentlessly cheerful. No matter what time we looked into her kitchen, there she was baking, weighing warmed flour, rinsing dried fruit, kneading large balls of dough, and constantly checking the color of the loaves in the oven. Every day Sandra started at 5 A.M., finishing well after midnight, baking batch after batch of pungent saffron buns, which are her specialty, along with a few dozen pasties, and her standard white and whole-wheat loaves. We returned late after a day of photography to discover that, although Sandra had had a massive and shiny new oven installed after breakfast, she had not missed a beat with her baking.

Saffron is used a good deal in Cornish baking, despite the fact that the local saying "as dear as saffron" is all too apt. Good saffron is fabulously expensive because each saffron crocus produces only three stamens, which have to be laboriously plucked out with tweezers, and 4,000 stamens weigh only one ounce. Although nearly all our saffron now comes from Spain, until a hundred years ago it was grown extensively in England around the towns of Saffron Walden, in Essex, and Stratton, in Cornwall. For centuries, this expensive flavoring was used to make breads and cakes look and taste wonderfully rich. The best saffron buns, like these, are generously flecked with saffron filaments. As this dough is enriched with a fair quantity of butter, it takes quite a bit of time to rise, but the result is light textured, fine crumbed, rich, and highly aromatic. Eat the buns within two days of baking, spread with butter. These buns do not freeze well.

Put the saffron strands onto a heatproof saucer or in a small ovenproof skillet and toast in a 350F oven for 10 to 15 minutes, or until their color darkens. Soak the saffron strands in the lukewarm water in a cup for at least 1 hour – it is best if you can leave it overnight.

Stir together the flour and salt in a large bowl. Stir in all but 1 teaspoon of the granulated sugar, all the dried fruit, and the mixed candied citrus peel. Rub in the butter with your fingertips until the mixture resembles fine crumbs.

Make a well in the center of the flour. Crumble the fresh yeast into a small bowl. Stir in the reserved 1 teaspoon sugar and half of the lukewarm milk. Let the yeast mixture stand for about 5 minutes, or until it starts to becomes foamy. If using dry yeast, mix the granules and the reserved 1 teaspoon sugar with half the lukewarm milk and let stand until foamy, 5 to 10 minutes (page 18).

Golden yellow and studded with dark and golden raisins and currants, these saffron-flavored buns are best spread with creamy, unsalted butter or with cream cheese. The dough can also be shaped into one large loaf, which is ideal for slicing and toasting.

Above
SHAPE EACH PIECE OF DOUGH INTO A NEAT BUN BY ROLLING IT BETWEEN YOUR FLOURED PALMS.

Top
KNEAD THE DOUGH IN THE BOWL UNTIL IT IS VERY SMOOTH AND ELASTIC. PULL OFF FOURTEEN PIECES OF DOUGH.

Pour the saffron, its soaking liquid, and the yeast mixture into the well in the flour, adding most of the remaining lukewarm milk. Using your hand, mix the flour mixture from the bowl into the liquid in the well until the dough comes together. If the dough is dry and crumbly, gradually add more lukewarm milk, 1 tablespoon at a time; the dough should be soft, but not sticky. Knead the dough in the bowl for 10 minutes, working it thoroughly against the side of the bowl, until it is very smooth and elastic. Cover with a damp dish towel and let rise, away from drafts, until doubled in size. This heavy dough is slow to rise and can take as long as overnight in a cool room, or 3 to 4 hours in a warm kitchen.

Punch down the dough. Using lightly floured hands, one at a time, pull off fourteen equal-size pieces of dough and roll each between your palms to form neat buns. Or, roll the dough into a fat rope and cut into fourteen equal pieces. Using floured hands, shape each portion into a bun. Put on the prepared baking sheets, spaced well apart. Cover with a damp towel and let rise at warm room temperature (about 75F) until doubled in size, about 2 hours. During the last 15 minutes of rising, heat the oven to 375F.

Bake the buns for 15 minutes. Then lower the oven temperature to 350F and bake for 5 minutes longer, or until the buns sound hollow when tapped underneath. Brush the hot buns with melted butter and sprinkle with the coarse sugar. Then bake for 3 minutes longer. Transfer to wire racks to cool completely.

NOTE: You can also make a saffron loaf, instead of buns. After the first rising, shape the dough into a loaf (page 24) and put it, seam side down, into a well-greased 9 × 5 × 3-inch loaf pan. Let rise as above, then bake in a 375F oven 40 minutes. Lower the oven temperature to 350F and bake for 15 to 20 minutes longer, or until the loaf sounds hollow when unmolded and tapped underneath. Brush with melted butter and sprinkle with the coarse sugar. Then bake 3 minutes longer. Unmold onto a wire rack to cool.

GENTLY WORK THE GLACÉ FRUIT AND ALMONDS INTO THE SOFT, RICH DOUGH.

ABOVE RIGHT
Serve slices of sugar-crusted pougno for a delicious breakfast.

POUGNO

This bread, generously studded with glacé (candied) fruit, comes from the Provence region of southern France. The region is justly famous for preserving whole fruit, such as strawberries, mandarins, figs, tiny whole pineapples, and greengage plums, which are cooked in sugar syrup and glazed. These are eaten with a knife and fork at the end of a festive meal, usually Christmas. Provence also produces fruit confits, in which fruits such as pineapple rings, lemon and orange slices, and melon and pumpkin pieces are preserved with sugar, but left unglazed. They are sold in the region's best grocers and confiseurs, and used for making cakes, breads, and pastries. Unfortunately, they are not available in America.

Quality glacé fruits are expensive because the preserving process is time-consuming and often done by hand. For the best flavor, do not use citrus peel from the supermarket. If you cannot get good glacé fruit, use raisins. In Provence, pougno is eaten for breakfast with bowls of very milky, strong coffee. It is best eaten within four days of baking, and it can be frozen for up to one month.

INGREDIENTS

Makes one small loaf.

- $1\frac{1}{2}$ cups white bread flour (preferably unbleached and stone-ground)
- $\frac{1}{2}$ teaspoon kosher salt or flaked sea salt
- 1 cake compressed fresh yeast (0.6 ounce) or 1 envelope active dry yeast ($2\frac{1}{2}$ teaspoons)
- 3 tablespoons granulated sugar
- 2 tablespoons lukewarm milk (95F to 105F)
- 3 large eggs, at room temperature, lightly beaten
- 4 tablespoons ($\frac{1}{2}$ stick) unsalted butter, diced and softened
- finely grated rinds of 1 large lemon and 1 medium-size orange (about $1\frac{1}{2}$ teaspoons each)
- $\frac{1}{2}$ cup (3 ounces) finely chopped glacé (or candied; see introduction) fruit (use a mixture of pineapple, figs, orange slices, pear, apricot, and peach, if possible)
- $\frac{1}{2}$ cup blanched almonds, coarsely chopped
- granulated sugar, for dredging

a baking sheet, greased

Stir together the flour and salt in a warmed medium-size bowl and make a well in the center of the flour. Crumble the fresh yeast into a small bowl. Stir in the sugar and lukewarm milk until smooth. Let the yeast mixture stand for about 5 minutes, or until it starts to become foamy. If using dry yeast, mix the granules and the sugar with the lukewarm milk and let stand until foamy, 5 to 10 minutes (page 18).

Pour the eggs and the yeast mixture into the well in the flour. Mix in the flour from the bowl with your hand or a wooden spoon to make a soft dough. Beat the dough in the bowl with your hand for 10 minutes, or until it becomes smooth, shiny, and elastic.

Using your hand, with fingertips splayed, gently beat the butter into the dough until incorporated. Add the grated lemon and orange rinds, working in the same way.

Scrape out the dough onto a lightly floured work surface and shape it into a ball. Wash, dry, and oil the bowl. Return the dough to the bowl, and turn the dough over so the top is oiled. Cover with a damp dish towel and let rise at room temperature, away from drafts, until doubled in size, about 2 hours.

Turn out the dough onto a lightly floured surface (there's no need to punch it down). Gently work in the glacé fruit and almonds until thoroughly incorporated. Shape the dough into a disk about $1\frac{1}{2}$ inches thick and put it on the prepared baking sheet. Cover lightly with a damp dish towel and let rise at warm room temperature (about 75F) until doubled in size, about 1 hour. During the last 15 minutes of rising, heat the oven to 375F. Bake the loaf for 20 to 25 minutes, or until it is golden and sounds hollow when tapped underneath. Dredge in the sugar, then transfer to a wire rack to cool completely.

VIOLA'S CARAMEL CINNAMON ROLLS

INGREDIENTS

Makes fifteen rolls.

DOUGH:

- 1 cake compressed fresh yeast (0.6 ounce) or 1 envelope active dry yeast (2½ teaspoons)
- ½ cup lukewarm water (95F to 105F)
- 1 teaspoon granulated sugar
- 4 tablespoons (½ stick) cold unsalted butter, diced
- ¼ cup granulated sugar
- ¾ teaspoon kosher salt or flaked sea salt
- 1¼ cups hot water (about 130F)
- 4½ to 5 cups white bread flour (preferably unbleached and stone-ground)
- 1 tablespoon plus 1½ teaspoons vital wheat gluten (optional)
- 1 large egg, at room temperature

FILLING:

- 6 tablespoons (¾ stick) unsalted butter, softened
- ½ cup firmly packed dark brown sugar
- 1 tablespoon ground cinnamon, or to taste

CARAMEL TOPPING:

- 1 cup firmly packed dark brown sugar
- ½ cup heavy cream

- a 13 × 9-inch baking pan, well buttered
- a baking sheet

The lightest, moistest, and gooiest sticky buns ever! Viola Unruh (page 45) says the secret to these rolls is to let the sweet, rich, and airy dough rise three times. This old-fashioned American prairie kitchen recipe, her husband Henry's favorite, is an absolute treasure. The vital wheat gluten Viola includes in every batch is unobtainable in Great Britain, yet may be purchased at health-food stores or by mail order in the States (page 187). However, the results are just as enjoyable when the dough is made without it. In England I use good-quality unrefined Barbados muscovado sugar, but dark brown sugar works well, too. This recipe makes plenty of caramel topping. When the rolls have cooled, store them, well wrapped, at room temperature, and eat them within two days.

To make the dough: Crumble the fresh yeast into a small bowl. Stir in the lukewarm water and the 1 teaspoon granulated sugar until smooth. Let the yeast mixture stand for 5 to 10 minutes, or until it starts to become foamy.

If using dry yeast, mix the granules and the sugar with the lukewarm water and let stand until foamy, 5 to 10 minutes (page 18).

Meanwhile, put the butter, the ¼ cup granulated sugar, and the salt into a large bowl. Pour in the hot water and stir until the butter melts. Add 1½ cups of the flour and the vital wheat gluten, if using, and beat together well with a wooden spoon until the mixture is very smooth. Pour in the yeast mixture and the egg and beat for 1 minute until well blended. Cover with a damp dish towel and let rest for 10 minutes.

Working in the bowl, gradually knead in about 3 cups of the remaining flour to make a soft dough. Turn out the dough onto a lightly floured work surface and knead for 10 minutes, gradually working in as much of the remaining flour as is necessary, a handful at a time, to make a soft, but not sticky dough. Wash, dry, and oil the bowl.

Return the dough to the bowl, and turn the dough over to oil the top. Cover with a damp dish towel and let rise at room temperature, away from drafts, until doubled in size, about 1 hour. Punch down the dough. Leave the dough in the bowl, cover again and let rise again at warm room temperature (about 75F) until almost doubled in size, about 1 hour.

Punch down the dough. Turn out onto a lightly floured work surface and knead for 1 minute. Cover with the upturned bowl and let rest for 10 minutes.

Meanwhile, make the filling: Beat the butter with the dark brown sugar and cinnamon in a medium-size bowl with a spoon or electric mixer until light and fluffy.

Roll out the dough on a lightly floured work surface with a lightly floured rolling pin into a 15 × 10-inch rectangle with a short side facing you. Gently spread the filling over the rectangle, trying not to stretch the dough, spreading all the way to the edges. Then roll up tightly from a short side, like a jelly-roll. Cut the roll into fifteen even slices, each about 1 inch thick. Arrange the slices, with a cut side down, in the prepared baking pan, with the sides just touching. Cover with a damp dish towel and let rise at room temperature until doubled in size, about 45 minutes. (If the temperature is too warm, the filling will ooze out.) During the last 15 minutes of rising, heat the oven to 350F.

Bake the rolls for 30 to 35 minutes, or until the rolls are well risen and golden brown. (Viola recommends that you do not bake these too near the bottom of the oven.)

Meanwhile, make the caramel topping: Whisk the dark brown sugar and cream together in a small bowl until no lumps remain. Turn out the buns in one piece onto the baking sheet.

Pour the caramel topping into the baking pan. Tilt the pan so the topping covers the bottom evenly. Then slide the buns, upside-down, back into the pan on top of the caramel mixture. Return to the oven and bake 10 minutes longer. Remove from the oven and let the buns cool in the pan for 30 minutes. Serve the rolls from the pan, spooning the caramel sauce over them, or invert the pan onto a baking sheet, so the caramel sauce is on top of the rolls. Pull the rolls apart to serve.

INVERT THE ROLLS ONTO A BAKING SHEET AND PULL APART TO SERVE.

BARM BRACK

This spicy loaf, dotted with currants, is from Ireland, where it was originally baked in a cast-iron pot suspended over a fire. Although now baked in conventional ovens, the bread is still made in a traditional round shape rather than as a loaf. The word "barm" in the name comes from the liquid ale yeast that was used to raise the dough before blocks of compressed yeast made bread-making easier.

Barm brack is a close cousin to bara brith (opposite), but it is sweeter and more cake-like. It keeps, well wrapped, for four or five days, or can be frozen for up to one month.

INGREDIENTS

Makes one loaf.

- $3\frac{1}{4}$ cups white bread flour (preferably unbleached and stone-ground)
- $\frac{3}{4}$ cup firmly packed light brown sugar or granulated white sugar
- $1\frac{1}{2}$ teaspoons ground cinnamon
- $1\frac{1}{2}$ teaspoons pumpkin-pie spice, or 1 teaspoon freshly ground spice mixture (page 140)
- 1 teaspoon kosher salt or flaked sea salt
- one and a half 0.6-ounce cakes compressed fresh yeast or $1\frac{1}{2}$ envelopes active dry yeast (1 tablespoon plus $\frac{3}{4}$ teaspoon)
- $\frac{1}{2}$ cup lukewarm milk (95F to 105F)
- 10 tablespoons ($1\frac{1}{4}$ sticks) unsalted butter, melted
- 3 large eggs, at room temperature, lightly beaten
- 2 cups (10 ounces) currants
- 2 tablespoons firmly packed light brown sugar dissolved in 3 tablespoons boiling water, for glazing

an 8-inch-round cake pan, with sides 3 inches deep, greased

ABOVE
Rich with currants, barm brack is served in Ireland for afternoon tea. It is just as delicious with a cup of coffee for a mid-morning snack.

RIGHT
Rural Ireland, where you can still see milk being transported by horse and cart, has a rich baking heritage. Accomplished home bakers keep traditional recipes alive, of which barm brack remains one of the most popular. More variations include golden raisins and candied citrus peel; if you wish, replace some of the currants with a tablespoon or two of diced candied peel.

Place the flour, sugar (reserve 1 teaspoon if using dry yeast), cinnamon, pumpkin-pie spice, and salt into a large bowl. Rub the sugar into the flour with your fingers to break up any lumps and to mix the ingredients. Make a well in the center of the flour mixture.

Crumble the fresh yeast into a small bowl. Stir in the lukewarm milk until smooth. If using dry yeast, mix the granules and the reserved 1 teaspoon sugar with the lukewarm milk and let stand until foamy, 5 to 10 minutes (page 18). Pour the yeast mixture into the well in the flour. Mix in enough of the flour in the bowl with your hand or a wooden spoon to make a thin, smooth batter. Let stand 15 minutes until spongy. Add the melted butter and the beaten eggs to the sponge and beat with a small whisk or your hand.

Mix the flour from the bowl into the spongy mixture to make a soft, but not sticky dough. If the dough is dry and crumbly, add more milk or water, 1 tablespoon at a time. If the dough sticks to your fingers, add more flour, 1 tablespoon at a time.

Turn out the dough onto a lightly floured work surface and knead for about 10 minutes, until smooth and elastic. Gradually knead in the currants until evenly distributed, 4 to 5 minutes. Return the dough to the bowl (there is no need to oil the bowl for this recipe). Cover with a damp dish towel and let rise at room temperature, away from drafts, until doubled in size, 2 to $2\frac{1}{2}$ hours.

Punch down the dough. Turn it out onto a floured surface and shape the soft dough into a round to fit the pan. Put the round, seam side down, into the prepared pan. Cover with a damp dish towel and let rise at room temperature, away from drafts, until doubled in size, 1 to $1\frac{1}{2}$ hours. During the last 15 minutes, heat the oven to 400F.

Bake the loaf for 25 minutes. Lower the oven temperature to 375F and bake for 15 minutes longer, or until it is browned and a skewer inserted in the center comes out clean. If the loaf is browning too quickly, cover loosely with butter wrappers or a sheet of foil. Remove from the oven and brush immediately with the hot, sweet glaze. Place the pan on a wire rack and let the bread cool completely before turning it out.

A farmhouse afternoon tea: Teacakes For Toasting (page 128), Bara Brith, and Barm Brack (opposite).

BARA BRITH

The name of this speckled loaf from Wales means currant bread. I've also added dark and golden raisins and a bit of candied citrus peel for extra flavor. To avoid over-baking the loaf, be sure to check it after 30 minutes.

INGREDIENTS

Makes one large loaf.

- $1\frac{1}{3}$ cups mixed dried fruit, such as currants and dark and golden raisins
- $\frac{1}{3}$ cup ($1\frac{1}{2}$ ounces) chopped candied citrus peel (preferably orange and lemon peel)
- $1\frac{1}{4}$ cups strong hot tea, strained, if necessary
- $3\frac{1}{4}$ cups white bread flour (preferably unbleached and stone-ground)
- $\frac{1}{3}$ cup firmly packed light brown sugar
- 1 teaspoon kosher salt or flaked sea salt
- $\frac{1}{2}$ teaspoon pumpkin-pie spice or freshly ground spice mixture (page 140)
- one and a half 0.6-ounce cakes compressed fresh yeast or $1\frac{1}{2}$ envelopes active dry yeast (1 tablespoon plus $\frac{3}{4}$ teaspoon)
- 2 tablespoons lukewarm milk (95F to 105F)
- 4 tablespoons ($\frac{1}{2}$ stick) unsalted butter, melted

a 9 × 5 × 3-inch loaf pan, greased

Put the mixed dried fruit and candied citrus peel into a medium-size bowl. Add the hot tea and stir well. Cover with plastic wrap and let soak overnight at room temperature.

The next day, place the flour, brown sugar (reserve 1 teaspoon if using dry yeast), the salt, and the spice into a large bowl. Rub the brown sugar into the flour with your fingers to break up any lumps and to mix the ingredients. Make a well in the center of the flour mixture. Crumble the fresh yeast into a small bowl. Stir in the lukewarm milk until smooth. If using dry yeast, mix the granules and the reserved 1 teaspoon brown sugar with the lukewarm milk and let stand until foamy, 5 to 10 minutes (page 18). Pour the yeast mixture into the well in the flour. Mix in enough of the flour in the bowl with your hand or a wooden spoon to make a thin, smooth batter. Let stand 15 minutes until spongy. Stir the fruit mixture, soaking liquid, and melted butter into the sponge.

Mix the flour from the bowl into the sponge to make a soft dough. If the dough is dry and crumbly, add milk or water, 1 tablespoon at a time. If the dough sticks to your fingers, add more flour, 1 tablespoon at a time.

Gently knead the dough in the bowl for 5 minutes, or until the fruit is evenly distributed and the dough is elastic; it will be quite soft. Turn out the dough onto a sheet of waxed paper and wash, dry, and oil the mixing bowl. Return the dough to the bowl, and turn the dough over so the top is oiled. Cover with a damp dish towel and let rise at room temperature, away from drafts, until doubled in size, $1\frac{1}{2}$ to 2 hours.

Punch down the dough. Turn out the dough onto a floured surface and shape into a loaf to fit the prepared pan (page 24). Put the loaf, seam side down, into the pan. Cover with a damp towel and let rise at room temperature, away from drafts, until doubled in size. Heat the oven to 400F. Bake the loaf for 40 minutes, or until it sounds hollow when unmolded and tapped underneath. If the loaf is browning too quickly, cover it with foil. Turn the loaf out of the pan onto a wire rack to cool.

Right
REMOVE THE TEACAKES FROM THE OVEN WHEN THEY ARE GOLDEN BROWN AND PUFFED UP.
Far right
SERVE TOASTED TEACAKES SPREAD WITH BUTTER. TO TOAST THEM UNDER A HOT BROILER, TOAST THE TOP AND THE BOTTOM. SPLIT THE TEACAKES IN HALF AND TOAST THE CUT SURFACES.

TEACAKES FOR TOASTING

INGREDIENTS

Makes eight teacakes.
- ½ cup currants
- ¼ cup (1 ounce) diced candied citrus peel (preferably orange and lemon peel)
- ½ cup strong hot tea, strained, if necessary
- about ½ cup milk
- 1 cake compressed fresh yeast (0.6 ounce) or 1 envelope active dry yeast (2½ teaspoons)
- 3¼ cups white bread flour (preferably unbleached and stone-ground)
- 1 teaspoon kosher salt or flaked sea salt
- ¼ cup cold diced lard or cold unsalted butter, diced
- 2 tablespoons granulated sugar
- milk, for brushing

two or three baking sheets, greased

My mother, like her mother before her, comes into her own at teatime. She possesses a china cupboard stacked from floor to ceiling with exquisite tea services, including some porcelain so eggshell-thin it is almost transparent; she enjoys using it, despite the hazards. Each day, teatime is an important ritual, even if it is "just family."

My American husband is greatly amused by the quaintness of this almost bygone English custom, although he has succumbed to their soothing comforts – even if he does insist on black coffee, instead of tea.

The best way to toast teacakes is under a very hot broiler, or over the red-hot embers of an open fire. These teacakes stale quickly so eat within one day, or you can keep for two days if you plan to toast them. They can also be frozen for up to one month. Thaw at room temperature before toasting.

Put the currants and candied citrus peel into a small bowl. Pour in the hot tea, stir well, and let steep for 1 hour. Drain the fruit in a strainer set over a measuring cup. Add enough milk to the tea soaking liquid to make 1 cup.

Crumble the fresh yeast into a small bowl. Stir in the tea mixture until smooth. If using dry yeast, note the amount of tea soaking liquid left after the fruit is strained out. Reserve the tea. Measure an amount of milk that when added to the tea will total 1 cup of liquid. Heat the measured amount of milk in a small saucepan to lukewarm (95F to 105F). Mix the dry yeast granules and 1 tablespoon of the granulated sugar with the lukewarm milk and let stand until foamy, 5 to 10 minutes (page 18). Then stir in the tea soaking liquid.

Mix together the flour and salt in a large bowl. Rub in the lard or butter with your fingertips until the mixture resembles fine crumbs. Stir in the sugar (the remaining 1 tablespoon, if using the dry yeast) and the soaked currants and candied citrus peel. Make a well in the center of the flour mixture.

Pour the yeast mixture into the well. Mix the flour from the bowl into the liquid in the well with your hand or a wooden spoon to make a soft dough. Turn out the dough onto a lightly floured work surface and knead for 10 minutes until smooth and elastic.

Return the dough to the bowl. (There is no need to oil the bowl.) Cover with a damp dish towel and let rise at room temperature, away from drafts, until doubled in size, 1½ to 2½ hours, depending on the weather and the temperature of the room.

Gently punch down the dough. Turn out the dough onto a lightly floured work surface. Weigh the dough and divide it into eight equal pieces, or roll it into a fat rope and cut it into eight equal pieces. Shape each portion into a neat roll (see Oatmeal Rolls, page 25). Flatten each roll so it is about 5 inches wide and ¾ inch thick. Arrange the teacakes on the prepared baking sheets, spaced well apart. Cover loosely with a damp dish towel and let rise at room temperature until almost doubled in size, about 45 minutes. During the last 15 minutes of rising, heat the oven to 400F.

Glaze the teacakes with milk. Bake them for about 20 minutes until they are golden brown and puffed up.

Transfer to wire racks. Lightly dust each teacake with flour, then cover loosely with dry dish towels to keep the crust soft. Let them cool completely.

CHELSEA BUNS

INGREDIENTS

Makes nine buns.

DOUGH:

- $3\frac{1}{4}$ cups white bread flour (preferably unbleached and stone-ground)
- 1 teaspoon kosher salt or flaked sea salt
- 3 tablespoons granulated sugar
- 1 cake compressed fresh yeast (0.6 ounce) or 1 envelope active dry yeast ($2\frac{1}{2}$ teaspoons)
- $\frac{1}{2}$ cup lukewarm milk (95F to 105F)
- 1 extra-large egg, lightly beaten
- 4 tablespoons ($\frac{1}{2}$ stick) unsalted butter, melted

FILLING:

- 3 tablespoons unsalted butter, melted
- $\frac{1}{3}$ cup firmly packed light or dark brown sugar
- $\frac{3}{4}$ cup mixed dried fruit, such as currants and dark and golden raisins
- $\frac{1}{4}$ cup (1 ounce) diced candied citrus peel (preferably orange and lemon peel)

STICKY GLAZE:

- $\frac{1}{2}$ cup firmly packed light brown sugar
- 4 tablespoons ($\frac{1}{2}$ stick) unsalted butter
- $\frac{1}{4}$ cup milk
- 2 tablespoons honey

an 8- to 9-inch-square cake pan, about $1\frac{1}{2}$ inches deep, greased

For about a hundred years, until its demise in 1839, the Chelsea Bun House was famous for its spicy, sugary, sticky buns. Situated in Bunhouse Place, off Pimlico Road, in London, the bakery was hugely fashionable, the place to be seen standing in line to buy a Chelsea bun. The owners also claimed to have invented the hot cross bun. In fact, the bakery's hot cross buns were in such demand that one Good Friday, thousands of people, including King George III, thronged down Ebury Street toward the shop. Eat these within two days of baking.

To make the dough: Mix together the flour, salt, and half the sugar in a large bowl. Make a well in the center of the flour mixture. Crumble the fresh yeast into a small bowl. Stir in the remaining sugar and the lukewarm milk until smooth. If using dry yeast, mix the granules and half the sugar with the lukewarm milk and let stand until foamy, 5 to 10 minutes (page 18).

Pour the yeast mixture into the well in the flour and mix enough flour from the bowl into the liquid with your hand or a wooden spoon to make a thick batter. Let stand until spongy, about 10 minutes. Beat the egg and melted butter into the spongy mixture with your hand or a small whisk. Gradually work in the flour from the bowl to make a soft, but not sticky dough. If the dough is dry, add water or milk, 1 tablespoon at a time.

Turn out the dough onto a lightly floured work surface and knead for 10 minutes until very smooth, elastic, and satiny. Wash, dry, and oil the bowl. Return the dough to the bowl, and turn the dough over so the top is oiled. Cover with a damp dish towel and let rise at room temperature, away from drafts, until doubled in size, about $1\frac{1}{2}$ hours.

Punch down the dough. Turn out the dough onto a floured work surface and roll out with a floured rolling pin into a 16 × 9-inch rectangle, with a long side facing you.

For the filling: Brush the dough with the melted butter. Then sprinkle with the sugar, followed by the mixed dried fruit and the candied citrus peel, leaving a $\frac{1}{2}$-inch border all around the edge. Starting from a long side, roll up the dough fairly tightly, like a jelly roll. Cut the roll into nine even pieces and arrange them, cut side down, in the prepared pan, touching but not squashed together. Cover the pan with a damp dish towel and let rise at room temperature, away from drafts, until almost doubled in size, 30 to 40 minutes. During the last 15 minutes of rising, heat the oven to 400F.

To make the sticky glaze: Combine the brown sugar, butter, milk, and honey in a small saucepan and heat over moderately low heat, stirring frequently, until the butter melts and the sugar dissolves. Bring to the boil, then simmer for 1 minute. Pour the glaze over the risen buns. Bake the buns for 20 minutes. Lower the oven temperature to 350F, cover the buns with a sheet of foil, and bake about 10 minutes longer, or until the buns are golden brown. Cool in the pan for about 10 minutes, or until the topping is firm, but not set. Then transfer the buns to a wire rack set over a sheet of foil and let cool. If the topping is left too long and welds onto the pan, put the pan back in the oven until the topping softens again. Pull or tear the buns apart when they have cooled.

POUR THE STICKY GLAZE OVER THE RISEN BUNS, THEN BAKE.

COOL THE BUNS ON A WIRE RACK, THEN PULL OR TEAR APART TO SERVE.

GERMAN PEAR LOAF

INGREDIENTS

Makes one loaf.
- $\frac{2}{3}$ cup chopped dried pears
- $\frac{1}{2}$ cup chopped dried figs
- $\frac{1}{2}$ cup chopped pitted prunes
- 1 cup apple juice or prune juice
- $\frac{1}{2}$ cup water
- $2\frac{1}{4}$ cups white bread flour (preferably unbleached and stone-ground)
- $\frac{3}{4}$ cup rye flour
- $\frac{1}{3}$ cup firmly packed light brown sugar
- $\frac{1}{4}$ cup granulated sugar
- 1 teaspoon kosher salt or flaked sea salt
- 2 cakes compressed fresh yeast (0.6 ounce each) or 2 envelopes active dry yeast ($2\frac{1}{2}$ teaspoons each)
- 2 tablespoons lukewarm water (95F to 105F)
- $\frac{1}{2}$ cup chopped, toasted, skinned hazelnuts
- $\frac{1}{3}$ cup chopped, toasted, blanched almonds
- grated rind of 1 large lemon (about $1\frac{1}{2}$ teaspoons)

a heavy baking sheet, greased

A loaf packed with dried fruit and nuts, but not as rich, heavy, or moist as the densely fruited Hutzelbrot from Nuremberg (page 141). This is traditionally served with a glass of kirsch or fruit liqueur, but is equally good with coffee for breakfast. Eat within one week of baking, or freeze for up to one month.

Mix together the pears, figs, and prunes in a medium-size bowl. Add the apple or prune juice and the $\frac{1}{2}$ cup water and stir well. Cover with plastic wrap and soak overnight.

The next day, put the two flours, the two sugars (if using dry yeast, reserve 1 teaspoon of the granulated sugar), and the salt into a large bowl. Rub the ingredients together with your fingers to break up any lumps of brown sugar and to combine the ingredients. Make a well in the center of the flour mixture.

Crumble fresh yeast into a small bowl. Stir in the 2 tablespoons lukewarm water until smooth. If using dry yeast, mix the granules and the reserved 1 teaspoon granulated sugar with the lukewarm water and let stand until foamy, 5 to 10 minutes (page 18).

Pour the yeast mixture into the well in the flour. Mix in enough flour from the bowl with your hand or a wooden spoon to make a thin, smooth batter. Let stand 15 minutes until spongy. Stir the fruit mixture, any soaking liquid, the nuts, and the lemon rind into the sponge. Mix the flour from the bowl with your hand into the sponge to make a rather damp, sticky dough. If the dough is extremely sticky, add white bread flour, 1 tablespoon at a time. If the dough is dry, add water, 1 tablespoon at a time. It is easiest to knead this dough in the bowl, squeezing it between your fingers, until the fruit is well distributed and the dough is elastic, about 5 minutes.

Cover with a damp dish towel and let rise at room temperature, until the dough increases in size by half, 2 to $2\frac{1}{2}$ hours. (This dough will not double in size.)

OPPOSITE
Dried fruit sweetens and flavors the Hazelnut, Apricot, and Honey Loaf and the German Pear Loaf (center). I prefer to purchase dried fruits from a health-food store with a fast turnover (also see mail-order sources in the List of Suppliers, page 187). Look for moist, pliable fruit with a slightly tart, intense, fruity flavor, otherwise, the breads will be too sweet.

Punch down the dough and turn it out onto a floured surface. Gently knead for 30 seconds. Shape the dough into an oval loaf (see The Basic Loaf, page 17) about 10 inches long. Place the loaf seam side down on the prepared baking sheet. Cover with a damp dish towel and let rise at warm room temperature (about 75F), away from drafts, until it again increases in size by half, 2 to 2½ hours. During the last 15 minutes of rising, heat the oven to 350F. Bake the loaf for 50 minutes to 1 hour, or until it is browned and sounds hollow when tapped underneath. Transfer to a wire rack to cool completely.

HAZELNUT, APRICOT, AND HONEY LOAF

This recipe uses hazelnut oil, more expected on salads than in breads, along with a flavorful honey, such as orange blossom, heather, or wildflower. I was given this recipe by Shaun Hill of Gidleigh Park, in Devon, England. Eat this loaf within three days, or toast and serve with butter or cheese. It can be frozen for one month.

INGREDIENTS

Makes one loaf.

- 1 cake compressed fresh yeast (0.6 ounce) or 1 envelope active dry yeast (2½ teaspoons)
- ½ cup lukewarm milk (95F to 105F)
- ¼ cup flavorful honey (see introduction)
- ¾ cup coarsely chopped dried apricots
- ½ cup boiling water
- 3 to 3¼ cups white bread flour (preferably unbleached and stone-ground)
- a scant ⅔ cup hazelnuts, toasted, skinned, and halved or coarsely chopped
- 1 teaspoon kosher salt or flaked sea salt
- 2 tablespoons hazelnut oil, or 2 tablespoons unsalted butter, melted
- rye flour for dusting (optional)

a 9 × 5 × 3-inch loaf pan, greased

NOTE: If desired, bake in two 8½ × 4½ × 2¾ inch loaf pans. Decrease baking time to about 40 minutes or until the loaves are golden brown.

Crumble the fresh yeast into a small bowl. Stir in the lukewarm milk and honey until smooth. Let the yeast mixture stand 5 to 10 minutes, or until it starts to become foamy. If using dry yeast, mix the granules with the lukewarm milk and the honey and let stand until foamy, 5 to 10 minutes (page 18). Meanwhile, put the apricots into a small bowl. Pour in the boiling water and let soak for about 10 minutes, or until the fruit has plumped up and the water cooled to lukewarm. Mix together 3 cups of the flour, the hazelnuts, and the salt in a large bowl and make a well in the center.

Pour the yeast mixture into the well in the flour mixture, followed by the hazelnut oil or melted butter, and the apricots and their soaking liquid. Mix all the ingredients in the well together with your hand or a wooden spoon. Then gradually work in the flour from the bowl into the liquid in the well to make a soft, but not sticky dough. If the dough sticks to your fingers, work in the rest of the flour, as needed, 1 tablespoon at a time.

Turn out the dough onto a lightly floured work surface and knead for 10 minutes until smooth and fairly firm. Return the dough to the bowl (there is no need to oil the bowl). Cover with a damp dish towel and let rise at room temperature, away from drafts, until doubled in size, 1½ to 2 hours.

Punch down the dough. Turn it out onto a floured surface and knead 1 minute in the rye dough, if using. Shape into a loaf (see A Plain White Loaf, page 24). Put the loaf, seam side down, into the prepared pan. Cover with a damp dish towel and let rise at room temperature until almost doubled in size, about 1 hour. During the last 15 minutes, heat the oven to 375F.

Bake the loaf for about 1 hour, or until it is golden brown and sounds hollow when unmolded and tapped underneath. Turn out onto a wire rack to cool completely.

LET THE LOAVES, OR LOAF, RISE IN THE PAN UNTIL ALMOST DOUBLED IN SIZE.

This twisted ring with its unusual fruit and nut filling can be served as a coffee cake, or as a winter dessert. It is especially good with pouring cream, or vanilla-scented, lightly whipped heavy cream. The intricate-looking shape is surprisingly easy to make, but you should allow yourself plenty of time for your first attempt.

PEACH COURONNE

Dried peaches plus raisins and walnuts make a deliciously tart filling for this pretty ring. The dried peaches can be replaced by an equal quantity of dried apricots, if you wish. Serve the couronne warm as a dessert, with cream if you like, or at teatime. Eat within one day, or freeze for only one week.

Place the peaches in a small bowl. Pour in the orange juice and let soak overnight.

To prepare the dough: Mix the flour and salt in a medium-size bowl. Rub in the butter until the mixture resembles fine crumbs. Make a well in the center of the flour mixture. Crumble the fresh yeast into a small bowl. Stir in the lukewarm milk until smooth. If using dry yeast, mix the granules and the ½ teaspoon sugar with the lukewarm milk and let stand until foamy, 5 to 10 minutes (page 18). Mix the egg into the yeast mixture.

Pour the yeast mixture into the well. With your hand, gradually work the flour from the bowl into the liquid to make a soft, but not sticky dough. Turn out the dough onto a

INGREDIENTS

Makes one large ring.

½ cup chopped dried peaches
½ cup orange juice

DOUGH:

1½ cups white bread flour (preferably unbleached and stone-ground)
½ teaspoon kosher salt or flaked sea salt
3 tablespoons cold unsalted butter, diced
two-thirds of a 0.6-ounce cake of compressed fresh yeast, or 2 teaspoons active dry yeast from a 2½-teaspoon envelope plus ½ teaspoon granulated sugar
¼ cup lukewarm milk (95F to 105F)
1 large egg, lightly beaten

FILLING:

6 tablespoons (¾ stick) unsalted butter, softened
¼ cup firmly packed light brown sugar
¼ cup all-purpose white flour (preferably unbleached)
⅔ cup walnuts, chopped
½ cup raisins
grated rind of 1 medium-size orange (about 1½ teaspoons)

2 tablespoons granulated sugar, for glazing

a baking sheet, greased

floured work surface and knead for 10 minutes until smooth, elastic, and satiny.

Shape the dough into a ball. Return it to the bowl. Cover with a damp dish towel and let rise at room temperature, away from drafts, until doubled in size, 1 to 1½ hours.

Meanwhile, prepare the filling: Drain the peaches, reserving the soaking liquid. Beat the butter and brown sugar in a medium-size bowl with an electric mixer on medium-high speed until fluffy. On low speed, beat in the flour, then the walnuts, raisins, orange rind, and peaches. Or, stir them in with a wooden spoon.

Punch down the dough. Turn out the dough onto a floured work surface and with a floured rolling pin roll out into a 12 × 9-inch rectangle. Spread the filling evenly over the dough. Roll the dough up fairly tightly from a long side, like a jelly roll. Gently roll the dough back and forth, stretching it, until it is 20 inches long.

Carefully cut the dough in half lengthwise. Working with the cut sides facing up, place the two lengths of dough side by side. Braid the two lengths together by holding them at one end and carefully lifting the right length of dough over the left length; arrange them so the two are roughly parallel. Do not twist the lengths, to avoid spilling out the filling. Lift the right length over the left length as before, and continue this process until the two lengths are braided together. Very gently slide the prepared baking sheet under the braided dough. Then shape the braid into a neat ring, twisting and pinching the ends together to close the ring. Cover loosely and let rise at room temperature, away from drafts, until doubled in size, about 1 hour. During the last 15 minutes of rising, heat the oven to 400F.

Bake the ring for 20 to 25 minutes, or until firm and golden. Stir the remaining 2 tablespoons of sugar into 2 tablespoons of the reserved peach soaking liquid in a small saucepan and bring to a boil, stirring to dissolve the sugar. Remove the couronne from the oven and immediately brush with the hot glaze. Slide onto a wire rack to cool.

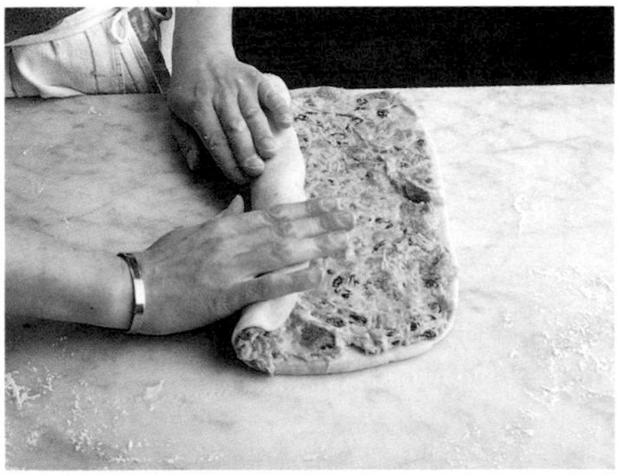

SPREAD THE FILLING EVENLY OVER THE DOUGH. ROLL UP THE DOUGH FROM A LONG SIDE, AS FOR A JELLY ROLL.

USING A VERY SHARP KNIFE, CAREFULLY CUT THE DOUGH IN HALF LENGTHWISE.

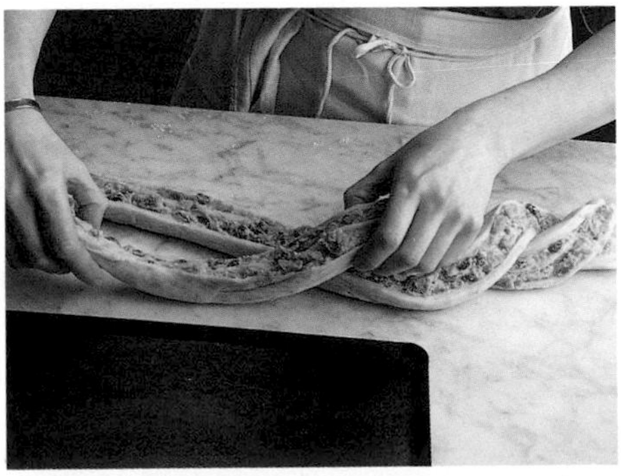

WITHOUT TWISTING THE HALVES, JOIN THEM TOGETHER BY LIFTING THE RIGHT OVER THE LEFT. KEEP THEM PARALLEL. CONTINUE UNTIL BRAIDED TOGETHER.

BRING THE ENDS OF THE DOUGH TOGETHER TO CLOSE THE RING. PINCH THEM TO SEAL.

LOIS'S FRUIT SLICE

INGREDIENTS

Makes two large coffee cakes.

DOUGH:

- 1 cake compressed fresh yeast (0.6 ounce) or 1 envelope active dry yeast ($2\frac{1}{2}$ teaspoons)
- 2 teaspoons granulated sugar
- $\frac{3}{4}$ cup lukewarm water (95F to 105F)
- 1 cup heavy cream
- $\frac{1}{2}$ cup granulated sugar
- 1 teaspoon kosher salt or flaked sea salt
- 2 large eggs
- 2 tablespoons unsalted butter, melted
- about $4\frac{3}{4}$ cups white bread flour (preferably unbleached and stone-ground)

FILLING:

- $1\frac{1}{2}$ pounds prune plums, halved and pitted, or $1\frac{1}{4}$ pounds fresh berries, such as blueberries, blackberries, raspberries, or pitted sour cherries
- 1 tablespoon plus $1\frac{1}{2}$ teaspoons cornstarch or 2 tablespoons tapioca
- about $1\frac{1}{2}$ cups granulated sugar, to taste

CRUMBLE TOPPING:

- $\frac{3}{4}$ cup all-purpose white flour (preferably unbleached)
- $\frac{2}{3}$ cup granulated sugar
- $\frac{1}{2}$ cup (1 stick) unsalted butter, diced, softened

two baking sheets with edges or two jelly-roll pans, about 14 × 8 inches, greased

Lois Keller with a freshly baked fruit slice.

Here is another recipe from Lois Keller (page 99), who lives in the heart of America – indeed, she is almost exactly at America's center, if you fold the map in fourths. This recipe, from her husband's German family, uses white flour, and is one of the few recipes Lois makes with refined flour. (She prefers to grind her own flour from whole wheat kernels.) Lois likes to use the wild berries that grow around her farm, or the German purple-blue plums she also grows, which are packed with flavor. You may use the European type of plums called prune plums. Prune plums are small, dark purple, and usually freestone plums with pointed, not rounded, ends. Grown in California, the Pacific Northwest, Michigan, and New York State, they become available in August. This coffee cake is eaten with coffee for breakfast or mid-afternoon tea. It is best eaten within two days of baking.

To prepare the dough: Crumble the fresh yeast into a large bowl. Stir in the 2 teaspoons sugar and the lukewarm water until smooth. If using dry yeast, mix the granules and the 2 teaspoons sugar with the lukewarm water and let stand until foamy, 5 to 10 minutes (page 18). In a medium-size bowl, whisk the cream with the $\frac{1}{2}$ cup sugar and the salt just until mixed. Whisk in the eggs and melted butter until well blended.

Add $1\frac{1}{4}$ cups of the flour to the yeast mixture and mix in with your hand. Stir in the cream mixture. Then work in enough of the remaining flour to make a very soft dough. If the dough seems too sticky, work in a little extra flour, 1 tablespoon at a time. If the dough is dry and crumbly, work in a little extra water, 1 tablespoon at a time. Turn out the dough onto a lightly floured work surface and knead with floured hands for 10 minutes to form a smooth and satiny ball. The dough should be soft rather than dry or tough. Return the dough to the bowl. Cover with a damp dish towel and let rise at room temperature, away from drafts, until doubled in size, about 1 hour. During the last 15 minutes of rising, heat the oven to 350F.

Meanwhile, prepare the filling. Mix together the plums, berries, or cherries, the cornstarch or tapioca, and sugar to taste in a large bowl. (If the fruit is very sweet you'll need less sugar than listed.) Cover and let stand while the dough is rising.

To prepare the crumble topping: Mix together the flour and sugar in a medium-size bowl. Using a fork, work in the butter to make coarse crumbs. Set aside.

Punch down the dough. Turn out the dough onto a floured surface and knead for 30 seconds. Divide the dough in half. Roll out each portion on a floured work surface with a floured rolling pin into a rectangle about $\frac{1}{4}$ inch thick, the same size as the prepared baking sheets or jelly-roll pans. Roll up the dough loosely on the rolling pin and unroll onto the sheets or pans, patting the dough with your hands into the corners, forming a slight rim on all sides. Spoon half the fruit filling evenly over each piece of dough. If using plums, arrange them cut-side up on the dough. Sprinkle half of the crumble topping evenly over each coffee cake. Bake the cakes for 35 to 40 minutes, or until the pastry rims are golden and firm. Serve warm with cream.

WALNUT BREAD

Toasting the walnut halves until lightly browned gives this loaf a dense, nutty flavor. Some bakers also add a tablespoon or two of walnut oil or melted butter with the last of the water. Eat this loaf within three days of baking, or freeze for up to one month.

Stir together the whole-wheat and white flours and the salt in a large bowl and make a well in the center. Crumble the fresh yeast into a small bowl. Stir in $\frac{3}{4}$ cup of the lukewarm water and the honey until smooth. If using dry yeast, mix the granules and the honey with $\frac{3}{4}$ cup of the lukewarm water and let stand until foamy, 5 to 10 minutes (page 18).

Walnut Bread variations in this photo include sliced Raisin Bread.

INGREDIENTS

Makes two medium-size loaves.

- 3½ cups whole-wheat bread flour (preferably stone-ground)
- 1½ cups white bread flour (preferably unbleached and stone-ground)
- 1¾ teaspoons kosher salt or flaked sea salt
- 1 cake compressed fresh yeast (0.6 ounce) or 1 envelope active dry yeast (2½ teaspoons)
- 1½ cups lukewarm water (95F to 105F)
- 1 tablespoon plus 1½ teaspoons flavorful honey
- 1 tablespoon walnut oil or melted unsalted butter (optional)
- 2½ cups walnuts, lightly toasted, cooled, and coarsely chopped

one very large baking sheet (18 × 12 inches) or two regular-size baking sheets, greased

Pour the yeast mixture into the well in the flour. Mix in enough flour from the bowl with your hand to make a thick batter. Let stand until spongy, 10 to 15 minutes.

If necessary, reheat the remaining ¾ cup water to lukewarm. Pour the water into the sponge, along with the oil or melted butter, if using. With your hand or a wooden spoon, gradually work the flour from the bowl into the sponge to make a soft, but not sticky dough. If the dough sticks to your fingers, work in a little extra flour, 1 tablespoon at a time. If the dough is dry and crumbly, work in a little extra water, 1 tablespoon at a time. Turn out the dough onto a lightly floured work surface and knead for 10 minutes until smooth and elastic. Gently knead the walnuts into the dough until they are evenly distributed, about 2 minutes. Wash, dry, and oil the bowl.

Shape the dough into a ball. Return the dough to the bowl, and turn the dough over so the top is oiled. Cover with a damp dish towel and let rise at room temperature, away from drafts, until doubled in size, about 2 hours.

Punch down the dough. Turn it out onto a floured surface and knead gently for 1 minute. Divide in half. Shape each half into a neat ball and place on the prepared baking sheet(s). Cover with a damp dish towel and let rise at room temperature, away from drafts, until doubled in size, about 1½ hours. During the last 15 minutes of rising, heat the oven to 425F. Cut three shallow slashes in the top of each loaf. Bake the loaves for 15 minutes. Then lower the oven temperature to 375F and bake for 20 to 30 minutes longer, or until the loaves sound hollow when tapped underneath. Cool on wire racks.

VARIATIONS: PECAN BREAD Use 2½ cups *each* whole-wheat bread flour (preferably stone-ground) and white bread flour (preferably unbleached and stone-ground) and prepare the dough as for the Walnut Bread. Replace the walnuts with an equal amount of coarsely chopped, untoasted pecans. Proceed with the recipe.

MIXED NUT BREAD Prepare the dough as for the Walnut Bread. Replace the walnuts with 2½ cups coarsely chopped, toasted mixed nuts, such as walnuts, skinned hazelnuts, pecans, and/or macadamia nuts. Proceed with the recipe.

RAISIN BREAD Prepare the dough as for the Walnut Bread, replacing up to ¾ cup of the whole-wheat flour with rye flour, if you wish. Replace the walnuts with 1¼ cups raisins.

FRUIT AND NUT BREAD Prepare the dough as for the Walnut Bread. Replace the walnuts with 1½ cups dark or golden raisins and 1½ cups coarsely chopped toasted walnuts. Proceed with the recipe.

CINDY'S PORTUGUESE SWEET BREADS

INGREDIENTS

Makes two loaves.
$\frac{1}{3}$ cup currants
1 tablespoon orange juice, rum, Madeira, sherry, or hot water
2 cakes compressed fresh yeast (0.6 ounce each) or 2 envelopes active dry yeast ($2\frac{1}{2}$ teaspoons each)
1 cup lukewarm water (95F to 105F)
$\frac{1}{2}$ cup plus 3 tablespoons granulated sugar
$\frac{1}{4}$ cup nonfat dry milk powder
$5\frac{1}{2}$ to $6\frac{1}{4}$ cups white bread flour (preferably unbleached and stone-ground)
3 large eggs, at room temperature
$\frac{1}{2}$ cup (1 stick) unsalted butter, softened
1 teaspoon kosher salt or flaked sea salt
1 large egg, beaten with a pinch of kosher salt or flaked sea salt, for glazing
coarse "raw" brown sugar, demerara sugar, or granulated sugar, for sprinkling

2 large baking sheets, one greased
a 9-inch-round cake pan, greased

Called pao doce *in Portuguese, this recipe makes two loaves, one with currants and braided, and the other shaped like a small snail, called* caracois.

Cindy Falk (page 51) was given this recipe by a colleague in the Kansas Wheat Commission, and now her eleven-year-old daughter Laura uses it to win baking competitions. Laura makes the neatest braid I have ever seen. To ensure a good shape to your loaf, do not let the shaped dough over-rise, or leave it in too warm a place to rise.

Eat this bread sliced and buttered within two days of baking. If you do not plan to eat both loaves, wrap and freeze one loaf for up to two months.

Put the currants in a small bowl. Add the 1 tablespoon of the liquid of your choice and let stand for 1 hour, or until the currants are softened.

Crumble the fresh yeast into the bowl of an electric mixer fitted with a dough hook, or into a large bowl. Mix in $\frac{1}{4}$ cup of the lukewarm water and 1 teaspoon of the granulated sugar until smooth. Let stand about 5 minutes, or until it starts to become foamy. If using dry yeast, mix the granules and 1 teaspoon of the granulated sugar with $\frac{1}{4}$ cup of the lukewarm water and let stand until foamy, 5 to 10 minutes (page 18). Add the rest of the water and the sugar, the milk powder, and $2\frac{1}{2}$ cups of the flour. Beat on medium speed with a dough hook for 2 minutes, or with your hand or a wooden spoon for 4 minutes, until it is a smooth, thick batter.

With the mixer on low speed, gradually add the eggs, one at a time, the butter, and the salt and mix until thoroughly combined, or mix in the ingredients with your hand or a wooden spoon. Add enough of the rest of the flour, a handful at a time, to make a soft, but not sticky dough that gathers in a ball around the dough hook or comes together and leaves the sides of the bowl cleanly. Knead the dough on slow speed for 5 minutes until it is smooth and feels "as silky as a baby's behind," as Cindy says. Or, turn out the dough onto a floured work surface and knead for about 10 minutes until smooth and soft.

Wash, dry, and oil the bowl. Return the dough to the bowl, and turn the dough over so the top is oiled. Place the bowl in a large greased plastic bag and tie closed, or cover the bowl with a damp dish towel and let rise at room temperature, away from drafts, until doubled in size, about 2 hours.

Punch down the dough. Turn it out onto a lightly floured work surface and divide into two equal portions. With lightly floured hands, knead the softened currants and any soaking liquid that has not been absorbed into one portion of the dough. Cover both portions of dough with a damp dish towel and let rest at room temperature, away from drafts, for 20 minutes.

Shape the plain portion of dough into the snail loaf: Roll out the dough with your lightly floured hands into a rope 25 inches long and $1\frac{1}{2}$ inches thick. Coil the rope in the

LET THE BRAIDED LOAF RISE AT ROOM TEMPERATURE, AWAY FROM DRAFTS, UNTIL DOUBLED IN SIZE, ABOUT 1 HOUR.

TO MAKE CINDY'S SPECIAL BRAID, ARRANGE TWO OF THE DOUGH ROPES IN A CROSS ON THE PREPARED BAKING SHEET. PLACE THE THIRD ROPE STRAIGHT THROUGH THE MIDDLE, TO MAKE A STAR SHAPE. BEGIN BRAIDING, FOLLOWING THE DIRECTIONS IN THE NOTE (BELOW RIGHT).

TOP
A selection of breads baked by Cindy Falk (page 51), including the highly glazed Portuguese Sweet Breads shaped into a long braid and as a snail. Other loaves include her Multi-grain Harvest Bread (page 51), which was baked in a loaf pan, and two round Pioneer Breads (page 53). For this photograph, Cindy slashed the Pioneer Breads with a checkerboard design, rather than the star shape suggested in the recipe.

prepared cake pan, starting in the center and twisting the dough as you coil it around to form a snail shape, and tuck the ends under. Place the pan in a large greased plastic bag and tie closed, or cover with a damp dish towel, and let rise at room temperature, away from drafts, until doubled in size, about 1 hour.

After you've shaped the snail loaf, make the braided loaf. On a lightly floured work surface, divide the currant dough into three equal pieces. Roll out each piece of dough with floured hands into a 16-inch-long rope. Lay the three ropes side-by-side on the prepared baking sheet, then braid the strands together neatly, but not too tightly. (See page 30 and the Note.) Tuck the ends under and pinch to seal. Cover with a damp dish towel and let rise at room temperature, away from drafts, until doubled in size, about 1 hour. During the last 15 minutes of rising, heat the oven to 350F.

When each loaf has doubled in size, brush with the egg glaze, taking care not to let it dribble down the sides or "glue" the dough to the pan or baking sheet. Sprinkle each with the coarse sugar. The snail loaf will probably be ready to bake before the braid, depending on how warm your kitchen is and how quickly you formed the braid. Slide another baking sheet under the sheet holding the braid to prevent the bottom of the loaf from browning. Put each loaf into the oven when it is ready; the baking times will overlap. Bake each loaf for 30 to 40 minutes, or until it is golden brown and sounds hollows when tapped underneath. Cover the loaves with foil during baking if they appear to be burning too quickly. Transfer to wire racks to cool completely.

NOTE: Another way to braid the loaf is to arrange two of the ropes in a cross shape on the prepared baking sheet. Place the third rope straight through the middle, to make a star shape. Braid the three ropes facing toward you, then turn the baking sheet around and braid the three other ends. This gives a slightly more unusual shape to the loaf. Pinch the ends together and tuck under to give a neat shape.

CELEBRATION BREADS

These elaborate, lightly textured, and richly flavored breads are intended to be a contrast to everyday breads. They often take a special place of pride on tables around the world during Christmas, Easter, the Jewish Sabbath, and Christian harvest celebrations. Made with generous quantities of expensive butter and eggs, these loaves are flavored with spices, honey, candied fruit peels, dried fruits, and nuts. You could be forgiven for thinking the loaves in this chapter are more like cakes than breads.

Yet it is not just the taste that lets you know these breads are out of the ordinary. They look special. Alice's Christmas Loaf (page 148) from Czechoslovakia and the Jewish challahs (page 154) are lovingly braided, using up to nine strands of dough to create intricate patterns. The Alsatian Kugelhopf (page 142), and the Italian Panettone (page 145) are baked in molds that instantly herald a celebration. My husband says my towering Panettone reminds him of a monument. (The Leaning Tower of Pisa, perhaps?) Fluted kugelhopf molds are so attractive that they often double as kitchen decorations in Alsace.

OPPOSITE
A Bulgarian farmer's harvest loaf.
ABOVE *An altar harvest loaf.*

Even the more familiar English Hot Cross Buns (page 150) are finished with a flour and water paste to make them special for Good Friday observances. Loaves shaped to look like sheaves of wheat (page 152) have been made by generations of British country bakers to mark a successful harvest. Served at harvest suppers held in church halls, this decorative loaf came to symbolize the end of hard labor for farm workers and a time of plenty for most farms. This custom is still followed throughout Europe, as you can see from the decorated round loaf proudly displayed by the jovial Bulgarian farmer (opposite). That loaf was made by the local bakery to celebrate a bountiful wine harvest. You can make such a loaf to eat at a Thanksgiving meal; or, bake it for much longer in a very low oven to create an attractive, nonedible decoration (page 153).

Some of the loaves in this chapter can be very time-consuming to make, so if you want to make a celebration bread in a hurry, I suggest you try Bishops Bread (page 150). This is a quick bread as it is not yeast-raised and therefore has no lengthy rising times.

If you do have some free time to spare, however, I hope you will try one of the more elaborately braided loaves, or the Harvest Wheat Sheaf (page 152). These are delicious breads, and not as difficult to make as they look, although they do require time and patience, especially for the first attempt. Anyone who does not feel confident at braiding dough should try Caroll's Twisted Ring (page 156). Strips of the dough are simply braided together, then the loaf is baked in a tube pan so it does not loose its shape.

Like many good bakers, Brigitte prefers the pungency of freshly ground spices. Here she crushes cardamom seeds to add a subtle, yet distinctive, flavor to the stollens.

SPICE MIXTURES

Fragrant spices are important ingredients in these recipes. And if, like me, you have tired of the blandness of commercial ground mixed spices, you will take great pleasure in making your own blends.

Even in 1907, Master Baker John Kirkland (page 65) was writing about the importance of "giving your spice mixture special considerations." His formula was 6 tablespoons each of ground coriander, ground cinnamon, and ground ginger; 2 tablespoons plus 2 teaspoons freshly grated nutmeg; and 2 tablespoons ground white peppercorns or ground allspice.

More recently, Elizabeth David suggested grinding together 4 teaspoons freshly grated nutmeg (about one large nutmeg), 1 tablespoon whole white peppercorns or ground allspice, 30 whole cloves, 1½ teaspoons ground ginger, and ½ teaspoon cumin seed. Store spice mixtures in airtight containers.

You will notice that both these combinations make a small quantity. I suggest you make up a batch when you need it, rather than storing a large amount.

BRESLAU STOLLEN

INGREDIENTS

Makes two large loaves.

- about 7½ cups white bread flour
- 1 tablespoon kosher salt or flaked sea salt
- 7 cakes compressed fresh yeast (0.6 ounce each), or two 2-ounce blocks and one-third 0.6-ounce cake compressed fresh yeast, or 7 envelopes active dry yeast (2¼ teaspoons each)
- 1¼ cups granulated sugar
- ⅔ cup lukewarm milk (95F to 105F)
- 2¼ cups whole blanched almonds, chopped
- 4 cups (1 pound, 2 ounces) raisins
- 1¾ cup (8¾ ounces) diced candied citrus peel (preferably orange and lemon)
- 1¼ cups currants
- grated rind of 2 large lemons (about 1 tablespoon)
- 2 teaspoons freshly grated nutmeg
- ¾ teaspoon ground cardamom
- 1¾ cups (3½ sticks) unsalted butter, softened
- 6 large eggs, lightly beaten
- 3 cups (6 sticks) unsalted butter, for brushing
- confectioners' sugar, for sprinkling

two large, heavy baking sheets, one lined with three layers of parchment paper

Breslau, in Silesia, formerly part of Germany but now in Poland, is where my friend Brigitte Friis's mother came from. Brigitte's mother always made these extravagant weihnachtsstollens *several weeks before Christmas. The cardamom is an inspired touch. Liberal applications of melted butter brushed over the stollens after baking are traditional – the stollens absorb the butter, resulting in a moist, ultrarich, cakelike taste and texture.*

Sift the flour and salt in a very large bowl. Make a well in the center of the flour. Crumble the fresh yeast into a medium-size bowl. Stir in 1 tablespoon of the sugar and the lukewarm milk until smooth. If using dry yeast, mix the granules and 1 tablespoon of the sugar with the lukewarm milk and let stand until foamy, 5 to 10 minutes (page 18).

Pour the yeast mixture into the well. Work a little of the flour into the yeast mixture to make a thick batter. Sprinkle with a little flour to prevent a skin forming. Cover with a dry dish towel and let stand in a warm place (about 75F) for 15 to 20 minutes until spongy.

In a medium-size bowl, mix the almonds, raisins, candied citrus peel, currants, and the lemon rind. Add 2 tablespoons flour and toss to coat. Stir in the spices. Mix the remaining sugar into the sponge. Add the butter and mix it with the sponge and the flour in the bowl by gently turning the mixture over with your hand until the flour is almost worked in. Add the eggs, about 2 at a time, and work the mixture with your hand until it forms a soft dough that holds its shape. If the dough is too sticky, add flour, 1 tablespoon at a time. If the dough is too dry, add milk, 1 tablespoon at a time.

Turn out the dough onto a well-floured work surface and "knead until it begins to show bubbles," says Brigitte. Large bubbles or blisters should appear after 10 minutes. Re-flour the work surfaces as necessary. The dough will become firmer and more pliable.

Pat out the dough with floured hands on a well-floured work surface into an 18 × 12-inch rectangle, about ¾-inch thick, with a long side facing you. Sprinkle one-quarter of the fruit and nut mixture across the center of the dough, from one short side to the other. Fold in the two long edges so they meet in the center. Fold the ends in. Fold the right-hand side of the dough over the left half to make a small package. If any of the filling oozes out, press it back in. Give the rectangle a quarter turn. Press out the dough again into an 18 × 12-inch rectangle, flouring the surface as needed. Spread another one-quarter of the filling across the center as before. Repeat the folding, as above. Give the

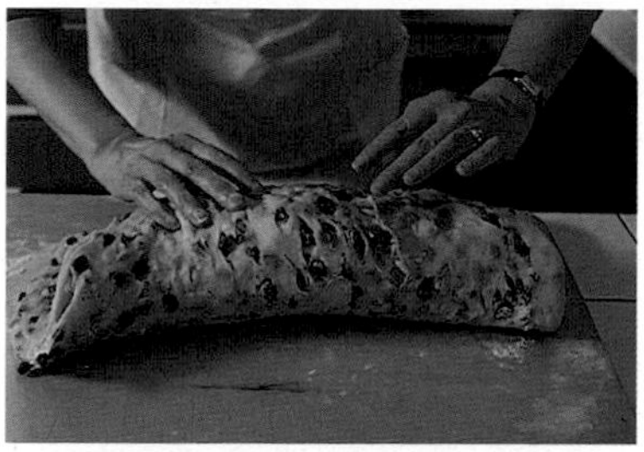

BRIGITTE FOLDS DOWN THE TOP THIRD OF THE DOUGH TO MAKE A THREE-LAYER RECTANGULAR DOUGH SANDWICH.

AFTER THE DOUGH HAS RISEN THE SECOND TIME, IT WILL BE DOUBLE IN SIZE AND BE READY TO BAKE.

rectangle a quarter turn again and repeat the patting, filling, and folding twice more. After all the fruit has been added, continue folding the dough over and over on itself, pressing down on it very lightly, and giving the dough a quarter turn after each fold.

Brigitte incorporates the fruit this way, instead of kneading it into the dough. It takes at least 5 minutes and must be done gently. The dough should not be streaky or sticky, and it will be very soft. Shape the dough into a ball and dust lightly with flour. Return the dough to the bowl if it is large enough, or leave the dough on the floured surface. Cover it with dry dish towels. Let rise at warm room temperature (about 75F), away from drafts, until doubled in size, about 2 hours.

Turn out the dough onto the floured surface (if it is in the bowl). Punch down the dough. You should hear the air being expelled as you do this. Knead it for 1 minute. Divide the dough in half. Pat out each piece of dough with floured hands into a 10 × 6-inch rectangle, $1\frac{1}{4}$ inches thick, with a short side facing you. Fold the bottom third of the dough up and fold the top third down, to make a three-layer rectangular dough sandwich. (Now, a long side will be facing you.) Pat to round the corners for a neat shape. Slide a second baking sheet under the prepared baking sheet to prevent the stollens from browning too much on the bottom. Transfer the stollens to the prepared baking sheet. Cover each with a dry dish towel and let rise at warm room temperature, away from drafts, until doubled in size, about 2 hours. During the last 15 minutes of rising, heat the oven to 325F.

Place the baking sheet of stollens on an oven rack set in the middle position. Bake for 45 minutes. Cover the stollens loosely with foil to prevent overbrowning, and rotate the baking sheet from front to back. Bake another 30 minutes, or until the stollens are golden brown and firm to the touch, and a skewer inserted into the center comes out clean.

Melt 1 cup of the butter. As soon as the stollens come out of the oven, brush the butter over each one. They should gradually absorb all this butter. Transfer to wire racks and let cool completely. When cool, wrap in foil and leave at room temperature.

The next day, heat the oven to 350F and melt $1\frac{1}{3}$ sticks of butter. Place the stollens, still wrapped, on a baking sheet. Warm them for 10 minutes. Remove the stollens from the oven, unwrap them, and brush with the butter until the loaves will not absorb any more. Transfer to wire racks to cool. Then wrap in foil. Repeat this procedure for the next two days. On the last day, brush the butter on the bottom of the stollens. When the stollens have cooled, sift a thick layer of confectioners' sugar over the tops. Keep the stollens in a cool place, but not the refrigerator, for at least two weeks, but not more than six weeks, until ready to serve.

Fruity and spicy, this butter-rich stollen is ideal for holiday entertaining. If you prefer, these stollens may be buttered only once with the melted 1 cup of butter, just after they are baked.

For easier mixing and kneading, you can transfer the flour mixture to a stationary mixer fitted with a dough hook before you add the eggs. Add the eggs, then knead on low speed for 5 to 10 minutes, until the dough becomes firm and pliable.

KUGELHOPF

INGREDIENTS

Makes one large loaf.

about 2 tablespoons unsalted butter, very soft, for buttering the mold
$\frac{3}{4}$ cup sliced unblanched almonds
$2\frac{3}{4}$ cups white bread flour (preferably unbleached and stone-ground)
$\frac{1}{2}$ teaspoon kosher salt or flaked sea salt
1 cake compressed fresh yeast (0.6 ounce) or 1 envelope active dry yeast ($2\frac{1}{2}$ teaspoons)
$\frac{1}{3}$ cup granulated sugar
$\frac{3}{4}$ cup lukewarm milk (95F to 105F)
3 large eggs, at room temperature, lightly beaten
grated rind of 1 medium-size lemon (about 1 teaspoon)
7 tablespoons unsalted butter, diced and softened
$\frac{1}{4}$ cup golden raisins
$\frac{1}{4}$ cup dark raisins
confectioners' sugar, for dusting

a 9- to 10-inch kugelhopf mold (see introduction)

Kugelhopfs are easy to identify with their distinctive shapes.

These pretty, almond-topped, fluted loaves can be found in Austria and Germany, as well as in Alsace, France, where the recipe originated. Clarisse Deiss, whose husband Jean-Michel makes the most exquisite wines at Bergheim, in Alsace, became both my culinary guide to the region and wine tutor.

Kugelhopf is the region's traditional celebration cake, baked for weddings, baptisms, wine harvests, and Christmas. The dough is similar to that used for brioche, but the kugelhopf is studded with fruit and sometimes flavored with lemon rind. At Easter, the sweet dough is baked in the shape of a fish or a lamb, and its richness depends on how much butter is included. "If you buy a kugelhopf, always go to a pâtisserie, rather than a boulangerie, because it will contain more butter," Clarisse advised.

The traditional, high-fluted mold is made of earthenware with a hole in the center, which allows the heat to penetrate to the middle of the dough for more even and thorough baking. Molds that are highly decorated on the outside are used for kitchen ornaments when not being used in the oven. Indeed, an elaborate mold was once an essential part of a woman's trousseau. On the wedding day, the bride would be given the family kugelhopf recipe by her mother.

I bought a selection of earthenware molds, some unglazed and plain on the outside, at Ribeauvillé, France, from a shop within sight of the town's famous local attraction – nesting storks. I should add that an equally important event is the town's kugelhopf festival, held each June. Although the earthenware molds are perhaps the prettiest, nonstick, glass, and metal heatproof molds can also be used. But remember, metal molds bake the quickest – a kugelhopf made in an earthenware mold will take about 10 minutes longer to bake than one made in a metal mold. This will keep for up to one week if tightly wrapped in foil, or it can be frozen for one month.

Thickly coat the mold with the 2 tablespoons butter. Evenly line the mold with the almonds by pressing them against the base and sides so they stick. Chill the mold while preparing the dough.

Mix together the flour and salt in a medium-size bowl and make a well in the center. Crumble the fresh yeast into a small bowl. Stir in the sugar and the lukewarm milk until smooth. If using dry yeast, mix the granules and $\frac{1}{2}$ teaspoon of the sugar with $\frac{1}{2}$ cup of the lukewarm milk and let stand until foamy, 5 to 10 minutes (page 18). Stir in the

The best of Alsace — a glass of Jean-Michel Deiss' finest, crisp white wine, a kugelhopf, and a thick, moist pear loaf, another regional specialty. (This one is darker than my recipe for pear loaf on page 130.) The kugelhopf was baked by Clarisse Deiss. She used an old family recipe and baked it in the unglazed, earthenware mold she was given on her wedding day as tradition dictates.

remaining sugar and lukewarm milk.

Pour the yeast mixture into the well in the flour. With your hand, work enough flour from the bowl into the yeast mixture to make a thick batter. Cover with a damp dish towel and let stand at room temperature until spongy, about 30 minutes (page 16).

Add the eggs and lemon rind to the sponge in the well and mix together with a small whisk or your hand. Gradually mix the flour from the bowl into the sponge with your hand or a wooden spoon to make a very soft and sticky dough. Beat the dough in the bowl with your hand in a circular motion for 5 minutes, or until it becomes firmer, smooth, very elastic, and glossy.

Beat in the butter, beating the dough until the butter is evenly incorporated. Gently mix in the fruit with your hand until evenly incorporated.

Carefully spoon the dough into the chilled mold without dislodging the almonds. The mold should be half full. Cover with a damp dish towel and let rise at warm room temperature (about 75F), away from drafts, until the dough has almost doubled in size and has risen to about 1 inch below the mold's rim, 40 to 50 minutes. During the last 15 minutes of rising, heat the oven to 400F.

Bake the kugelhopf for 35 to 40 minutes, or until the loaf is golden brown and a skewer inserted in the center comes out clean. Cover the loaf loosely with foil if it appears to be browning too quickly during baking. Cool the loaf in the mold for 5 minutes. Then carefully turn it out onto a wire rack to cool completely. To serve, dust with confectioners' sugar by sifting it over the cake. Offer slices of kugelhopf with a glass of Alsatian wine, such as a Tokay Pinot Grise.

SAVORY KUGELHOPF

Clarisse Deiss (opposite) also makes kugelhopfs without the sugar and dried fruit, using bacon or ham instead. The region of Alsace is renowned for cured pork, and one of Alsace's famous dishes, choucroute garni, *is rich with smoked or salted pork, bacon, and meaty sausages.*

This savory kugelhopf is served in Alsace with an aperitif such as a glass of Riesling or Gewurztraminer before dinner. Eat this loaf within three days of baking.

INGREDIENTS

Makes one large loaf.

- about 2 tablespoons unsalted butter, very soft, for buttering the mold
- $\frac{2}{3}$ cup walnut halves
- $2\frac{3}{4}$ cups white bread flour (preferably unbleached and stone-ground)
- 1 teaspoon kosher salt or flaked sea salt
- several grinds of fresh black pepper
- 1 cake compressed fresh yeast (0.6 ounce), or 1 envelope active dry yeast ($2\frac{1}{2}$ teaspoons) plus $\frac{1}{2}$ teaspoon granulated sugar
- 1 cup lukewarm milk (95F to 105F)
- 3 large eggs, at room temperature, lightly beaten
- 7 tablespoons unsalted butter, diced and softened
- 4 ounces thick-sliced lean bacon, diced, or 4 ounces diced cooked flavorful ham, such as York, Westphalian, or Smithfield

a 9- to 10-inch kugelhopf mold (see opposite)

Thickly coat the mold with the 2 tablespoons butter. Evenly line the inside of the mold with the walnuts, pressing the pieces against the base and sides so they stick. Chill the mold while preparing the dough.

Prepare the dough as for the Kugelhopf (opposite), using the flour, salt, pepper (adding the pepper to the flour), yeast, milk, eggs, and butter. Since this is a savory kugelhopf, the sugar and lemon rind are omitted.

If using dry yeast, mix the granules and the $\frac{1}{2}$ teaspoon granulated sugar with $\frac{1}{2}$ cup of the lukewarm milk and let stand until foamy, 5 to 10 minutes (page 18). Stir in the remaining lukewarm milk.

Meanwhile, while the dough is "sponging," fry the bacon (if using it) in a medium-size skillet over medium heat until crisp, but not too brown. Remove the bacon pieces with a slotted spoon to paper towels to drain well and cool. Fold in the bacon or ham after beating the butter into the dough.

Carefully spoon the dough into the mold without dislodging the walnuts. Cover with a damp dish towel and let rise at warm room temperature (about 75F) until the dough has almost doubled in size and has risen to about 1 inch below the mold's rim, 40 to 50 minutes.

During the last 15 minutes of rising, heat the oven to 400F. Bake as for the Kugelhopf (opposite), but omit the dusting of confectioners' sugar. Cool the loaf in the mold for 5 minutes. Then carefully turn it out onto a wire rack to cool completely.

Twinkling lights and traditional decorations herald the start of the Christmas season in Nuremberg's Christkindelmarket. Shoppers buy slices of spicy hutzelbrot to nibble as they browse for gifts, or they purchase whole loaves to share with family and friends.

HUTZELBROT

This Bavarian Christmas bread is packed with dried fruits and nuts. It is sold in the traditional Advent markets held in town squares throughout southern Germany.

The oldest of these markets is the Nuremberg Christkindelmarkt. It is held from the Friday before the beginning of Advent until Christmas Eve. The market – with food, toys, and decorations – began about 1639. With row upon row of red-and-white striped stalls, all iced with snow, the market is decorated with tiny white lights, fir tree garlands, and Christmas motifs.

The chilly air is laced with enticing smells – frying sausages, hot spicy gluhwein, caramelized almonds, and roasting chestnuts. Rich and fruity hutzelbrots are sold by the slice, so even their fragrant aroma adds to the atmosphere. Eat this bread sliced and buttered, toasted, or with honey.

Mix together the pears, prunes, figs, dark and golden raisins, dates, kirsch or brandy, and lemon rind in a large bowl. Pour in enough of the boiling water to cover the fruit. Stir

INGREDIENTS

Makes two loaves.

- $1\frac{1}{3}$ cups chopped dried pears
- $1\frac{1}{3}$ cups chopped pitted prunes
- $\frac{2}{3}$ cup chopped dried figs
- $\frac{1}{2}$ cup dark raisins
- $\frac{1}{2}$ cup golden raisins
- $\frac{1}{4}$ cup chopped pitted dried dates
- 2 tablespoons kirsch or brandy
- grated rind of 1 small lemon (about $\frac{3}{4}$ teaspoon)
- about $\frac{3}{4}$ cup boiling water
- about $2\frac{3}{4}$ cups white bread flour (preferably unbleached and stone-ground)
- 1 teaspoon ground cinnamon
- $\frac{1}{2}$ teaspoon kosher salt or flaked sea salt
- good pinch each ground cloves and ground aniseed
- one and one-half 0.6-ounce cakes compressed fresh yeast or $1\frac{1}{2}$ envelopes active dry yeast (1 tablespoon plus $\frac{3}{4}$ teaspoon)
- about 1 cup lukewarm water (95F to 105F)
- 2 tablespoons firmly packed light brown sugar
- 1 tablespoon honey
- $\frac{2}{3}$ cup blanched almonds, lightly toasted and chopped
- $\frac{2}{3}$ cup hazelnuts, lightly toasted, skinned, and chopped
- milk, for brushing (optional)
- $\frac{2}{3}$ cup sliced unblanched almonds, for decorating (optional)

a large, heavy baking sheet, greased

well, cover, and let soak overnight.

The next day, drain the fruit, reserving any liquid, although most should have been absorbed. Set the fruit aside, covered.

Sift together the flour, cinnamon, salt, cloves, and aniseed in a large bowl. Make a well in the center of the flour mixture. Crumble the fresh yeast into a small bowl. Mix together the fruit soaking liquid, if any, and enough lukewarm water to measure 1 cup. If necessary, heat the fruit liquid mixture in a small saucepan until lukewarm (95F to 105F). Stir the brown sugar and the fruit liquid mixture into the yeast until smooth. If using dry yeast, mix the granules and the brown sugar with the lukewarm fruit liquid mixture and let stand until foamy, 5 to 10 minutes (page 18).

Pour the yeast mixture into the well in the flour along with the honey. Mix these ingredients together briefly with a small whisk or your hands. Then mix the flour from the bowl into the yeast mixture with your hand or a wooden spoon to make a soft, but not sticky dough. If the dough is too sticky, work in a little extra flour, 1 tablespoon at a time. If the dough is dry and crumbly, work in a little extra water, 1 tablespoon at a time.

Turn out the dough onto a lightly floured work surface and knead for 10 minutes until smooth and elastic. Return the dough to the bowl (no need to wash or oil the bowl). Cover with a damp dish towel and let rise at room temperature, away from drafts, until doubled in size, about $1\frac{1}{2}$ hours.

Punch down the dough. Turn out the dough onto a lightly floured work surface. Sprinkle one-quarter of the soaked fruit and of the chopped almonds and hazelnuts over the dough and gently knead for 2 to 3 minutes until they are evenly distributed. Repeat this process three more times, using a quarter of the fruit and nuts each time. Divide the dough into two equal portions and shape each portion into an oval (see The Basic Loaf, page 17). Arrange the loaves on the prepared baking sheet. Cover with a damp dish towel and let rise at room temperature, away from drafts, until doubled in size, about $1\frac{1}{2}$ hours. During the last 15 minutes of rising, heat the oven to 400F.

To decorate the loaves, if you wish, brush them with the milk, then gently press the sliced almonds lightly on the surface. Bake the loaves for 30 to 40 minutes, or until they are golden brown and sound hollow when tapped underneath. Loosely cover the loaves with foil if they are browning too quickly during baking. Transfer the loaves to wire racks to cool completely. Wrap the cooled loaves in plastic wrap and overwrap in foil and keep at room temperature for at least 2 days, or up to 1 week, before slicing. This helps the flavor to develop. After slicing, it stays fresh for five days.

PANETTONE

You can find panettone – prettily wrapped in cellophane, tied and hung by ribbons – in every Italian delicatessen in England (as well as in the States) as Christmas approaches. It is a specialty of Milan, where bakers vie to make the tallest, lightest, most delicate butter-rich loaf.

Since the classic tall, cylindrical panettone molds are difficult to find, some bakers use large 2-pound coffee cans. I prefer to use a 6-inch-round cake pan that has sides 3 inches high. I extend the pan about 4 inches upward by wrapping it on the outside with a stiff collar made of doubled heavy-duty foil that I secure with a paper clip, and on the inside with a sheet of buttered parchment paper, as if lining a soufflé dish.

For the best results, buy large pieces of candied orange and lemon peel and chop them yourself, as the flavor is much fresher than the ready-chopped variety from supermarkets.

Valentina Harris, the Italian food writer, once served me an excellent festive pudding made with panettone. She sliced off the domed top of the panettone, hollowed out the center slightly, filled it with a warm zabaglione, and replaced the top. You can also eat this loaf simply sliced into wedges like a cake within a week of baking. For the first couple of days after it is baked, this panettone will be moister than those bought from the bakery.

INGREDIENTS

Makes one loaf.

- 2½ cups white bread flour (preferably unbleached and stone-ground)
- ½ teaspoon kosher salt or flaked sea salt
- 1 cake compressed fresh yeast (0.6 ounce) or 1 envelope active dry yeast (2½ teaspoons)
- 3 tablespoons lukewarm water (95F to 105F)
- ⅓ cup granulated sugar
- 3 large eggs, at room temperature, lightly beaten
- 3 large egg yolks
- grated rind of 1 large lemon (about 1½ teaspoons)
- few drops vanilla extract
- ¾ cup (1½ sticks) unsalted butter, diced and softened
- ⅔ cup golden raisins
- ⅓ cup (2 ounces) finely chopped candied citrus peel (preferably orange and lemon peel)
- about 2 tablespoons unsalted butter
- a panettone mold, greased, or a greased 6-inch-round cake pan, with sides 3 inches high, wrapped with heavy-duty foil and lined with buttered parchment paper (see introduction)

At holiday time, a buttery, fruit-studded panettone makes a lovely gift, especially when wrapped in cellophane and festooned with ribbons.

Mix together 2 cups of the flour and the salt in a medium-size bowl and make a well in the center of the flour mixture. Crumble the fresh yeast into a small bowl. Stir in the lukewarm water until smooth. If using dry yeast, mix the granules and ½ teaspoon of the granulated sugar with the lukewarm water and let stand until foamy, 5 to 10 minutes (page 18).

Pour the yeast mixture into the well in the flour. Add the sugar and beaten whole eggs to the well. Mix together these ingredients in the well with a small whisk or your hand. Then, with your hand or a wooden spoon, mix enough flour from the bowl into the mixture in the well to make a thick batter. Sprinkle the top with a little of the flour to prevent a skin forming. Let stand at room temperature, away from drafts, until spongy, 45 minutes to 1 hour (page 16).

Add the egg yolks, lemon rind, and vanilla extract to the sponge. Mix together these ingredients in the well. With your hand, gradually beat the remaining flour from the bowl into the sponge to make a soft and very sticky dough. Again using your hand, gradually beat the butter into the dough until thoroughly incorporated.

Turn out the dough onto a lightly floured work surface and knead, working in the remaining ½ cup flour, for 10 minutes, or until soft, satiny, and pliable.

Return the dough to the bowl (no need to wash and oil the bowl). Cover with a damp dish towel and let rise at room temperature, away from drafts, until almost doubled in size, 2 to 2½ hours.

Punch down the dough. Cover with a damp dish towel and let rise again at room temperature, away from drafts, until doubled in size, 1 to 1½ hours.

Punch down the dough. Turn out onto a lightly floured work surface. Toss the golden raisins and chopped candied citrus peel with 1 teaspoon flour in a small bowl to prevent them from sticking together. Sprinkle half of the raisins and peel over the dough and gently knead in with lightly floured hands until the fruit is evenly distributed, 2 to 3 minutes. Repeat with the remaining fruit.

Shape the dough into a ball and drop it into the prepared panettone mold or the lined cake pan. Using the tip of a long, sharp knife, score a cross in the top of the dough.

Cover with a piece of plastic wrap and let rise at room temperature, away from drafts, until doubled in size, about 1 hour.

During the last 15 minutes of rising, heat the oven to 400F.

Melt 1 tablespoon of the remaining butter in a small saucepan. Brush the top of the panettone with some of the melted butter. Put the other tablespoon of butter in the center of the cross.

Bake the panettone for 10 to 12 minutes, or until it begins to color. Then brush the top again with the rest of the butter. Lower the oven temperature to 350F and bake for 30 to 40 minutes longer, or until the loaf is golden brown and a skewer inserted in the center comes out clean.

Remove the panettone from the oven. It will be fragile, so stand the mold on a wire rack for 5 minutes while the loaf firms up. Gently unmold the loaf and place it upright on the wire rack to cool completely.

PLACE REMAINING BUTTER IN THE CENTER OF THE CROSS.

WHEN THE TOP BEGINS TO BROWN, BRUSH AGAIN WITH BUTTER.

I suggest using a mild-flavored olive oil for these decorative Provençal breads, rather than the heavier, fruity extra-virgin oil I more often use in breads. I think it is vital to use good-quality candied orange peel from gourmet shops or by mail order (page 187). It comes in large pieces and has more flavor than the ready-chopped variety from supermarkets. You can chop the peel as finely as you like. To keep it from sticking to the knife, sprinkle the peel with a little flour before you start.

FOUGASSES

This flat-bread recipe comes from Provence, where you find the best candied oranges and orange flower water. Fougasse usually forms the central part of the thirteen desserts (symbolizing the twelve disciples and Christ) that are served for the Christmas Eve meal in Provence. The meal usually begins with fish and vegetable dishes followed by a salad. Then come the thirteen desserts, which include a selection of nougats, raisins, dried figs, glacé fruits, and fresh fruits, such as figs, grapes, apples, clementines, and pears. All these are accompanied by a dessert wine.

Use a mild olive oil in this bread, and good-quality candied orange peel from a gourmet shop (you can buy the orange flower water there, too).

Eat the fougasses the day they are baked.

INGREDIENTS

Makes eight fougasses.

- $4\frac{3}{4}$ cups white bread flour (preferably unbleached and stone-ground)
- $\frac{3}{4}$ cup granulated sugar
- $1\frac{1}{2}$ teaspoons kosher salt or flaked sea salt
- 1 cake compressed fresh yeast (0.6 ounce), or 1 envelope active dry yeast ($2\frac{1}{2}$ teaspoons) plus $\frac{1}{2}$ teaspoon granulated sugar
- $\frac{1}{4}$ cup lukewarm water (95F to 105F)
- 2 large eggs
- $\frac{1}{3}$ cup plus 1 tablespoon mild olive oil
- grated rind and juice of 1 large orange (about 4 teaspoons rind and a scant $\frac{1}{2}$ cup juice)
- 1 tablespoon orange flower water
- $\frac{3}{4}$ cup (3 ounces) diced candied orange peel
- additional mild olive oil, for brushing

several baking sheets, oiled with olive oil

CUT EIGHT OR NINE SLITS IN EACH TOP, IN A HERRINGBONE DESIGN

Mix the flour, sugar, and salt in a large bowl and make a well in the center. Crumble the fresh yeast into a small bowl. Stir in the lukewarm water until smooth. If using dry yeast, mix the granules and the $\frac{1}{2}$ teaspoon sugar with the lukewarm water and let stand until foamy, 5 to 10 minutes (page 18). Pour the yeast mixture into the well in the flour. Mix enough flour from the bowl into the liquid with your hand to make a thick batter. Let stand until spongy, about 10 minutes (page 16).

Meanwhile, whisk the eggs, oil, the orange rind and juice, and orange flower water in a medium-size bowl. Add to the sponge in the well and mix together with your hand. Gradually work in the flour from the bowl to make a soft, but not sticky dough. If the dough is dry, add extra water, 1 tablespoon at a time. If the dough sticks to your fingers, add extra flour, 1 tablespoon at a time.

Turn out the dough onto a lightly floured work surface and knead for 10 minutes until smooth and elastic. Wash, dry, and oil the bowl. Return the dough to the bowl, and turn it over to oil the top. Cover with a damp dish towel and let rise at room temperature, away from drafts, until doubled in size, about $1\frac{1}{2}$ to 2 hours.

Punch down the dough. Turn it out onto a floured surface and knead in the candied orange peel until distributed, about 5 minutes. Divide the dough into eight equal pieces. Roll out each piece to a $\frac{1}{2}$-inch thick oval. Cut eight or nine slits in the top, in a herringbone design. Arrange the fougasses, spaced well apart, on the prepared baking sheets. Lightly cover and let rise until almost doubled in size, about 1 hour. During the last 15 minutes of rising, heat the oven to 400F. Lightly brush the fougasses with olive oil. Place each baking sheet on another sheet to prevent the bottoms from burning. Bake for 15 to 20 minutes, or until the fougasses are golden brown and sound hollow when tapped on the bottom.

Transfer to wire racks to cool completely.

Nine strands of dough are braided together to make this elaborate, almond-studded loaf. Using a freshly ground spice mixture (page 148), instead of pumpkin-pie spice, adds a fresh flavor.

If you don't have time to make the braid, shape the dough into rolls instead. It will make about 25 rolls; follow shaping instructions for Oatmeal Rolls, page 25. Brush the shaped rolls with egg glaze, top each with a halved almond, and let rise, uncovered, at cool room temperature until almost doubled in size, 30–45 minutes. Gently glaze again, then bake at 375F for about 25 minutes, or until the rolls are golden brown and sound hollow when tapped underneath. Cool on wire racks.

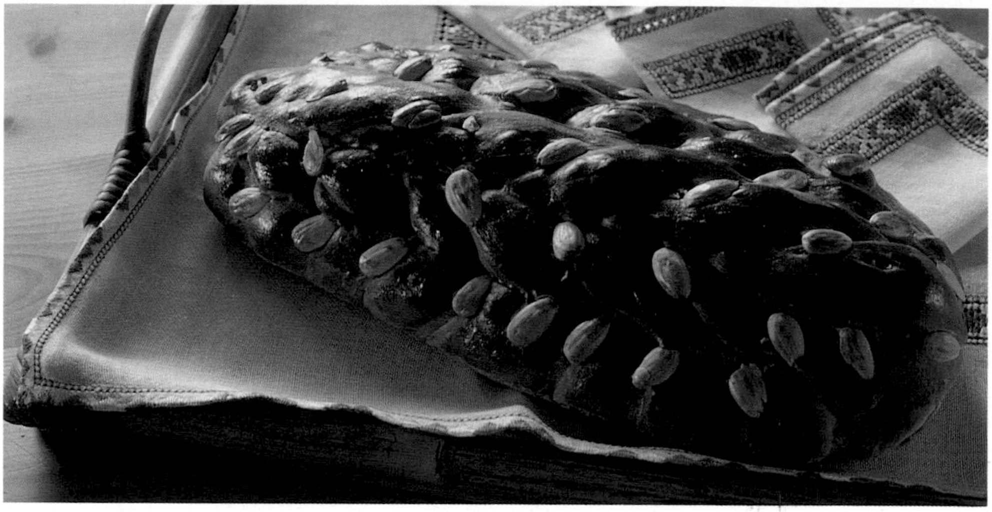

ALICE'S CHRISTMAS LOAF

INGREDIENTS

Makes one large loaf.

- 2 cups whole-wheat bread flour (preferably stone-ground)
- 1 cake compressed fresh yeast (0.6 ounce) or 1 envelope active dry yeast ($2\frac{1}{2}$ teaspoons)
- 1 tablespoon firmly packed light brown sugar
- $1\frac{1}{4}$ cups milk, water, or a mixture of both, lukewarm (95F to 105F)
- $3\frac{1}{4}$ cups white bread flour (preferably unbleached and stone-ground)
- $\frac{1}{2}$ cup granulated sugar
- 2 teaspoons kosher salt or flaked sea salt
- $\frac{1}{2}$ cup (1 stick) cold unsalted butter, diced
- 1 teaspoon ground cinnamon, or to taste
- 1 teaspoon freshly ground spice mixture (page 140) or pumpkin-pie spice, or to taste
- grated rind of 1 large lemon (about 2 teaspoons)
- 2 large eggs, lightly beaten
- $\frac{1}{2}$ cup each dark and golden raisins, mixed
- 1 large egg beaten with a pinch of salt, for glazing
- about $\frac{3}{4}$ cup halved or sliced unblanched almonds, for decorating
- two large, heavy baking sheets, one lined with parchment paper
- three 10- to 12-inch-long thin bamboo skewers

While Anthony Blake and I were visiting Mary Curtis in Ireland (page 86), she took us to meet her friends Gerry and Alice Turner. While Gerry makes wonderful sourdough bread for everyday (page 164), Alice bakes for special occasions with family recipes, including this elaborate Czech loaf with nine strands of dough braided together. Her trick of securing the shape of the braid with bamboo skewers while it rises should be useful to anyone new to shaping dough braids. Look for the skewers in Asian shops. Eat this loaf within four days.

Put the whole-wheat flour into a medium-size bowl and make a well in the center. Crumble the fresh yeast into a small bowl. Stir in the brown sugar and the lukewarm liquid until smooth. If using dry yeast, mix the granules and the brown sugar with $\frac{3}{4}$ cup of the lukewarm liquid and let stand until foamy, 5 to 10 minutes (page 18). Stir in the remaining $\frac{1}{2}$ cup lukewarm liquid. Pour the yeast mixture into the flour. Work the flour from the bowl into the yeast mixture to make a thick batter. Cover with a damp towel and let stand at room temperature, away from drafts, until spongy, about 1 hour.

Mix together the white flour, granulated sugar, and salt in a large bowl. Rub in the butter with your fingertips until the mixture looks like fine crumbs. Stir in the cinnamon, the spice mixture or pumpkin-pie spice, and the lemon rind. Make a well in the flour mixture. Add the eggs. Then pour in the sponge. Mix the ingredients in the well with a small whisk. Then, with your hand, mix the flour from the bowl into the yeast mixture to make a soft, but not sticky dough. If the dough is dry and crumbly, add milk, 1 tablespoon at a time. If the dough is too sticky, add flour, 1 tablespoon at a time.

Turn out the dough onto a floured surface and knead for 10 minutes until firm, pliable, and smooth. Return it to the bowl. Cover with a damp dish towel and let rest at room temperature for 30 minutes.

Turn out the dough onto a floured surface. Roll out the dough, rolling away from you with a floured rolling pin, into a 12 × 9-inch rectangle, about $1\frac{1}{2}$ inches thick, with a short side facing you. Sprinkle one-third of the raisins over the dough, leaving a $\frac{1}{2}$-inch border at the edges. Fold up the bottom third of the dough, then fold down the top third to make a three-layer dough sandwich, as for the Aberdeen Butteries (page 180). Give it a quarter turn to the left so the completely enclosed side is to your left. Roll out to a 12 × 9-inch rectangle. Sprinkle with another one-third of the raisins, and proceed as above. Repeat the process to incorporate the remaining raisins. Knead the dough just enough to form a ball. Be careful not to overwork the dough. Return the dough to the bowl and cover. Let rise at cool room temperature until doubled in size, 3 to 8 hours.

Punch down the dough. Roll it into a fat rope and cut it into nine pieces. To make the elaborate braid, first make a four-strand braid.

To make a four-strand braid: With your hands, roll out four pieces of dough into ropes 14 inches long and 1 inch thick. Pinch the ends together firmly at one end. Arrange the four strands side by side and slightly apart, with the unattached ends facing you. Move the strand on the far left under the two strands to its right. Twist the same strand over the last strand it went under, which was originally the third strand from the left. Move the strand on the far right under the twisted two strands in the center. Twist the same strand over the last strand it went under; it then becomes the third strand from the left.

Repeat this process until all the strands are braided. Pinch the ends together. Transfer the braid to the prepared baking sheet and tuck under the ends for a neat finish. Using the edge of your hand, make an indentation lengthwise down the center of the braid.

To make a three-strand braid: Roll out three of the remaining portions of dough into 16-inch-long ropes. Braid the three strands together as for the Braided Loaf (page 30). Carefully place the three-strand braid in the indentation on top of the four-strand braid. Tuck the top ends under the bottom braid for a neat finish. Using the edge of your hand, make an indentation lengthwise down the center of this braid.

Knead the remaining two pieces of dough together with your hands and roll out into a 20-inch-long rope. Place the index finger of your left hand in the center of the rope and press down to hold the rope. Fold the dough over your finger, then wind the two pieces of the strand together to make a twisted rope. Place this in the indentation on top of the assembled braid and tuck the loose ends of the twisted rope under itself.

Pat the loaf to make a neat, high, slim loaf. Insert bamboo skewers near each end and the center. Brush with the egg glaze. Decorate liberally with the almonds, pressing them into the surface. Let rise, uncovered, at cool room temperature until almost doubled in size, 30 minutes to 1 hour. Take care not to over-rise the dough. During the last 15 minutes, heat the oven to 400F. Brush the loaf with the egg glaze. Bake the loaf for 10 minutes. Lower the temperature to 350F, cover the loaf loosely with buttered foil, and bake for 25 to 35 minutes, or until it is firm and golden brown and a skewer inserted in the thickest part comes out clean. If the loaf starts to flop over during baking or a braid comes loose, pin it back together with a skewer, continue baking. Transfer to a wire rack to cool. Carefully remove the skewers.

TO TOP THE LOAF, ALICE WINDS THE TWO STRANDS OF DOUGH AROUND HER FINGER TO MAKE A TWISTED ROPE.

SHE GENTLY PLACES THE TWIST ON TOP OF THE ASSEMBLED BRAID.

ALICE BRUSHES THE LOAF A SECOND TIME WITH THE EGG GLAZE. THE SKEWERS HELP THE LOAF KEEP ITS SHAPE WHILE BAKING.

SPOON THE BRANDY OVER THE FRESHLY BAKED LOAF.

RIGHT
For easy entertaining over the Christmas holidays, make this fruit and nut loaf and serve it with liqueur or brandy.

BISHOPS BREAD

A friend in Australia sent me this recipe for a Christmas ring loaf, which seemed most peculiar at first glance. Almost solid with fruit and nuts, the loaf is held together with a little batterlike dough, and after baking is soused in brandy. Because it does not contain yeast and is not decorated or iced, it is a very quick recipe to make – which really is welcome with all the last-minute rush surrounding Christmas.

INGREDIENTS

Makes one loaf.
6 ounces glacé pineapple
$\frac{1}{3}$ cup (2 ounces) red glacé cherries
$\frac{1}{3}$ cup (2 ounces) crystallized ginger
$1\frac{1}{2}$ cups raisins
$1\frac{1}{2}$ cups all-purpose white flour (preferably unbleached)
$\frac{2}{3}$ cup walnuts
$\frac{1}{3}$ cup pecans
$\frac{1}{3}$ cup whole blanched almonds
$\frac{1}{3}$ cup Brazil nuts
1 teaspoon baking powder
$\frac{1}{4}$ teaspoon kosher salt or flaked sea salt
2 large eggs
$\frac{1}{3}$ cup firmly packed light brown sugar
$\frac{1}{4}$ cup brandy

a jelly-roll pan
an 8-inch-round cake pan with sides 3 inches deep, greased
a 15-ounce empty can, label removed and can cleaned, well greased on the outside (be sure the can is aluminum)

Heat the oven to 400F. To prepare the fruit and nuts: Rinse the pineapple, glacé cherries, and ginger in a strainer with hot water. Drain, and then dry well on paper towels. If necessary, cut the pineapple and ginger into small chunks. Halve the cherries. Mix the pineapple, cherries, and ginger with the raisins in a medium-size bowl. Then toss with 1 tablespoon of the flour to coat the fruit.

Spread the nuts in an even layer on the jelly-roll pan. Toast in the oven for about 10 minutes, or until very lightly browned, stirring occasionally. Let the nuts cool, but do not chop them. Lower the oven temperature to 300F.

Stir together the remaining flour, baking powder, and salt in a large bowl. Add the fruit mixture and cooled nuts and mix together well. Put the eggs and sugar in another large bowl and beat with an electric mixer on medium speed until pale and thick. By hand, stir in the flour mixture until well blended. You will have a stiff mixture of fruit and nuts bound together by a little batter. Position the well-greased can in the middle of the prepared cake pan. Spoon the batter into the cake pan around the can and smooth the surface with the back of the spoon.

Bake the bread for $1\frac{1}{4}$ hours, or until the loaf is firm and golden brown. Remove from the oven and immediately spoon the brandy evenly over the bread. Let the bread cool in the pan on a wire rack. Then turn out the bread. Store at room temperature, wrapped in waxed paper and overwrapped in foil. Eat within a week.

HOT CROSS BUNS

Betty Charlton, who gave me this recipe, lives near Norwich, in Norfolk, England. She is a great baker of yeast doughs and makes the best hot cross buns, according to Joy Skipper, who has assisted Anthony Blake and me with this book. Joy has diligently tasted every bread described in the recipes.

INGREDIENTS

Makes twenty-four buns.

- $6\frac{1}{2}$ cups white bread flour (preferably unbleached and stone-ground)
- $\frac{3}{4}$ to 1 cup granulated sugar
- 2 to 3 teaspoons (or to taste) freshly ground spice mixture (page 140) or pumpkin-pie spice
- 1 teaspoon kosher salt or flaked sea salt
- $2\frac{1}{4}$ cups mixed dried fruit, such as dark and golden raisins and currants
- $\frac{1}{4}$ cup diced candied citrus peel (preferably orange and lemon peel)
- 2 cakes compressed fresh yeast (0.6 ounce each) or 2 envelopes active dry yeast ($2\frac{1}{2}$ teaspoons each)
- 2 cups lukewarm water (95F to 105F)
- 1 cup nonfat dry milk powder
- $\frac{1}{2}$ cup (1 stick) unsalted butter or margarine, diced and softened
- 2 large eggs, at room temperature, lightly beaten

TOPPING:

- $\frac{1}{4}$ cup all-purpose flour
- 1 tablespoon granulated sugar
- 3 to 4 tablespoons water
- 1 large egg, beaten with 1 tablespoon milk, for glazing

a baking sheet, greased or lined with parchment paper

BETTY PIPES THE FLOUR PASTE OVER THE INDENTATION ON TOP OF EACH BUN.

Spicy and fruity hot cross buns are traditionally baked on Good Friday throughout the Christian world.

Betty likes to use all unbleached white bread flour from her local mill, Reads. You can, however, replace a portion of the white flour with stone-ground whole-wheat bread flour. These buns are very moist and light, packed with fruit and spice. They are delicious freshly baked on Good Friday, and are equally good for the rest of the Easter weekend when split, toasted, and buttered. If you do not eat all the buns within three days, they will freeze for up to one month. I've given a range on the sugar and spice used in the recipe to account for regional taste differences. The hot cross buns I tasted in the States were sweeter and less spicy than the British ones.

Heat the oven to its lowest setting. Mix together the flour, sugar (reserving 1 teaspoon if using dry yeast), spice, salt, mixed dried fruit, and candied citrus peel in a large bowl. Make a well in the center of the flour mixture. Put the bowl in the oven for 5 to 8 minutes to warm the ingredients while you prepare the yeast.

Crumble the fresh yeast into a medium-size bowl. Stir in the lukewarm water and nonfat dry milk powder until smooth. If using dry yeast, mix the granules and the reserved 1 teaspoon granulated sugar with $\frac{1}{2}$ cup of the lukewarm water and let stand until foamy, 5 to 10 minutes (page 18). Stir in the milk powder and the remaining $1\frac{1}{2}$ cups of the lukewarm water. Then stir in the butter or margarine until melted.

Pour the yeast mixture into the well in the warmed flour mixture. Add the eggs to the well and blend together with the yeast mixture with a small whisk or your hands. With your hand or a wooden spoon, gradually work the flour from the bowl into the yeast mixture to make a very soft, but not sticky dough. If the dough is dry and crumbly, work in water, 1 tablespoon at a time. If too sticky, work in flour, 1 tablespoon at a time.

Turn out the dough onto a floured surface and knead for 10 minutes, or until smooth and elastic. Return the dough to the bowl. Cover with a damp dish towel and let rise at warm room temperature (about 75F) until doubled in size, 30 minutes to 1 hour.

Punch down the dough. Turn out onto a lightly floured surface and knead gently for 5 minutes until very smooth and elastic. Weigh the dough and divide it into twenty-four equal portions, or roll it into a fat rope and cut it into twenty-four pieces. Shape each portion into a neat roll (see Oatmeal Rolls, page 25). Arrange fairly close together, but not touching, on the prepared baking sheet. Cover with a damp dish towel and let rise at warm room temperature until the buns have almost doubled in size and have joined together, 30 to 45 minutes. During the last 15 minutes of rising, heat the oven to 500F.

While the buns are rising, make the topping: In a small bowl, mix the flour and sugar with enough of the water to make a thick, smooth paste. Spoon the paste into a small pastry bag fitted with a narrow, plain tip. With the back of a table knife, make an indentation about $\frac{1}{4}$-inch deep in the shape of a cross on the top of each bun. Brush the buns with the egg glaze. Pipe a cross of the flour paste over the indentation on each bun.

Put the buns in the oven, then immediately lower the oven temperature to 400F and bake for 15 to 20 minutes, or until the buns are nicely golden brown. Transfer the buns to a wire rack to cool. When completely cool, pull the buns apart.

HARVEST WHEAT SHEAF

INGREDIENTS

Makes one large loaf.

$9\frac{1}{2}$ cups white bread flour (preferably unbleached and stone-ground)

4 teaspoons kosher salt or flaked sea salt

2 teaspoons granulated sugar

1 cake compressed fresh yeast (0.6 ounce) or 1 envelope active dry yeast ($2\frac{1}{2}$ teaspoons)

$2\frac{3}{4}$ to 3 cups lukewarm water (95F to 105F)

1 large egg, beaten with 1 teaspoon kosher salt or flaked sea salt, for glazing

one very heavy, large baking sheet, greased (see introduction)

"Toward the end of September or the beginning of October each year, bakers, especially in the southern parts of England, are frequently asked to supply large loaves as ornamental as the baker can make them for harvest festivals in churches," wrote Master Baker John Kirkland in 1907 (page 65). For him, a convenient size was a loaf made of an incredible 26 to 28 pounds of dough. And although he says an ordinary bread dough made a little firmer by adding less liquid will do, this lightly yeasted dough works better. This is a scaled-down version of his recipe to make a wheat sheaf about 17 × 13 inches.

You will need a kitchen scale to make this recipe. If you don't have a scale already, this provides a very good reason to purchase this very useful piece of kitchen equipment.

Mix together the flour, salt, and sugar (if using dry yeast, reserve $\frac{1}{2}$ teaspoon of the sugar) in a very large bowl. Make a well in the center of the flour mixture. Crumble the fresh yeast into a small bowl. Stir in $\frac{3}{4}$ cup of the lukewarm water until smooth. If using dry yeast, mix the granules and the reserved $\frac{1}{2}$ teaspoon sugar with $\frac{3}{4}$ cup of the lukewarm water and let stand until foamy, 5 to 10 minutes (page 18).

Pour the yeast mixture into the well in the flour. Add almost all the remaining 2 cups lukewarm water and mix well. With your hand or a wooden spoon, work the flour from the bowl into the yeast mixture in the well to make a soft dough. (John Kirkland said it should not be sticky, dry, or tough). If the dough is dry and crumbly, work in more of the water, 1 tablespoon at a time. If the dough is too sticky, work in extra flour, 1 tablespoon at a time.

Turn out the dough onto a lightly floured work surface and knead for 10 minutes, or until very elastic.

Wash, dry, and oil the bowl. Return the dough to the bowl and turn the dough over so the top is oiled. Cover with a damp dish towel and let rise at room temperature, away from drafts, until doubled in size, about 2 hours.

Punch down the dough. Turn it out onto a floured surface and knead for 2 minutes to work out the air bubbles. Cover with the upturned bowl and let rest for 10 minutes.

To shape the wheat sheaf: Cut off 10 ounces of the dough. Cover the remaining dough with a damp dish towel (see Note). Roll out the cut-off piece of dough on a lightly floured work surface with a lightly floured rolling pin into a 10 × 6-inch rectangle to form the base for the wheat stalks, patting the dough as necessary to keep the shape. Center a short side of the rectangle on a short side of the prepared baking sheet, so the dough is almost touching one edge of the sheet. (The space should be equal at both long sides, and there should be emply space above the sheaf.)

Roll or pat out 12 ounces of the remaining dough into a crescent shape with rounded ends, 11 inches wide across the crescent and longer than the rectangle. Position the crescent on top of the rectangle so it looks like a very large mushroom. Prick the dough all over with a fork and brush with water to prevent a crust forming.

To make the wheat stalks: Divide 14 ounces of the remaining dough into thirty equal pieces, by weight. Roll each piece on a floured surface with your hands into a thin rope about 10 inches long. Twist or braid three ropes together to make the sheaf band. Set this aside. Lay the remaining twenty-seven "stalks" side-by-side along the length of the stalk base, covering it, to create the sheaf. Place the twisted sheaf band across the center of the sheaf, curving it slightly. Do not press the band down onto the sheaf. Tuck the ends under the sheaf.

Set aside 1 ounce of the remaining dough to make the mouse. Weigh the remaining dough and divide into five equal portions. Divide each fifth into twenty equal pieces by weight, for a total of one hundred pieces. These will form the ears of wheat. Roll each piece with your hand on the floured work surface into a fat, oval-shaped roll. Pinch each roll at one end to make a point and round it at the other end. Using a small pair of kitchen

In autumn, fresh vegetables replace the more traditional flower decorations in Anglican churches throughout Britain to celebrate the harvest festivals. After the service of thanksgiving, many congregations enjoy a meal in the church hall, which can include a decorated loaf of bread, such as this wheat sheaf.

POSITION THE DOUGH CRESCENT OVER THE TOP OF THE STALK BASE AND PRICK THE DOUGH ALL OVER WITH A FORK.

TWIST THREE DOUGH ROPES TOGETHER TO MAKE THE SHEAF BAND.

ARRANGE THE WHEAT STALKS ON THE BASE. PLACE THE TWISTED SHEAF BAND ACROSS THE CENTER OF THE STALKS, CURVING THE BAND SLIGHTLY.

SNIP ANGLED SHALLOW CUTS DOWN THE CENTER OF EACH EAR. THEN SNIP ALONG EACH SIDE, ANGLING THE CUTS IN THE SAME DIRECTION.

ARRANGE THE EARS, A FEW AT A TIME, CLOSE TOGETHER BUT NOT TOUCHING ALONG THE TOP OF THE CRESCENT.

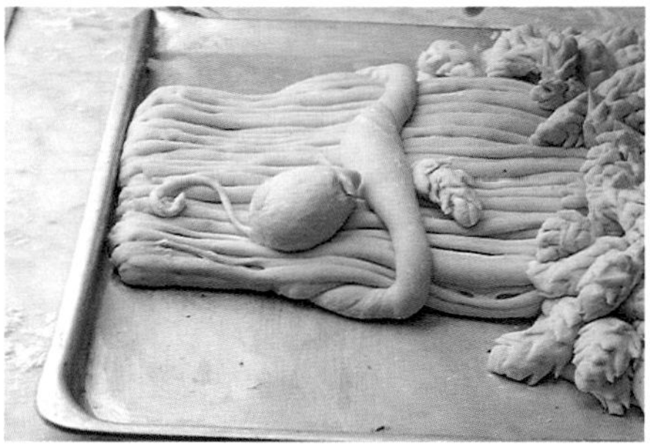

SHAPE THE DOUGH MOUSE, THEN POSITION IT ON THE STALKS AS IF IT IS CLIMBING UP THE SHEAF.

This decorative loaf looks attractive hanging on a kitchen wall, or makes a wonderful housewarming gift for a special friend. If you want to use the wheat sheaf purely for decoration, bake it an extra 6 hours at 250F.

scissors, snip angled, shallow cuts down the center of each ear (without cutting all the way through), working from the rounded end to the pointed end. Then make shallow cuts down each side of the first snips, positioning these cuts between the cuts of the center row.

Arrange the ears close together, but not touching, along the edges of the crescent. The next row should be arranged between these ears, leaving about $1\frac{1}{2}$ inches of the first row exposed. Do not arrange the ears too regularly, and leave one or two to droop slightly. Repeat until the crescent center has been filled and all the wheat ears used.

Shape the remaining 1 ounce dough into an egg-shaped mouse with a pointed nose and a long, thin tail.

Using small scissors, cut two small flaps toward the pointed end, then lift them up and forward to resemble ears. Make two small holes for the eyes.

Brush the underside with water and place it on the stalks as if it is climbing up the sheaf.

Heat the oven to 425F.

Carefully brush the wheat sheaf with the egg glaze. Then prick "in a good many places," according to Kirkland, with the tip of a pointed knife to prevent the loaf from cracking during baking. The knife holes should be made vertically, following the pattern of the stalks and ears, so there are no visible cuts.

Bake the bread for 15 minutes. Brush with more glaze. Then lower the oven temperature to 325F and continue baking for 25 minutes longer, or until the loaf is golden brown and very firm.

Let the loaf cool completely on the baking sheet.

NOTE: If your kitchen is warm, it is best to keep the portions of dough you are not using in the refrigerator, tightly covered with plastic wrap. If the dough rises too fast, the sheaf will lose its crisp shape.

CHALLAH

Challah is the Jewish white egg bread which is often braided into an elaborate loaf. It is regarded as an essential symbol for celebrating the Sabbath on Friday night. The word challah means dough offering in Hebrew. Its meaning dates back from the Temple period, about 380 BC, when a portion of the dough from the Sabbath loaf, generally made with finely-milled flour, rather than the coarse, everyday variety, was given to the temple priests. After the Temple was destroyed in 70 AD, Jews continued this practice symbolically, by throwing a small piece of the challah dough into the fire to burn while a blessing is recited.

Ashkenazi Jews, originally from central and Eastern Europe, often have two symbolic loaves of challah on their Sabbath dinner table. The loaves are covered with a special embroidered cloth, called a challah cover.

The elaborately braided challah, sometimes made with up to twelve strands of dough, was first baked by Central European Jews during the Middle Ages. This special, sweeter loaf was in complete contrast with the coarse, dark, slightly bitter bread eaten during the rest of the week. At the beginning of a Sabbath meal, the challah is blessed. Then, in some traditions, pieces are broken off, dipped in salt, and tossed unceremoniously to the diners, rather than being passed around, to symbolize the gift of bread from God.

Sephardic Jews, originally from Spain, Portugal, North Africa, and the Middle East, do not necessarily bake a special Sabbath loaf. Instead they use two of their everyday breads, such as pitas, or other flat breads. The breads are covered and placed on the Sabbath table to be blessed, and then sometimes broken and dipped in salt.

The symbolic challah made for Rosh Hashana, the Jewish New Year, is circular, or crown-shaped. It signifies peace, unity, and the creation of the Universe. In some communities, for Chanukah, the challah is shaped like a menorah, a seven-branched candle holder. Ukranian Jews may often bake three different shaped challahs: a bird-shaped challah for Yom Kippur, the Jewish day of Atonement; a spiral loaf for Rosh Hashana; and a key-shaped loaf for the Sabbath after Passover.

Some challahs are made with dark or golden raisins, nuts, and saffron, or other spices, depending on the traditions of the community.

The characteristic dark, shiny, reddish-brown color of the commercial varieties is achieved by glazing the loaf with egg yolk tinted with a few drops of red or yellow food coloring.

BRAIDED CHALLAH

This honey-sweetened, saffron-gold, rich dough can be braided into a twist using up to twelve strands, but I am giving only some of the simpler examples in this section. If you are attempting to shape a braid for the first time, you might like to try this tip from Alice Turner (page 148): Insert 10- to 12-inch thin bamboo skewers through the braided strands while the loaf is rising, to help retain the shape.

Traditional challah dough has three risings, but should never be left in too warm a place, or it will become too soft to shape. Glazing the braid twice with egg yolk gives a deeper-colored finish to the loaf. Eat the challah within three days, or freeze for up to one month.

INGREDIENTS

Makes one loaf.

- ¼ teaspoon saffron strands
- 1 cup boiling water
- 1 cake compressed fresh yeast (0.6 ounce) or 1 envelope active dry yeast (2½ teaspoons)
- 3 tablespoons honey
- about 4¾ cups white bread flour (preferably unbleached and stone-ground)
- 2 teaspoons kosher salt or flaked sea salt
- 3 large eggs, at room temperature, lightly beaten
- 6 tablespoons unsalted butter, melted and cooled
- 1 large egg yolk beaten with a pinch of kosher salt or flaked sea salt, for glazing

two heavy baking sheets, one greased

Crumble the saffron strands into a small bowl. Pour in the boiling water and let stand to infuse until the water cools to lukewarm (95F to 105F). Crumble the fresh yeast into a small bowl. Stir in the lukewarm saffron mixture and the honey until smooth. If using dry yeast, mix the granules and the honey with the lukewarm saffron mixture and let stand until foamy, 5 to 10 minutes (page 18).

Stir together the flour and salt in a large bowl and make a well in the center of the flour mixture. Pour the yeast mixture into the well in the flour, followed by the beaten eggs and melted butter. Mix together the ingredients in the well with a small whisk or your hand. Then, with your hand or a wooden spoon, gradually mix the flour from the bowl into the ingredients in the well to form a soft, but not sticky dough. If the dough is too sticky, add a little extra flour, 1 tablespoon at a time. If the dough is dry and crumbly, add a little extra lukewarm water, 1 tablespoon at a time.

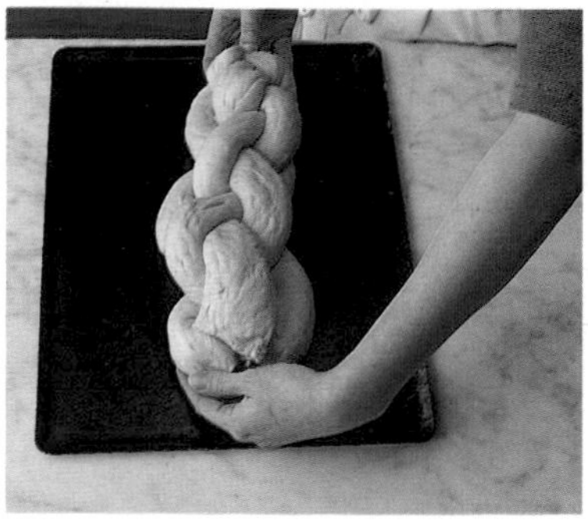

TUCK THE ENDS OF THE BRAID UNDER FOR A NEAT FINISH.

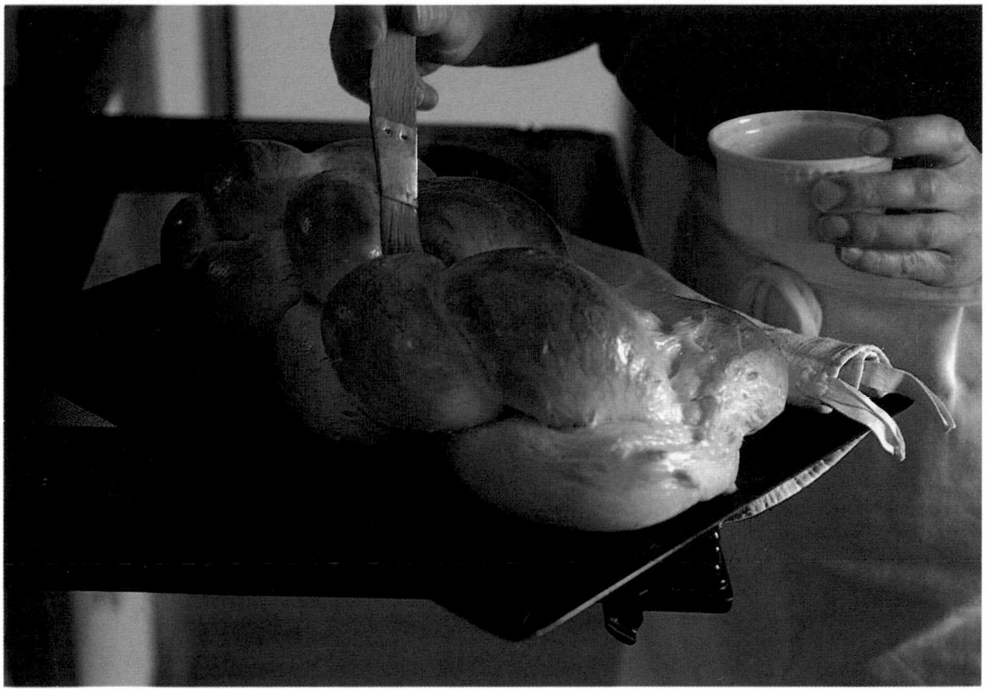

Right
BAKE THE CHALLAH FOR 10 MINUTES. THEN REMOVE IT FROM THE OVEN AND BRUSH A SECOND TIME WITH THE EGG AND SALT GLAZE.

Turn out the dough onto a lightly floured work surface. Knead for 10 minutes until smooth and elastic. Wash, dry, and oil the bowl. Return the dough to the bowl, and turn the dough over so the top is oiled. Cover with a damp dish towel and let rise at room temperature, away from drafts, until doubled in size, about $1\frac{1}{2}$ hours.

Punch down the dough in the bowl. Cover with a damp dish towel and let rise again at room temperature, away from drafts, until doubled in size, about 45 minutes.

Punch down the dough. Turn out the dough onto a very lightly floured work surface. Knead for about 1 minute until the dough is smooth and elastic. Cover the dough with the upturned bowl and let rest for 5 minutes.

To shape a two-strand twist, divide the dough into two equal portions. Using your hands, roll each portion into a 15-inch-long rope about 2 inches thick. Pinch the ropes together firmly at one end. Wind the two ropes together to make a neat twist. Pinch the ends together. Transfer to the prepared baking sheet and tuck the ends under to give a neat shape.

To shape a three-strand braid, see Braided Loaf, page 30.

To shape a four-strand braid, divide the dough into four equal portions. Using your hands, roll each portion into a 13-inch-long rope about 1 inch thick. Pinch the ropes together firmly at one end.

Arrange the four strands side by side and slightly apart, with the unattached ends facing you. Move the strand on the far left under the two strands to its right. Twist the same strand over the last strand it went under, which was originally the third strand from the left. Move the strand on the far right under the twisted two strands in the center. Twist the same strand over the last strand it went under; it then becomes the third strand from the left. Repeat this process until all the strands are braided. Pinch the ends together. Transfer to the prepared baking sheet and tuck under the ends for a neat finish.

To make a double braid, using nine strands, see Alice's Christmas Loaf, page 148.

Cover the shaped challah loosely with a damp dish towel and let rise at room temperature, away from drafts, until doubled in size, 45 minutes to 1 hour. During the last 15 minutes of rising, heat the oven to 425F.

Slide the second baking sheet under the first to prevent the bottom of the challah from overbrowning. Gently brush the risen challah with the egg glaze. Bake for 10 minutes. Remove from the oven and glaze it again. Return the loaf to the oven, lower the oven temperature to 375F, and bake for 20 to 35 minutes longer, with the thicker, more complicated braids taking the longer time, until the loaf is a good golden brown and sounds hollow when tapped underneath. If the loaf is browning too quickly, cover loosely with a sheet of foil. Transfer to a wire rack to cool completely.

NOTE: For its second rising, the dough can also be left overnight in the refrigerator.

CAROLL'S TWISTED RING

Caroll Boltin (page 69) uses her challah dough to make a braided ring loaf for family celebrations. But I enjoy this loaf for everyday eating with soup or cheese, especially a mature, runny Milleen from Veronica Steele's dairy in Ireland. Caroll recommends using this rich bread for French toast, or pain perdu. Eat within three days, or use for toast.

INGREDIENTS

Makes one loaf.

- *about 4¾ cups white bread flour (preferably unbleached and stone-ground)*
- *2 tablespoons granulated sugar*
- *2 teaspoons kosher salt or flaked sea salt*
- *1 cake compressed fresh yeast (0.6 ounce) or 1 envelope active dry yeast (2½ teaspoons)*
- *1 cup lukewarm water (95F to 105F)*
- *6 tablespoons unsalted butter, melted and cooled*
- *3 large eggs, at room temperature, lightly beaten*
- *1 large egg, separated*
- *1 teaspoon poppy seeds, for sprinkling*

a 9-inch tube pan, greased

Stir together 1¼ cups of the flour, the sugar (reserve ½ teaspoon of the sugar if using dry yeast), and the salt in the bowl of a heavy-duty stationary electric mixer fitted with a dough hook. Crumble the fresh yeast into a small bowl. Stir in the lukewarm water until smooth. If using dry yeast, mix the granules and the reserved ½ teaspoon sugar with ½ cup of the lukewarm water and let stand until foamy, 5 to 10 minutes (page 18). Stir in the remaining ½ cup lukewarm water.

Pour the yeast mixture and the melted butter into the flour mixture. Beat on medium speed for 2 minutes. Add the 3 whole eggs and the egg white. Beat on high speed for 2 minutes, or until the dough is very smooth. Gradually add enough of the remaining flour, with the machine on low speed, to make a soft, but not sticky dough that gathers into a ball around the dough hook and leaves the sides of the bowl cleanly. Knead the dough with the dough hook at medium speed for 10 minutes, or until the dough is satiny-smooth and elastic. If the dough is too sticky, add a little extra flour, 1 tablespoon at a time. If the dough is dry and crumbly, add a little extra water, 1 tablespoon at a time.

If you prefer, you can prepare the dough by hand: Mix together the 1¼ cups of the flour, the sugar, and the salt in a large bowl. Make a well in the center of the flour. Prepare the yeast mixture as above, using fresh or dry yeast. Pour the yeast mixture and the melted butter into the well in the flour. With your hand or a wooden spoon, gradually work the flour from the bowl into the liquid. Then beat the batter vigorously with your hand for 2 minutes. Add the 3 whole eggs and the egg white and beat with your hand for 4 minutes. Gradually mix in enough of the remaining flour to make a soft, but not sticky dough. Turn out the dough onto a lightly floured work surface and knead for 10 minutes until satiny-smooth and elastic.

CAROLL BRAIDS THE THREE FLAT STRIPS OF DOUGH TOGETHER.

AFTER THE DOUGH IS BRAIDED, CAROLL WILL PUT IT IN THE TUBE PAN.

This ring loaf is easier to shape than more elaborately braided challahs, yet it's attractive enough to make any celebration more special. Here Caroll has displayed her loaf with an arrangement of vegetables, a bowl of apples, and an old-fashioned, wooden candelabra.

Put the dough into a lightly oiled bowl, and turn the dough over so the top is oiled. Cover with a damp dish towel and let rise at room temperature, away from drafts, until doubled in size, 1 to $1\frac{1}{2}$ hours.

Punch down the dough. Turn out the dough onto a lightly floured work surface. With lightly floured knuckles, pat the dough out into a 22 × 10-inch rectangle, about 1 inch thick. (You may also roll out the dough with a lightly floured rolling pin.) Cut the rectangle lengthwise into four strips, unequal in width: three strips 3 inches wide, and one strip 1 inch wide.

Pinch the three wide strips together at one end. Braid as for the Braided Loaf (page 30) to make a flat, braided rope 18 to 20 inches long. Arrange the dough in the prepared ring mold, pinching the two ends together. Use the remaining narrow strip of dough to wrap like a strap around the point where the two ends meet and tuck underneath, so the loaf is an even thickness all the way around.

Beat the reserved egg yolk with 1 teaspoon water to make a glaze. Brush over the loaf, making sure not to glue the loaf to the mold. Sprinkle the top of the loaf evenly with the poppy seeds.

Cover with a damp dish towel and let rise at room temperature, away from drafts, until doubled in size, about 1 hour. Check from time to time to make sure the dough is not sticking to the cloth. During the last 15 minutes of rising, heat the oven to 400F.

Bake the loaf for 10 minutes. Then lower the oven temperature to 350F and bake 40 minutes longer, or until the loaf is golden brown and a skewer inserted in the center comes out clean.

Let the bread cool in the pan for a couple of minutes. Then carefully turn out onto a wire rack to cool completely.

SOURDOUGH AND RYE BREADS

One of the joys of baking bread is the miracle of yeast. Yeast is a living thing, needing food, some warmth, and pampering to survive – and to perform its job, which is to make a dough rise. What sets sourdough breads apart from other yeast breads is that much of their rising power comes from the wild yeasts that are naturally present in the air, rather than from commercial yeast.

Sourdoughs are not the types of bread that can be quickly made. A starter can take up to three days to develop. And once the starter is made, the dough can take as long as ten days to ferment, as in the German Friendship Cake (page 160). The rising times are often lengthy as well. Leaving the doughs for an extra hour or so will not cause them to over-rise, as is the case with most other doughs. This suits me. I like being able to shape a dough that has risen overnight while I boil the kettle for tea at breakfast, knowing that when I finish working in the evening, the dough will be ready for the oven.

OPPOSITE Lionel Poilâne with his sourdough loaves. ABOVE Poilâne bread for sale in Paris.

Rye breads are made with all or part rye flour, a dark gray flour, commonly used in Northern, Middle, and Eastern European baking, which has a distinctly tangy and slightly acidic taste. This taste is enhanced and heightened when the flour is combined with a sourdough starter.

Unlike wheat flours, rye flour contains very little gluten so doughs made exclusively with rye flour are heavy and sticky, and do not rise much. Consequently, rye-flour doughs are often lightened, and the gluten boosted by the addition of unbleached white bread flour or stone-ground whole-wheat flour. These combinations make the dough easier to work, but more importantly, I feel the taste is improved. It is worth searching out good, coarse, stone-ground rye flour from local mills, health-food stores, or through mail order (see page 187).

For a basic, heavy rye loaf, combine three parts rye flour to one part wheat flour. A light rye loaf is made with the reverse proportions: one part rye flour to three parts wheat flour. Anthony Blake bakes a loaf of rye bread to perfection every day. He uses equal proportions of rye flour, coarse stone-ground whole-wheat flour, and unbleached white bread flour. Gerry's Sourdough Rye Bread (page 164) also uses this combination of flours, but his recipe begins with a sourdough starter.

Some rye bread recipes, such as Scandinavian Rye Bread (page 167) include buttermilk to provide an extra tang. Molasses is used to impart color and an intense flavor to breads like the Pumpernickel Loaf (page 165).

The flavor of sourdough bread becomes distinctively tangy the longer it is left to rise at a cool temperature. The sourness also depends on the pungency of the starter.

Jeffrey Hamelman, of Hamelman's Bakery, in Brattleboro, Vermont, bakes the best sourdough bread I have tasted outside Europe. He makes 500 loaves of bread each day, and considers delicious, well-flavored sourdough bread to be the highest expression of a baker's skill.

"You learn by your mistakes. There are not any shortcuts to wonderful sourdough," he says. "The important thing to remember is that the dough is alive. The baker performs alchemy, and if he or she is successful the yeast becomes exuberant and more lively. If the baker does not supply the yeast's needs, it will be crippled."

Each afternoon before Jeffrey leaves his bakery, he combines a new batch of dough with a starter and leaves it to ferment for 16 hours. He then adds flour and water at regular intervals until the dough is finally baked 24 hours after it was first mixed. Just like home bakers, Jeffrey has to take account of weather conditions when he prepares his dough. In Vermont, the weather can change dramatically and the winters are very cold; the summers extremely hot.

Sourdough breads are slow to stale, and, as they mature, the flavors mellow and blend. Most sourdough breads will stay fresh for up to a week.

TIPS FOR MAKING SOURDOUGH BREADS:

– Flexibility is a key factor when making sourdough breads. The rising times can be variable and unpredictable and, unfortunately, there are times when a dough fails to thrive for no apparent reason. When this happens, you have to accept defeat. Throw away the dough and begin again. Flour and liquid quantities are never precise (as with most yeast breads) because of everyday variations in temperature and humidity and the quality of the flour. Work by feel, and treat the recipes as guides, adding the amounts of ingredients you feel the dough requires.

– There are certain signs that let you know that your starter has "died," is weak, or has gone off. If a starter smells bad, rather than sour, or if it has patches of mold throw it away. Check that it is "alive" by looking for bubbles on the surface and a distinct yeasty, or sour, smell. You will notice that the mixture gradually turns gray as it ferments – this is a good sign. A failed starter will produce a flat, dense loaf. If this happens your starter is not active; you must use a fresh starter for the next loaf.

– Do not use bleached flours. The best starters are made with unbleached, stone-ground flours in which yeasts thrive. The chemical treatment used to bleach flour seems to hinder the development of the starter and – even worse – it may produce a chlorine taste.

– Do not add salt to a starter mixture because it will inhibit the development of the yeast.

– I think a kitchen counter is the best location in the house to leave a starter while it is developing. The kitchen is often warmer than other rooms, and because it is the place where food is prepared, there seem to be more yeasts in the air. The best sourdough breads I have ever made were ones at Anthony Blake's studio, after a week of food photography.

– Do not cover the starter mixture, or the sponge, with plastic wrap, foil, or a lid. Use a damp thin dish towel, to provide a warm, moist enviroment which will attract the yeasts naturally present in the air and encourage them to multiply.

– When you are leaving a starter to ferment over several days, be sure to re-dampen the towel at least once a day.

– Starters develop at different rates depending on the season and the weather. You will find starters and doughs tend to develop most quickly in hot and humid conditions.

– In my recipes I specify how long you can keep a starter before you have to use it in another loaf. If, however, there is not an instruction in a recipe or you want to keep a portion of the dough to use as a starter for the next loaf for more than three days, you must "feed" it. Add about $\frac{1}{2}$ cup water from the cold tap and enough flour to make a soft dough every four days. Store the dough in a covered container in the refrigerator or in a cool pantry. Do not keep the starter longer than two weeks.

GERMAN FRIENDSHIP CAKE

I had heard a lot about friendship cakes, a sourdough loaf made from a starter that has been passed from friend to friend, but I had never tasted one until recently. One day, friend and fellow cookery writer Elaine Hallgarten arrived on my doorstep with a container of starter and some instructions that had been given to her. You certainly know who your friends are when you start making this recipe! Coincidentally, a letter from my mother-in-law in America containing a recipe for Amish friendship bread arrived in the next post. It was identical!

This loaf is delicious and simple to make, more like a crumb cake than a bread, but it does take ten days – once you've made the starter. I discovered it is a good idea to write down the date of Day 1, or you might lose your place in the recipe. After ten days, you will have enough starter to give two portions away and keep two portions for yourself: one to bake immediately and one to refrigerate. You cannot use active dry yeast to make this recipe; it simply doesn't work. Eat the bread within three days after baking, or freeze for up to one month.

INGREDIENTS

Makes one large loaf.

STARTER:
2 cups all-purpose white flour (preferably unbleached)
1 cake compressed fresh yeast (0.6 ounce)
2 cups water

FOR DAY 1:
1 cup granulated sugar
1 cup all-purpose flour (preferably unbleached)
1 cup milk

FOR DAY 5:
1 cup granulated sugar
1 cup all-purpose flour (preferably unbleached)
1 cup milk

TO MAKE THE DOUGH (DAY 10):
2 cups all-purpose flour (preferably unbleached)
1 cup granulated sugar
3 large Granny Smith apples, peeled, cored, and diced
$\frac{2}{3}$ cup golden raisins
$\frac{1}{2}$ cup vegetable oil
2 large eggs, lightly beaten
$\frac{1}{2}$ cup walnuts or $\frac{1}{3}$ cup pecans
2 teaspoons ground cinnamon
2 teaspoons baking powder
$\frac{1}{2}$ teaspoon kosher salt or flaked sea salt
few drops vanilla extract

TOPPING:
$\frac{3}{4}$ cup firmly packed light brown sugar
$\frac{1}{2}$ cup (1 stick) unsalted butter, melted and cooled
a 13 × 9-inch baking pan or roasting pan, well greased

The first time I made this fruit-filled sourdough loaf, I gave a portion of the starter to Joy Skipper, who has assisted on this book, and she has made a new loaf every ten days since then. She has also passed on portions of her starter to friends and neighbors in the small Norfolk village where she lives, and the starter is now making its way around Britain.

"Most sourdoughs are too sour to my taste," she says, "but this is delicious."

Joy has also experimented with different flavorings for this loaf, and recommends replacing the golden raisins and apples with finely grated orange rind and prunes.

To make the starter: Put the flour in a large nonmetallic bowl and make a well in the center of the flour. Crumble the fresh yeast into the well in the flour. Then pour the water into the well and stir with a wooden spoon or your hand until the mixture is smooth. Stir the flour from the bowl into the yeast mixture to make a sticky batter.

Cover with a damp dish towel and let stand on the kitchen table or counter, at room temperature, away from drafts, so the batter absorbs the natural yeasts in the air. Stir the batter once a day for each of the next three days and re-dampen the dish towel if it gets dry. The starter is ready to use when it is gray and foamy.

DAY 1 Stir the starter you have made, or the starter you have been given. Add the sugar, flour, and milk to the starter in the bowl. Stir well, cover with a damp dish towel, and let stand overnight at room temperature, away from drafts.

DAY 2 Stir the starter well and re-cover with a damp dish towel.

DAYS 3 and 4 Do nothing. If the dish towel is dry, re-dampen it.

DAY 5 Stir the starter well and add the sugar, flour, and milk. Stir well again, cover with a damp dish towel, and let stand overnight at room temperature, away from drafts.

DAY 6 Stir the starter well and re-cover with a damp dish towel.

DAYS 7, 8, and 9 Do nothing. Re-dampen the dish towel if it is dry.

DAY 10 Stir the starter well and divide the mixture into four equal portions. Give two portions to friends with instructions, keep one portion for your next batch (see below), and use one portion to make the loaf.

To make the dough: Heat the oven to 350F. Place one reserved portion of the starter in a very large mixing bowl. Add the flour, sugar, apples, golden raisins, oil, eggs, nuts, cinnamon, baking powder, salt, and vanilla to the starter. Mix with your hand or a wooden spoon. When all the ingredients are thoroughly combined, place the dough in the prepared pan and smooth the surface.

For topping: Sprinkle the top of the loaf with the brown sugar, then drizzle with the butter. Bake the loaf for 30 to 40 minutes, or until a wooden skewer inserted in the center comes out clean. Turn out onto a wire rack to cool completely.

TO KEEP A STARTER FOR THE NEXT BATCH: Add 1 teaspoon of granulated sugar to the portion of starter you are going to keep for your next loaf. Stir well, then store in a covered container in the refrigerator for up to one week. To make a fresh cake, begin at Day 1, using this starter.

FRENCH SOURDOUGH LOAF

INGREDIENTS

Makes one large loaf.

STARTER:

- $1\frac{1}{2}$ cups whole-wheat bread flour (preferably stone-ground)
- about 1 cup lukewarm water (95F to 105F)

SPONGE:

- $\frac{1}{2}$ cup lukewarm water (95F to 105F)
- 1 cup white bread flour (preferably unbleached and stone-ground)

DOUGH:

- $\frac{1}{4}$ cup lukewarm water (95F to 105F)
- 2 teaspoons kosher salt or flaked sea salt
- about 2 to $2\frac{1}{2}$ cups white bread flour (preferably unbleached and stone-ground)

one round wicker basket, about 9 inches wide and 4 inches high, lined with a heavily floured dry dish towel, and a baking sheet, heavily floured, or a 9 × 5 × 3-inch loaf pan, greased

This is my version of the delicious, thick-crusted, chewy loaf made popular by the Poilâne family in Paris. The huge loaves from their bakery in the rue du Cherche-Midi are baked in old, wood-fired ovens, which gives them a delicious, smoky flavor. The sourdough tang in this loaf is quite strong, and may not be to all tastes.

You can vary the flour in this recipe using any combination, including a little rye flour. The loaf is an excellent keeper, tasting better as it matures, and it is best thinly sliced. The first two or three batches will taste good, but will not rise as well as later batches when the starter is established. Eat within one week.

To make the starter: Mix together the flour and enough of the lukewarm water in a small bowl to make a very thick batter. Cover with a damp dish towel and let stand at room temperature, away from drafts, for three days, so it absorbs the yeasts in the air. (Re-dampen the dish towel when necessary.) After three days, the starter should be smelly, gray, and only slightly bubbly.

To make the sponge: Pour the starter into a large bowl. Then add the lukewarm water, stirring to dissolve any lumps in the starter. Add the white bread flour. Beat with your hand or a wooden spoon for about 1 minute to make a thick batter. Cover with a damp dish towel and let stand at room temperature, away from drafts, for 24 to 36 hours, or until it is spongy and slightly bubbly. (Re-dampen the dish towel when necessary.) The longer you leave the sponge, the more pronounced the sour taste will be.

To make the dough: Stir down the sponge. Beat in the lukewarm water and the salt. Then mix in enough white bread flour, about one handful at a time, to make a soft, but not sticky dough.

Turn out the dough onto a lightly floured work surface and knead for 10 minutes until firm, smooth, and elastic, adding more flour as needed. Return the dough to the bowl

OPPOSITE
I like to serve this country-style loaf with cheese and a full-bodied, dry red wine.

(no need to wash and oil the bowl). Cover with a damp dish towel and let rise at room temperature, away from drafts, until almost doubled in size, 8 to 12 hours.

Punch down the dough. Cut off 6 to 8 ounces of the dough (about 1 cup) and set aside for making the next starter (see below). Shape the rest of the dough into a ball and put into the cloth-lined basket, if using, or onto the prepared baking sheet. (The basket gives the loaf a nice round shape.) Or shape into a loaf to fit the prepared pan (see A Plain White Loaf, page 24). Cover with a damp dish towel and let rise at room temperature, away from drafts, until almost doubled in size, about 8 hours. Subsequent batches may take less time to rise.

To bake: Heat the oven to 425F. If you used the basket, invert the loaf from the basket onto the prepared baking sheet. Using a sharp knife or a razor blade, slash the top of the loaf four times, or make two diagonal slashes across the top if you are baking the loaf in a pan. Sprinkle with a little white flour. Bake the loaf for 20 minutes. Then lower the oven temperature to 375F and bake for 35 to 45 minutes longer, or until the loaf sounds hollow when tapped underneath. Transfer the loaf to a wire rack and cool completely.

TO KEEP A STARTER FOR THE NEXT BATCH: Put the reserved 6- to 8-ounce (about 1-cup) portion of dough into a greased plastic bag and store in the refrigerator for up to three days. Or place the dough in a small bowl, covered with a damp dish towel, and let stand at room temperature, away from drafts, for up to two days. (To keep the starter longer, see page 160.) To use for making a loaf, start at the sponging stage in the above recipe, and beat in a little extra lukewarm water to make a thick batter. Proceed with the recipe.

TO MAKE THE STARTER: STIR TOGETHER THE WHOLE-WHEAT BREAD FLOUR AND ABOUT 1 CUP LUKEWARM WATER TO MAKE A VERY THICK BATTER.

AFTER THREE DAYS, THE STARTER SHOULD BE SMELLY, GRAY, AND SLIGHTLY BUBBLY.

WHEN THE DOUGH HAS RISEN TO DOUBLE IN SIZE, HAVE READY THE BASKET WITH THE FLOURED CLOTH.

RESERVE 6 TO 8 OUNCES DOUGH FOR THE NEXT STARTER. SHAPE THE REST OF THE DOUGH INTO A BALL AND PUT IT INTO THE CLOTH-LINED BASKET.

AFTER THE DOUGH HAS RISEN AT NORMAL ROOM TEMPERATURE FOR ABOUT 8 HOURS IT WILL DOUBLE IN SIZE.

SLASH THE TOP OF THE LOAF FOUR TIMES, THEN SPRINKLE WITH FLOUR.

Gerry turns out his dough onto a floured surface for kneading.

GERRY'S SOURDOUGH RYE BREAD

INGREDIENTS

Makes one large loaf.

STARTER:

- 1½ cups rye flour (preferably stone-ground)
- about 1¼ cups lukewarm water (95F to 105F)

SPONGE:

- 1¼ cups lukewarm water (95F to 105F)
- about 1¼ cups rye flour (preferably stone-ground)

DOUGH:

- 1 tablespoon kosher salt or flaked sea salt
- 1 to 2 teaspoons ground caraway seeds, or to taste
- 2 tablespoons sunflower oil
- 1¼ cups whole-wheat bread flour (preferably stone-ground)
- 1¼ cups rye flour (preferably stone-ground)
- about 1½ to 2½ cups white bread flour (preferably unbleached and stone-ground)
- extra rye flour, for sprinkling

a large oval or round cast-iron casserole with lid (about 8 inches wide and 4 inches deep), greased, or an ovenproof enamel Dutch oven

"For me, the only bread worth eating is sourdough. Everything else tastes like cake," says Gerry Turner of Bree, County Wexford, in Ireland. Gerry started baking his own bread in 1981, when he moved to Ireland. He had lived in Prague, where he met his charming wife Alice (page 148), and where he developed a liking for rye bread, particularly the sourdough variety.

"I invented a loaf to satisfy our tastes. It was trial and error for many weeks," he says. Part of his technique is to bake the loaf in a covered cast-iron casserole.

Gerry saves a quarter of his prepared dough to use as the starter for the next loaf. His dough is uniquely flavored with ground caraway seeds. A mortar and pestle, a clean coffee grinder, or a spice grinder will do the job nicely.

To make the starter: Mix the flour and water in a large bowl to make a stiff batter. Cover with a damp dish towel and let stand at room temperature, away from drafts, for four days to absorb the natural yeasts in the air. Re-dampen the towel as necessary. After four days, the batter should be very gray and foamy. (Gerry says you need strong nerves, and a good sense of smell is a disadvantage, as the batter will smell dreadful.)

To make the sponge: Stir down the starter in the bowl with a wooden spoon or your hand. Then add the lukewarm water, stirring to dissolve any lumps in the starter. Add enough rye flour to make a very thick, sticky batter – about 1¼ cups, but the exact quantity will vary depending on your flour. Sprinkle the surface of the batter with a little more rye flour to prevent a crust from forming. Cover with a damp dish towel and let stand in a cool place, away from drafts, until smelly and bubbly, about 18 hours.

To make the dough: Sprinkle the salt, ground caraway seeds, and sunflower oil evenly onto the sponge. Mix to make a very sloppy batter. Mix in the whole-wheat flour, then the rye flour. Mix in enough of the white bread flour, a handful at a time, to make a soft, but not sticky dough. Turn out the dough onto a floured surface and knead for 10 minutes, or until firm and elastic, adding extra white flour as needed. Cut off one-quarter of the dough and set aside for making the next starter (see below).

Shape the larger piece of dough into an oval or a round to fit the prepared casserole. Put the dough into the casserole and sprinkle with a little rye flour. Cover with the lid and let rise at room temperature, away from drafts, until doubled in size, 1 to 6 hours, depending on the vigor of your dough and the room temperature. When ready to bake, heat the oven to 400F. Bake the loaf in the casserole, covered, for 50 to 70 minutes, or

OPPOSITE
A loaf just removed from the oven.

until the loaf sounds hollow when unmolded and tapped underneath. Turn the loaf out of the casserole onto a wire rack to cool.

TO KEEP A STARTER FOR THE NEXT BATCH: Grease the inside of a plastic bag. Put the reserved piece of dough in the bag and store in the refrigerator for up to three days to use for the next batch. (To keep the starter longer, see page 160.) To prepare the sponge: Put the reserved dough into a large bowl and pour in enough lukewarm water (95F to 105F) to cover. Let stand for 5 minutes. Then mix the water and dough together with your hands, squeezing the dough between your fingers. Beat in enough rye flour, about 1¼ cups, with your hand to make a very thick batter. Sprinkle the surface of the batter with a little rye flour to prevent a crust from forming. Cover with a damp dish towel and let stand in a cool place, away from drafts, until smelly and bubbly, about 18 hours. Proceed with the recipe.

PUMPERNICKEL LOAF

You cannot buy pumpernickel flour because it does not exist. Pumpernickel bread is actually made of a mixture of several flours, always including a high proportion of rye flour. The dark color of this dense, tasty bread is usually achieved both by tinting the dough with coffee, molasses, cocoa, or even liquid gravy browning and by long, slow baking. This loaf includes only a small amount of molasses, so it is lighter in color than breads made commercially. If you like a tangier-tasting loaf, replace some of the milk with an equal quantity of buttermilk. Across northern Europe, pumpernickel is enjoyed with cured or smoked fish or meats, cheese, and soups.

INGREDIENTS

Makes one large loaf or two smaller loaves.

- 2 cups rye flour (preferably coarsely stone-ground)
- 1 cup white bread flour (preferably unbleached and stone-ground)
- 1 cup whole-wheat bread flour (preferably stone-ground)
- 2 teaspoons kosher salt or flaked sea salt
- 1 cake compressed fresh yeast (0.6 ounce) or 1 envelope active dry yeast (2½ teaspoons)
- 1½ cups lukewarm water (95F to 105F)
- 1 tablespoon firmly packed light brown sugar
- ¼ cup molasses
- 1 tablespoon vegetable oil, or 1 tablespoon unsalted butter, melted
- 1 tablespoon potato starch
- 2 tablespoons cold water
- about ¾ cup boiling water, for glazing

one 9 × 5 × 3-inch loaf pan or two 8½ × 4½ × 2¾-inch loaf pans, greased

Mix together the flours and salt in a large bowl and make a well in the center of the flour mixture. Crumble the fresh yeast into a small bowl. Stir in the lukewarm water until smooth. If using dry yeast, mix the granules and the 1 tablespoon brown sugar with ¾ cup of the lukewarm water and let stand until foamy, 5 to 10 minutes (page 18). Stir in the remaining ¾ cup lukewarm water.

Pour the yeast mixture into the well in the flour. Add the sugar, molasses, and oil or melted butter to the well in the flour and mix these ingredients together with a small whisk or your hand. Mix the flour from the bowl into the liquid in the well with your hand or a wooden spoon to make a soft and slightly sticky dough. It will be difficult to work. Turn out the dough onto a lightly floured work surface and knead for 10 minutes until the dough becomes firm, smooth, and elastic. If necessary, add a little more rye and whole-wheat flours to prevent sticking. The dough will feel heavier than a non-rye dough. Return the dough to the bowl. Cover with a damp dish towel, and let rise at room temperature, away from drafts, until doubled in size, 2 to 3 hours.

Punch down the dough. Turn out the dough onto a lightly floured work surface and knead for 1 minute until it feels elastic. If making two loaves, divide the dough into two equal portions, otherwise, leave the dough in one piece. Shape the dough into a loaf (or loaves) to fit the prepared pan (or pans; see A Plain White Loaf, page 24). Put the shaped dough, seam side down, into the prepared pan (or pans). Cover with a damp dish towel and let rise at room temperature, away from drafts, until doubled in size, 1½ to 2 hours. During the last 15 minutes of rising, heat the oven to 400F.

Whisk together the potato starch and the 2 tablespoons cold water in a small bowl until smooth. Whisk in enough of the boiling water to make a thick, smooth glaze. Gently brush the risen loaves with the potato starch glaze. Bake the bread for 35 to 40 minutes, or until it is dark brown and sounds hollow when unmolded and tapped underneath. Turn out onto a wire rack to cool completely. Wrap in plastic wrap, overwrap with foil, and keep at room temperature for at least one day or up to one week before slicing thinly.

OPPOSITE
Use slices of Scandinavian Rye Bread to make colorful open-face sandwiches.

ONION AND CARAWAY RYE BREAD

Extremely good with pickled, cured, and smoked fish, this light rye loaf tastes best one or two days after it has been baked. Replace the caraway seeds with toasted cumin seeds for a spicier, more fragrant loaf. This bread is best made with fresh yeast, so I have not given any instructions using dry yeast. Eat within four days of baking.

INGREDIENTS

Makes one large loaf.

- about $2\frac{1}{2}$ cups white bread flour (preferably unbleached and stone-ground)
- $1\frac{2}{3}$ cups rye flour (preferably stone-ground)
- 1 tablespoon caraway seeds, or to taste
- 2 teaspoons kosher salt or flaked sea salt
- 1 cake compressed fresh yeast (0.6 ounce)
- 1 teaspoon firmly packed dark brown sugar
- $\frac{3}{4}$ cup lukewarm milk (95F to 105F)
- $\frac{3}{4}$ cup lukewarm water (95F to 105F)
- 1 medium-size yellow onion, finely chopped (about 1 cup)
- 2 tablespoons vegetable oil
- water for brushing
- extra caraway seeds for sprinkling

a 9 × 5 × 3-inch loaf pan, greased

Mix together the flours, caraway seeds, and salt in a large bowl and make a well in the center. Crumble the fresh yeast into a small bowl. Stir in the brown sugar and the lukewarm milk and water until smooth.

Pour the yeast mixture into the well in the flour. With your hand or a wooden spoon, mix enough of the flour from the bowl into the yeast mixture in the well to make a thick batter. Cover with a damp dish towel and let stand at room temperature, away from drafts, until spongy, about 20 minutes (page 16). Meanwhile, sauté the onion slowly in the oil in a skillet until softened, but not browned, about 10 minutes. Let cool.

Add the cooled onion and any remaining oil in the skillet to the sponge in the well and mix together with your hand or a wooden spoon. Gradually mix the flour from the bowl into the sponge with your hand or a wooden spoon to make a soft, but not sticky dough.

Turn out the dough onto a lightly floured surface and knead for 10 minutes until firm, smooth, and elastic. Return the dough to the bowl. Cover with a damp dish towel and let rise at room temperature, away from drafts, until doubled in size, 2 to 3 hours.

Punch down the dough. Turn it out onto a floured surface and shape into a loaf to fit the prepared pan (see A Plain White Loaf, page 24). Place the dough, seam side down, in the pan. Cover with a damp towel and let rise at room temperature, away from drafts, until doubled in size, $1\frac{1}{2}$ to 2 hours. During the last 15 minutes, heat the oven to 350F. Gently brush the loaf with water. Sprinkle the top with caraway seeds.

Bake the loaf for 35 to 45 minutes, or until the loaf sounds hollow when unmolded and tapped underneath. Transfer to a wire rack to cool completely.

ADD THE COOLED ONION AND ANY REMAINING OIL TO THE SPONGE.

SPRINKLE THE TOP WITH CARAWAY SEEDS JUST BEFORE BAKING.

SCANDINAVIAN RYE BREAD

Buttermilk and a high proportion of rye flour to white bread flour make this bread the strongest tasting and most densely textured in this chapter. The dough is quite sticky to work and it will feel heavier than even an all-whole-wheat dough – but it is worth the effort. Barley malt extract is found at well-stocked health-food stores.

Wrap the loaf in foil and keep for one day after baking. It will stay fresh for five days, or can be frozen for up to one month.

INGREDIENTS

Makes one loaf.

- $2\frac{1}{2}$ cups rye flour (preferably stone-ground)
- $1\frac{1}{4}$ cups white bread flour (preferably unbleached and stone-ground)
- 2 teaspoons kosher salt or flaked sea salt
- 2 tablespoons cold unsalted butter, diced
- one and one-half 0.6-ounce cakes compressed fresh yeast, or $1\frac{1}{2}$ envelopes active dry yeast (1 tablespoon plus $\frac{3}{4}$ teaspoon) plus $\frac{1}{2}$ teaspoon granulated sugar
- $\frac{1}{2}$ cup lukewarm milk (95F to 105F)
- 1 cup buttermilk
- 4 teaspoons barley malt extract
- 1 tablespoon black treacle or dark molasses

a baking sheet, greased

Mix together the flours and salt in a large bowl. Rub in the butter with your fingertips until the mixture looks like fine crumbs. Make a well in the center of the flour. Crumble the fresh yeast into a small bowl. Stir in the lukewarm milk until smooth. If using dry yeast, mix the granules and the $\frac{1}{2}$ teaspoon sugar with the lukewarm milk and let stand until foamy, 5 to 10 minutes (page 18).

Pour the yeast mixture into the well. Add the buttermilk, barley malt extract, and black treacle or molasses and mix these ingredients together. Mix the flour from the bowl into the liquid in the well with your hand or a wooden spoon to make a soft and sticky dough. If the dough is dry and crumbly, add a little more buttermilk, 1 tablespoon at a time. If the dough is too wet, add a little more white flour, 1 tablespoon at a time.

Turn out the dough onto a floured surface and knead for 10 minutes until firm, elastic, and smooth. Return the dough to the bowl. Cover with a damp dish towel and let rise at room temperature, away from drafts, until doubled in size, about 2 hours.

Punch down the dough. Turn out the dough onto a lightly floured work surface and shape into an oval loaf (see The Basic Loaf, page 17). Place the loaf on the prepared baking sheet. Using a sharp knife or a razor blade, slash the loaf down the center. Cover with a damp dish towel and let rise at room temperature, away from drafts, until doubled in size, about $1\frac{1}{2}$ hours. During the last 15 minutes of rising, heat the oven to 400F. Bake the loaf for 35 to 45 minutes, or until it sounds hollow when tapped underneath. Transfer to a wire rack to cool completely.

ENRICHED DOUGHS

Rich, rich, rich. These are extravagant recipes, where white yeast dough is transformed into luxurious pâtisserie by adding what appear to be extravagant quantities of butter, eggs, or cream. Technique is all-important in working with these doughs – pastry chefs may practice for years before they are satisfied. Equally important are the ingredients. Because of the large amounts of butter, lard, or cream incorporated into these doughs, they must be of the very best quality and really fresh, untainted by "refrigerator smells" or exposure to air. I think firm, pale, and creamy-tasting unsalted butter, or "sweet" butter is best for enriching doughs. Unsalted butter from the French regions of Normandy and Brittany is particularly prized by European pastry chefs. In the States, look for unsalted butter graded AA; it will have the best flavor. Buy butter from a store with a high turnover. Never try to substitute margarine for butter or coffee lightener for heavy cream, because the results will be disappointing, if not totally inedible. Whole-wheat flour does not lend itself to these recipes either. As these doughs contain such a high proportion of fat, they have more yeast in proportion to the flour than usual to help them rise. It is wise to let the doughs rise fairly slowly at normal to warm room temperature because, if the room is too hot, the fat will melt and ooze out, and a soggy, heavy dough will be your result. Some soft doughs such as the one for croissants, need to be chilled before shaping, while others, such as brioche dough, are so soft they also need a mold to give them shape. The numerous fairly slow risings in these recipes help to give the breads their fine textures: Aberdeen Butteries (page 180), Michel Roux's Croissants (page 170), and Danish Pastries (page 173) are made like puff pastry, with crisp, flaky layers that should not be damp or doughy; Michel Roux's Brioche (page 181) has an even, fine crumb; Sally Lunns (page 178) have a delicate texture similar to a rich sponge cake, while Rum Babas (page 184) and Savarin (page 185) develop a honeycomb structure, like a bath sponge, ready to absorb plenty of flavored syrup. Lardy Cake (page 177) is a rich, sweet cake with layers of flaky dough.

OPPOSITE Michel Roux and croissants. ABOVE A basket of freshly baked enriched breads

These recipes do take a lot of time and need a bit of practice, but the results are always worth eating and will provide you with a tremendous sense of achievement. You, too, can make croissants like Michel Roux!

MICHEL ROUX'S CROISSANTS

INGREDIENTS

Makes sixteen to eighteen croissants.

- 2 tablespoons plus 2 teaspoons granulated sugar
- 2 teaspoons kosher salt or flaked sea salt
- $1\frac{1}{4}$ cups cold water from the tap
- 1 cake compressed fresh yeast (0.6 ounce), or 1 envelope active dry yeast ($2\frac{1}{2}$ teaspoons) plus $\frac{1}{2}$ teaspoon granulated sugar
- 2 tablespoons nonfat dry milk powder
- $3\frac{1}{2}$ cups white bread flour (preferably unbleached and stone-ground)
- $1\frac{1}{4}$ cups ($2\frac{1}{2}$ sticks) unsalted butter
- 1 large egg yolk beaten with 1 tablespoon milk, to glaze

- a $6 \times 3\frac{1}{2}$-inch rectangle of heavy cardboard, cut in half diagonally to make two triangle templates, optional
- two baking sheets that will fit in your refrigerator, lightly greased

A Meilleur Ouvrier de France, 1976, Pâtissier-Confiseur, Michel Roux is one of France's finest pastry chefs. He is also the owner of a Michelin three-star restaurant in England, the Waterside Inn, at Bray-on-Thames.

As you might suspect, Michel is a perfectionist who cares passionately about his work. He spent many hours developing this exquisite croissant recipe so it can be made at home without specialized pastry training or equipment. Making successful croissants is a challenge for even the most experienced home baker, so remember Michel's warning that "only practice makes perfect," and take it from me that it is worth the effort required to make these. You will not find a better recipe anywhere.

If you want to have freshly baked croissants for breakfast, cover the shaped and glazed dough with plastic wrap and let it rise very slowly overnight in the refrigerator. (The croissants should slowly double in size.) In the morning, let the dough stand at room temperature for about 30 minutes, then glaze again and bake. If the refrigerator is very cold, the croissants may not rise sufficiently overnight. In that case you will have to leave them at room temperature longer, until they are doubled in size.

Croissants are best eaten warm, soon after baking, or at least on the day they are baked. If that is not possible, however, croissants and Petits Pains au Chocolat (page 173) freeze well for up to two weeks. After baking, while they are still warm, place them in freezer bags and freeze immediately. To use, remove them from the bags and place them, still frozen, on a baking sheet. Bake at 500F for 5 minutes, or until warmed through.

You can also freeze unbaked croissants for up to one week. Place the shaped croissants on a baking sheet as described below. Before glazing them and leaving them to rise, cover the baking sheet well with plastic wrap or a plastic bag and freeze. Then let them thaw in the refrigerator overnight, or at room temperature for 4 to 6 hours. When thawed, glaze and leave to rise until doubled in size. Glaze again and bake as in the recipe.

Dissolve the sugar and salt in one-third of the cold water. Crumble the fresh yeast into a small bowl. Stir in the remaining water until smooth, then beat in the milk powder. If using dry yeast, heat the remaining two-thirds of the water to lukewarm (95F to 105F).

MICHEL HAS ROLLED OUT THE DOUGH, LEAVING A ROUGH, 5-INCH SQUARE IN THE CENTER.

HE WRAPS THE DOUGH OVER THE BUTTER SO IT IS COMPLETELY ENCLOSED.

TO BEGIN FOLDING, HE TURNS THE DOUGH ON A LONG SIDE. HE THEN FOLDS THE RIGHT THIRD OVER INTO THE CENTER.

MICHEL THEN FOLDS OVER THE LEFT THIRD. THE COMPLETELY ENCLOSED SIDE OF THE DOUGH IS ON HIS LEFT.

AFTER THE THIRD CHILLING, HE ROLLS THE DOUGH INTO A 16 × 30-INCH RECTANGLE.

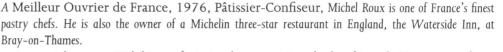

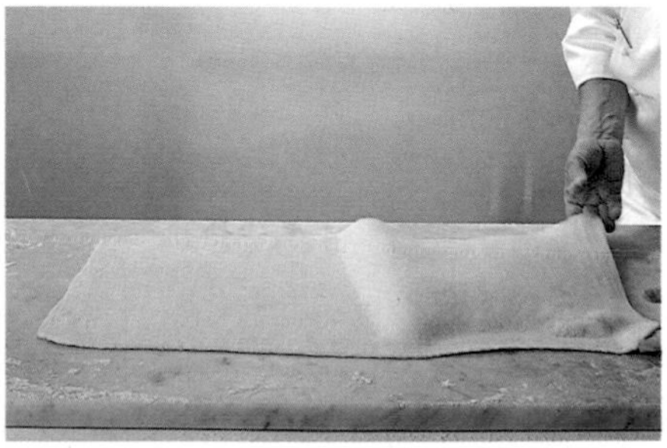

TO RELAX THE DOUGH, HE GENTLY LIFTS AND FLAPS IT AGAINST THE WORK SURFACE.

AFTER TRIMMING THE EDGES, MICHEL CUTS THE DOUGH LENGTHWISE INTO TWO STRIPS.

USING A LIGHTLY FLOURED KNIFE, HE CUTS EACH STRIP INTO EIGHT OR NINE TRIANGLES.

TO SHAPE A CROISSANT, MICHEL GENTLY STRETCHES OUT THE TWO SHORTER POINTS OF THE TRIANGLE.

STARTING FROM THE WIDE EDGE, HE ROLLS THE DOUGH TOWARD THE POINT. HE SHAPES IT INTO A CRESCENT AND PUTS IT ON A BAKING SHEET.

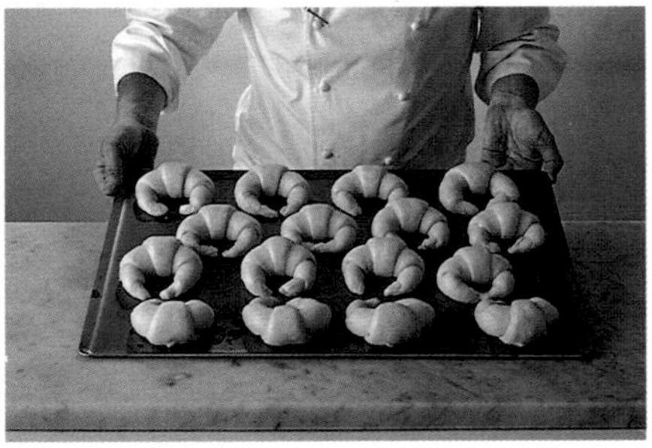

THE CROISSANTS THAT WILL BE CLOSEST TO THE OVEN'S HOT SPOTS ARE ARRANGED SO THE TIPS POINT TO THE CENTER OF THE BAKING SHEET.

BAKED CROISSANTS WILL BE WELL RISEN AND GOLDEN BROWN. MICHEL COOLS THEM ON A WIRE RACK.

Mix the yeast granules and the $\frac{1}{2}$ teaspoon sugar with the lukewarm water and let stand until foamy, 5 to 10 minutes (page 18). Beat in the milk powder.

Put the flour in the bowl of a heavy-duty stationary electric mixer. Using the dough hook and beating at low speed, beat in the sugar-salt liquid, then beat in the yeast mixture. Stop beating as soon as the ingredients are well mixed and the dough comes away from the sides of the bowl, which should not take longer than $1\frac{1}{2}$ minutes. The dough will be soft and sticky, and it is important not to overwork the dough at this stage. Or, combine the flour, sugar-salt liquid, and the yeast mixture in a large bowl and beat with a wooden spoon until the dough is soft and sticky and comes away from the sides of the bowl, which should not take longer than 3 minutes.

Cover the dough with a damp dish towel and let rise in a warm place (about 75F, but not more than 86F), away from drafts, until doubled in size, about 30 minutes.

Punch down the dough by quickly flipping it over in the bowl with your fingers to release the carbon-dioxide gases. Do not knead or overwork the dough, or the croissants will be heavy. Cover with plastic wrap and refrigerate for 6 to 8 hours, or until the dough slowly doubles in size. If the dough rises again after an hour, punch it down as above, re-cover, and return to the refrigerator.

If using sticks of butter, shape them into a 5-inch square by cutting the sticks in half lengthwise, arranging the pieces side by side, and mashing them together with your fingertips. Otherwise, using a rolling pin, gently roll and shape the butter into a 5-inch square. The butter must be firm, but still quite pliable, and about the same temperature as the dough when they are combined. If necessary, pound the butter between two sheets of waxed paper with a rolling pin to make it more pliable, or chill until it is firmer.

Punch down the dough. Turn it out onto a lightly floured work surface and shape it into a ball. Using a sharp knife, cut a cross in the top of the dough. Roll out the dough with a lightly floured rolling pin in four places, giving the dough a quarter turn to the left after each roll, making a rough circle with a thick, rough 5-inch square of dough in the center. Brush off any excess flour.

A French-style breakfast of freshly baked croissants and pains au chocolat. In France, butter-rich croissants are sometimes not shaped into crescents, but left straight like these. This custom developed after World War II when butter was in short supply and bakers were forced to make croissants with margarine instead. Shoppers were then able to tell at a glance what they were buying because a crescent shape indicated margarine had been used.

Put the butter on the rough square of dough. Fold the dough over the butter, tucking in the edges and making sure the butter is completely enclosed so it does not ooze out during the following rolling and folding processes.

Roll out the dough, rolling away from you, on a lightly floured surface with a floured rolling pin, into a 16 × 27-inch rectangle. Turn the dough rectangle so a long side faces you. Brush off any excess flour. Fold over the right third of the dough, then fold over the left third on top of the right third to make a three-layer dough sandwich with the completely enclosed side on your left. Use the rolling pin to seal the top, bottom, and right edges by pressing down on them. Wrap the dough in plastic wrap and chill for at least 20 minutes but no more than 45 minutes. Repeat the rolling, folding, and chilling twice more, turning the dough a quarter turn to the left so the enclosed side is on the bottom before each roll. Dust off excess flour.

After the third chilling, roll out the dough with a lightly floured rolling pin into a 16 × 30-inch rectangle, flouring the work surface very lightly as you roll.

Gently lift the dough and flap it against the work surface twice to relax it and prevent shrinkage during baking, taking care not to spoil the shape of the rectangle. Using a large, lightly floured knife, trim the edges of the dough rectangle to neaten it, then cut the dough lengthwise into two equal strips. You can use a ruler as a guide if you like. Do not re-roll the trimmings – just bake as they are to enjoy as nibbles.

Lay the short edge of one of the triangle templates along one long edge of the dough and mark the outline with the back of the knife. Continue this way, using both pieces of dough, until you have marked out a total of sixteen to eighteen triangles. Then cut out the dough triangles. Marking out the triangles first helps prevent mistakes. If you feel confident, cut out the triangles without using the templates, as Michel Roux does.

Arrange the triangles on the prepared baking sheets. Cover tightly with plastic wrap and refrigerate for a few moments: If the dough becomes too warm, it may soften and crack while the croissants are being shaped.

Place one dough triangle at a time on the floured work surface with the longest point toward you. (Keep the rest refrigerated.) Gently stretch out the two shorter points. Then, starting from the edge opposite the long point, roll up the triangle toward you; use one hand to roll the dough and the other to gently pull the long point. Make sure that this pointed end is in the center and tucked underneath it, so it will not rise up during baking.

As soon as the croissant is shaped, place it on a lightly greased baking sheet, turning the ends in the same direction in which you rolled the dough to make a curved crescent shape. Space the croissants about 2 inches apart. If your oven has a "hot spot," such as the back, arrange the row of croissants closest to it with the tips pointing towards the center of the sheet or the tips may dry out and burn.

Lightly brush the croissants with the egg glaze, brushing upward from the inside of the crescent, so the layers of dough do not stick together and prevent the croissant from rising properly during baking. Let the croissants rise, uncovered, in a warm (about 75F), humid place, away from drafts, until doubled in size, 1 to 2 hours. During the last 15 minutes of rising, heat the oven to 450F.

Very lightly brush the croissants in the same direction again with the egg glaze. Then bake for 15 minutes until golden brown, well risen, and slightly crisp. Lower the oven temperature to 400F if the croissants are browning too quickly. Transfer them immediately to wire racks to cool, making sure they are not touching.

VARIATION: PETITS PAINS AU CHOCOLAT Croissant dough is also used to make these classic French breakfast rolls, which have a rich, dark chocolate filling. When you are in France, look out for the long, thin bars of *couverture* chocolate traditionally used for making these. Otherwise, use a good-quality semisweet chocolate.

After the third rolling, folding, and chilling, roll out the dough as for the croissants. Cut the dough into 6 × 4-inch rectangles. Place one or two 1-ounce squares of semisweet chocolate on one short end. Fold over the dough loosely to make a small, flattish cylinder. Arrange on a lightly greased baking sheet. Glaze with egg glaze. Let rise, uncovered, then glaze again, and bake as for Michel Roux's Croissants (above). Do not re-roll the trimmings – just bake them as they are to enjoy as nibbles.

DANISH PASTRIES

In Denmark, these crisp and flaky filled sweet pastries are called Vienna bread, or wienerbrot. *This is because the method of interleaving yeast-bread dough with butter was brought to Denmark about 150 years ago by Austrian pastry chefs, who, in turn, had learned the technique from Turkish bakers working in Vienna. It was the Danes who added the sweet fillings to the pastries. The three fillings given here are the ones I like best, and you'll need to make all three to fill the four different Danish pastry shapes this recipe makes. If you prefer, you can create your own fillings: Try using a good conserve or jam; sweetened ground walnuts; almond paste; or cottage or farmers' cheese flavored with grated lemon rind and sugar. Vary the fillings and shapes to suit your fancy.*

Whatever the filling, the baked pastries should be crisp, light, and flaky, not spongy or cake-like. After the dough has been rolled out, folded, and chilled three times, it can be wrapped well and left in the refrigerator for one day, or frozen for up to two weeks. These are best eaten on the day they are baked.

Golden Danish pastries shaped into twists, windmills, pinwheels, and envelopes.

INGREDIENTS

Makes twenty-eight pastries.

- $3\frac{1}{4}$ cups white bread flour (preferably unbleached and stone-ground)
- 1 teaspoon kosher salt or flaked sea salt
- 1 cake compressed fresh yeast (0.6 ounce), or 1 envelope active dry yeast ($2\frac{1}{2}$ teaspoons) plus $\frac{1}{2}$ teaspoon granulated sugar
- $\frac{3}{4}$ cup lukewarm water (95F to 105F)
- $\frac{1}{4}$ cup diced cold lard, chilled solid white vegetable shortening, or cold unsalted butter, diced
- 2 large eggs, lightly beaten
- 1 cup (2 sticks) unsalted butter
- Almond Filling, see page 176
- Vanilla Cream Filling, see page 176
- Apricot Filling, see page 176
- 1 large egg, lightly beaten, to glaze
- about $\frac{1}{3}$ cup sliced almonds
- strained, warmed apricot jam, optional
- Glacé Icing, see page 176, optional

several baking sheets, greased

Stir together the flour and salt in a large bowl. Crumble the fresh yeast into a small bowl. Stir in the lukewarm water until smooth. If using dry yeast, mix the granules and the $\frac{1}{2}$ teaspoon sugar with the water and let stand until foamy, 5 to 10 minutes (page 18).

Rub the lard, shortening, or $\frac{1}{4}$ cup butter into the flour with your fingertips until the mixture looks like fine crumbs, lifting your hand well above the bowl to toss and aerate the mixture. Make a well in the center of the flour. Add the yeast mixture to the well. Then mix the eggs into the yeast mixture in the well. Work in the flour from the bowl with your hand or a wooden spoon to make a soft, but not sticky dough. Turn out the dough onto a lightly floured work surface and gently knead for 2 minutes only. Wash and dry the bowl and oil it lightly. Return the dough to the bowl and turn the dough over so the top is oiled. Cover the bowl with a damp dish towel. Let the dough rise at room temperature, away from drafts, until doubled in size, about 1 hour.

Punch down the dough in the bowl. Cover with plastic wrap and chill in the refrigerator for 2 to 4 hours until firmer and chilled, but not hard.

If using sticks of butter, shape them into a 5-inch square by cutting the sticks in half lengthwise, arranging the pieces side by side, and mashing them together with your fingertips. Otherwise, using a rolling pin, roll and shape the butter into a 5-inch square. The butter must be quite firm, but still pliable, and about the same temperature as the dough when they are combined. If necessary, pound the butter between two sheets of waxed paper with a rolling pin to make it more pliable, or chill until it is firmer.

Turn out the dough onto a lightly floured work surface and shape it into a ball. Using a sharp knife, mark four evenly spaced points around the sides of the ball of dough. At each point, cut through the dough toward the center, stopping about $1\frac{1}{2}$ inches from the center. Roll out the four sections of dough with a lightly floured rolling pin, giving the dough a quarter turn after each roll and leaving a thick, rough 5-inch square of dough in the center. Brush off any excess flour.

Put the butter on top of the rough square of dough. Fold the dough over the butter, tucking in the edges and making sure the butter is completely enclosed so it does not ooze out during the following rolling and folding processes.

Roll out the dough, rolling away from you, on a lightly floured surface with a lightly

FOR THE ENVELOPES, SPOON VANILLA CREAM FILLING IN THE CENTER OF EACH SQUARE.

BRING THE CORNERS UP OVER THE FILLING TO MEET IN THE CENTER. PINCH THE ENDS TOGETHER FIRMLY.

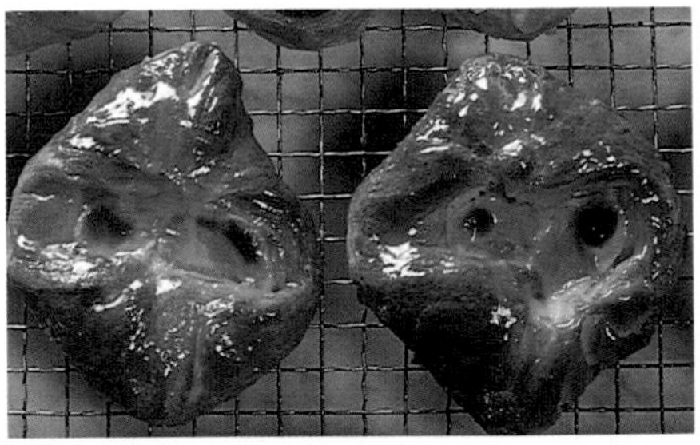

THE BAKED ENVELOPES WILL HAVE A SHINY FINISH IF THEY ARE GLAZED WITH APRICOT JAM.

FOR THE TWISTS, CUT THE FILLED, FOLDED DOUGH INTO NINE STRIPS.

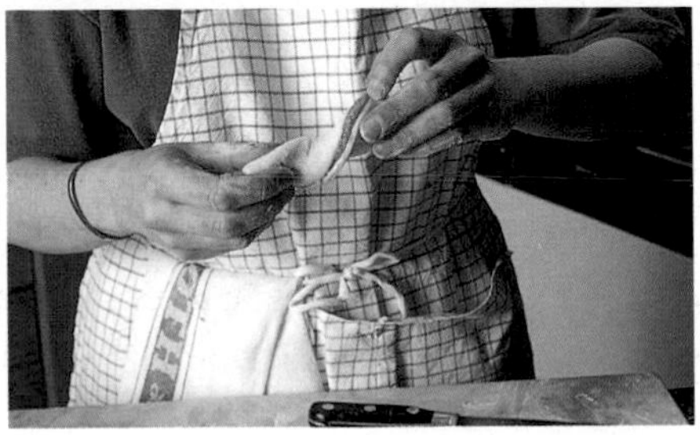

TO SHAPE THEM, TWIST EACH STRIP FIRMLY, TURNING THE ENDS IN OPPOSITE DIRECTIONS.

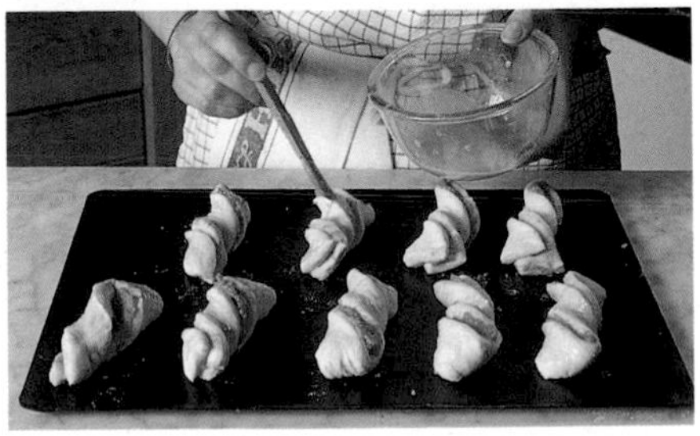

LET THE TWISTS RISE UNTIL ALMOST DOUBLED IN SIZE. THEN BRUSH WITH THE BEATEN EGG GLAZE.

TO SHAPE PINWHEELS, ROLL UP THE FILLED DOUGH FROM A LONG SIDE, LIKE A JELLY ROLL.

USING A LIGHTLY FLOURED KNIFE, CUT THE ROLL INTO ELEVEN EVEN SLICES. ARRANGE ON A BAKING SHEET.

AFTER THE DOUGH HAS RISEN, BRUSH WITH THE EGG GLAZE AND SPRINKLE WITH SLICED ALMONDS.

BRUSH THE EDGES OF THE FILLED WINDMILLS LIGHTLY WITH BEATEN EGG GLAZE.

FOLD EVERY OTHER CORNER INTO THE CENTER. TWIST THE ENDS TOGETHER FIRMLY.

ARRANGE ON A BAKING SHEET, THEN LET THEM RISE UNTIL THEY ARE ALMOST DOUBLED IN SIZE.

floured rolling pin, into an 18 × 6-inch rectangle, with a short edge facing you. Brush off any excess flour from the dough's surface. Fold up the bottom third of the dough, then fold down the top third to make a three-layer dough sandwich that is 6 inches square with the completely enclosed side at the top. Use the rolling pin to seal the side and bottom edges. Wrap in plastic wrap and chill for 15 minutes. Repeat the rolling, folding, and chilling processes twice more. Each time, roll out the dough with the completely enclosed or folded side on your left.

Divide the dough into four equal squares. Then shape and fill the pastries, covering and chilling the portions you are not working with. Here are the shapes and fillings I used for the photographs.

To shape pinwheels, roll out one portion of the dough with a rolling pin to a 9 × 6-inch rectangle, with a long side facing you. Spread evenly with the Almond Filling, leaving a ½-inch border at the edges. Then roll up loosely from the long side, like a jelly roll. Using a lightly floured knife, cut into eleven even slices. Arrange with a cut side up on a greased baking sheet and cover with plastic wrap. Let rise at warm room temperature (about 75F), away from drafts, until almost doubled in size, 45 minutes to 1 hour.

To shape envelopes, roll out one portion of the dough with a rolling pin into an 8-inch square. With a lightly floured knife, cut into four equal squares. Put one-quarter of the Vanilla Cream Filling in the center of each square. Brush the corners with a little of the beaten egg glaze, then bring the corners over the filling to meet in the center. Pinch together firmly with your fingers to seal and enclose the filling. Arrange on a greased baking sheet and cover with plastic wrap. Let rise at warm room temperature (about 75F), away from drafts, until almost doubled in size, 45 minutes to 1 hour.

To shape windmills, roll out one portion of the dough with a rolling pin to an 8-inch square. Cut into four equal squares. Using half the Apricot Filling, put 1 heaping teaspoonful in the center of each square. With a lightly floured knife, make a cut diagonally from each corner to within ½ inch of the center. Brush the edges with a little of the beaten egg glaze. Fold every other corner into the center and twist them together firmly to seal and partially enclose the filling. Arrange on a greased baking sheet and cover with plastic wrap. Let rise at warm room temperature (about 75F), away from drafts, until almost doubled in size, 45 minutes to 1 hour.

To shape twists, roll out one portion of the dough with a rolling pin to an 8-inch square. Spread evenly with the other half of the Apricot Filling, leaving a ½-inch border at the edges. Fold the dough in half. With a lightly floured knife, cut crosswise into nine equal strips. Twist each strip firmly (some filling may ooze out), then arrange on a greased baking sheet. Cover with plastic wrap. Let rise at warm room temperature (about 75F), away from drafts, until doubled in size, 45 minutes to 1 hour.

During the last 15 minutes of rising, heat the oven to 425F. Lightly brush each pastry with the egg glaze, avoiding the cut edges. Sprinkle the pinwheels and twists with sliced almonds. Bake for 10 to 12 minutes, or until well risen and golden. Transfer to a wire rack to cool. You can leave them plain, or brush with a thin layer of strained, warm apricot jam and/or drizzle with Glacé Icing.

Almond Filling

Whisk 1 large egg white in a bowl until stiff peaks form. Fold in 2 tablespoons granulated sugar, 1½ ounces ground almonds, and 1 teaspoon kirsch or light rum, or a few drops of almond extract. Cover and refrigerate for up to one day until ready to use. Makes enough to fill eleven pinwheels, or four envelopes, or four windmills, or nine twists.

Vanilla Cream Filling

Heat ¾ cup half-and-half with half a split vanilla bean in a small heavy saucepan until scalding (bubbles will appear around the edges). Remove from the heat, cover, and let stand to infuse for 15 minutes. Meanwhile, beat together 1 large egg yolk with 1 tablespoon granulated sugar and 1 tablespoon unbleached all-purpose flour in a small bowl until very thick and almost paste-like. Remove the vanilla bean from the half-and-half, scrape the seeds with the tip of a small knife into the half-and-half, and discard the bean. Whisk the warm half-and-half into the egg mixture. Rinse and dry the saucepan. Return the mixture to the saucepan and simmer over low heat, stirring constantly, until thick enough to coat the back of the spoon. Do not let the mixture boil. Scrape it into a small bowl and cover the surface with plastic wrap to prevent a skin forming. Let cool. Refrigerate for up to one day. Makes enough to fill four windmills or four envelopes; do not use for pinwheels or twists.

After the pastries have cooled, you can drizzle them with Glacé Icing, if you like. Here I am decorating baked pinwheels.

Apricot Filling

Drain an 8½-ounce can of apricots and purée the fruit in a blender or food processor. Put the purée in a small, heavy saucepan and simmer over medium heat until very thick, stirring frequently to prevent scorching. Let cool. Beat together 2 tablespoons softened unsalted butter, 1 tablespoon granulated sugar, and ½ teaspoon ground cinnamon in a small bowl until soft and smooth. Then beat in the purée. Add a few drops of lemon juice and extra cinnamon to taste, if you wish. Cover and refrigerate for up to one day until ready to use. Makes enough to fill eight windmills or eight envelopes; or eighteen twists; or four windmills and four envelopes and nine twists.

Glacé Icing

Mix 6 tablespoons sifted confectioners' sugar with 1 tablespoon cold water in a small bowl to make a smooth icing that leaves a trail when you lift the spoon. Makes enough to decorate eleven pinwheel Danish pastries.

An old-fashioned, British teatime favorite, yeasted Lardy Cakes are utterly delicious. The outside is crisp, crunchy, and slightly caramelized, while the layered inside is moist and flaky without being too sweet or heavy.

LARDY CAKES

INGREDIENTS

Makes two cakes.

- $3\frac{1}{2}$ cups white bread flour (preferably unbleached and stone-ground)
- 2 teaspoons kosher salt or flaked sea salt
- 1 cake compressed fresh yeast (0.6 ounce) or 1 envelope active dry yeast ($2\frac{1}{2}$ teaspoons)
- 1 teaspoon granulated sugar
- 1 cup lukewarm milk (95F to 105F)
- 1 large egg, lightly beaten
- 1 cup cold diced lard, or $\frac{1}{2}$ cup (1 stick) cold, diced, unsalted butter and $\frac{1}{2}$ cup cold diced lard, mixed
- 1 cup granulated sugar
- $1\frac{2}{3}$ cups golden raisins and currants, mixed

two 8- to $8\frac{1}{2}$-inch-round layer-cake or springform pans, greased
two jelly-roll pans

In the North of England, a good pinch of mixed sweet spice (akin to pumpkin-pie spice in the U.S.) is often added to this dough. In the West Country (the region in southwestern England that includes the counties of Devon, Somerset, and Cornwall), recipes insist on using good pork lard, a holdover from when lardy cake was a luxury saved for feasts, harvest suppers, and farm celebrations. Along with some bakers, I prefer to use half butter and half lard for a lighter texture and richer taste. The calories, however, remain the same.

For many years, I regularly bought lardy cakes from Wreford's, a small, old-fashioned bakery situated right on highway A303 near West Camel in Somerset. Just before their baker Chris Wreford retired, he showed me how to make his especially delicious lardies. This is his recipe, as he learned it from his father.

The cakes should be eaten within two days of baking, but are best warm from the oven, served thickly sliced. Lardy cake is also good toasted, and if you do not eat the second cake right away, it can be frozen, tightly wrapped in plastic wrap or a freezer bag, for up to one month. Thaw at room temperature for 4 to 6 hours, then unwrap, place on a baking sheet, and warm thoroughly in a 350F oven for 10 minutes.

Mix together the flour and salt in a medium-size bowl. Make a well in the center of the flour. Crumble the fresh yeast into a small bowl. Stir in the sugar and lukewarm milk until smooth. If using dry yeast, mix the granules and the 1 teaspoon sugar with the lukewarm milk and let stand until foamy, 5 to 10 minutes (page 18). Add the yeast mixture to the well in the flour. Work in just enough of the flour from the bowl with a small whisk or a spoon to make a thin, smooth batter. Sprinkle the batter with a little of the flour to prevent a skin forming. Cover the bowl with a dish towel and let stand at room temperature until the batter becomes spongy and frothy, 20 to 30 minutes.

Add the egg to the batter. Then gradually work in the remaining flour from the bowl with your hands or a wooden spoon to make a soft, but not sticky dough.

Turn out the dough onto a lightly floured work surface and knead for 10 minutes until smooth and elastic. Wash, dry, and lightly oil the bowl. Put the dough back into the bowl, then turn the dough over so the top is oiled. Cover with a dry dish towel and let rise at room temperature, away from drafts, until doubled in size, 1 to $1\frac{1}{2}$ hours.

Punch down the dough and turn out onto a lightly floured work surface. Divide the dough into two equal pieces and cover one piece and set aside. Divide the lard (or the butter and lard mixture), the sugar, and the dried fruit into two equal batches.

AFTER FOLDING UP THE BOTTOM THIRD OF THE DOUGH OVER HALF THE FILLING, FOLD DOWN THE TOP THIRD TO MAKE A THREE-LAYER DOUGH SANDWICH.

Roll out the uncovered piece of dough on a lightly floured surface with a lightly floured rolling pin into a 10 × 6-inch rectangle, with a short side facing you. Dot the top two-thirds of the dough rectangle with one-third of the first batch of lard, leaving a 1-inch border at the edges of the dough. Sprinkle with one-third of the first batch of sugar and one-third of the first batch of dried fruit. Fold up the uncovered bottom third of the dough over half the filling. Then fold down the top third of the dough to make a three-layer dough sandwich. Use the rolling pin to seal side and bottom edges. Give the dough a quarter turn to the left, so the completely enclosed side is on your left. Then repeat the whole procedure twice more, to make a total of three rollings, fillings, and foldings. Make sure to give the dough a quarter turn to the left each time.

Let the dough rest, uncovered, at room temperature for 5 to 10 minutes. Meanwhile, roll, fill, and fold the second piece of dough the same way, using the remaining batch of lard, sugar, and dried fruit.

Roll out each piece of dough on a lightly floured surface with a lightly floured rolling pin into an 8-inch square. Put a piece of dough into each prepared layer-cake or springform pan, tucking under the corners, so the dough roughly fits the pan. Cover each pan with a damp dish towel and let rise at room temperature, away from drafts, until the dough has almost doubled in size and expanded to fit the pans, 45 minutes to 1 hour. During the last 15 minutes of rising, heat the oven to 425F.

Just before baking, using the tip of a sharp knife or a razor blade, score the surface of each cake in a criss-cross pattern. Place each cake pan on a jelly-roll pan to catch any fat that may run out of the pans. Bake the cakes for 25 to 30 minutes until golden brown and crisp. Lower the oven temperature to 375F if the cakes are browning too quickly. Unmold the cakes onto the jelly-roll pans, leaving them upside down. Bake for 5 minutes longer so the fat seeps downward and the bases (which are now on the top) have a chance to get crispy. Turn out onto wire racks to cool.

SALLY LUNNS

INGREDIENTS

Makes two cakes.

a large pinch of saffron threads
¼ cup milk
3½ cups white bread flour (preferably unbleached and stone-ground)
2 teaspoons kosher salt or flaked sea salt
1 cake compressed fresh yeast (0.6 ounce) or 1 envelope active dry yeast (2¼ teaspoons)
1 teaspoon granulated sugar
1 cup heavy cream
4 large eggs, lightly beaten
3 tablespoons granulated sugar dissolved in 3 tablespoons milk and brought to a boil, to glaze
1 cup clotted cream, or lightly whipped cream, or about ½ cup softened unsalted butter, to fill the cakes

two 6-inch-round, deep cake pans (see Note), or two 6-inch copper saucepans, well greased

This very rich, sponge-like cake is similar to the kugelhopf of Alsace (page 142). The dough is so soft it is worked in the bowl and must be baked in a deep pan, as it will not hold a shape.

Who or what was Sally Lunn? All sorts of tales surround the origin of the cake – that Sally Lunn sold cakes along the fashionable streets of Bath, England, in the 18th century; that she was a Bath pastry chef with a shop in Lilliput Alley; or that Sally Lunn is a corruption of "Soleil Lune," the French sun-and-moon cake, a yellow layer cake filled with white clotted cream. There are many versions of the recipe as well, all claiming authenticity. Some enrich the dough with eggs and melted butter, others add milk too, and some use cream. Saffron, the West Country's favorite spice, is often added, and Elizabeth David recommends grated lemon rind or ground mixed sweet spice in her recipe.

This is my favorite recipe for Sally Lunn. In the 18th century, 5-inch cakes were popular, but the larger pans I use in this recipe are easier to come by nowadays. Slices of this are delicious toasted. If you prefer, you may freeze the second cake. Before splitting and filling it, wrap the cooled cake well in plastic wrap and then in foil, or place it in a freezer bag. The cake will keep in the freezer for up to one month. Thaw, wrapped, at room temperature for 4 to 6 hours. Then unwrap, place on a baking sheet, and heat for 5 minutes in a 350F oven. When the cake is warm, split and fill it as described.

Crumble the saffron into a small bowl. Heat the milk in a small saucepan until scalding (bubbles will appear around the edge). Then pour it onto the saffron, stir, and let stand to infuse until the milk is lukewarm (95F to 105F).

Mix together the flour and salt in a large bowl. Crumble the fresh yeast into the saffron liquid. Then stir in the sugar until smooth. If using dry yeast, mix the granules and the sugar with the lukewarm milk mixture and let stand until foamy, 5 to 10 minutes (page

18). Make a well in the center of the flour. Add the yeast mixture to the well. Mix in enough flour from the bowl with your hand or a wooden spoon to make a thick, smooth batter. Sprinkle the batter with a little flour to prevent a skin forming. Cover the bowl with a damp dish towel and let the batter sponge and become frothy, about 15 minutes.

Whisk the cream and eggs together in a medium-size bowl, then add to the well in the flour. With a small whisk or a spoon, blend the cream and egg mixture into the yeast mixture. When thoroughly combined, gradually work in the flour from the bowl to make a very soft, sticky dough. Using your fingers, work the dough in the bowl for 5 minutes, or until it is firm, glossy, smooth, elastic, and no longer sticks to your fingers.

Divide the dough in half. With lightly floured hands, shape each portion into a ball and place one in each of the prepared cake pans or saucepans. Cover them with damp dish towels and let rise at room temperature, away from drafts, until doubled in size, $1\frac{1}{2}$ to 2 hours. During the last 15 minutes of rising, heat the oven to 400F.

Bake the cakes for about 25 minutes until golden brown and firm. Cover the cakes with a piece of foil or parchment paper if they brown too quickly while baking. When turned out, a completely baked cake will sound hollow if tapped underneath. Turn out the cakes onto a wire rack, and immediately brush with the boiling hot sweet glaze. Let stand until warm, then slice each cake horizontally into three layers. Spread each layer with clotted cream, whipped cream, or good unsalted butter and reassemble. Eat immediately.

NOTE: The 6-inch cake pans called for in this recipe may be purchased at cookware or specialty bakeware stores that sell supplies for making wedding cakes, or by mail order. See List of Suppliers (page 187).

With its rich, sponge-like texture, Sally Lunn can be served plain, or sliced into layers and filled with clotted cream or whipped cream. A more simple presentation would be to spread unsalted butter between the layers.

A delicious Scottish breakfast of warm butteries served with homemade preserves and a pot of tea.

ABERDEEN BUTTERIES

These Scottish pastries are best served warm. Make the dough a day ahead.

INGREDIENTS

Makes sixteen to twenty butteries.

- $4\frac{3}{4}$ cups white bread flour (preferably unbleached and stone-ground)
- 1 tablespoon kosher salt or flaked sea salt
- 1 cake compressed fresh yeast (0.6 ounce) or 1 envelope active dry yeast ($2\frac{1}{2}$ teaspoons)
- 2 cups lukewarm water (95F to 105F)
- 1 tablespoon granulated sugar
- $\frac{3}{4}$ cup ($1\frac{1}{2}$ sticks) cold unsalted butter, diced
- $\frac{1}{2}$ cup cold diced lard
- milk for glazing

- 3-inch round or oval biscuit or cookie cutter
- two or three baking sheets, lightly floured

Stir together the flour and salt in a large bowl. Crumble the fresh yeast into a small bowl. Stir in the lukewarm water and sugar until smooth. If using dry yeast, mix the granules and the sugar with the lukewarm water and let stand until foamy, 5 to 10 minutes (page 18). Make a well in the center of the flour. Add the yeast mixture to the well. Work in the flour from the bowl and mix to make a soft, but not sticky dough.

Turn out the dough onto a lightly floured work surface and knead gently for 2 minutes, or until the dough just comes together and is slightly smooth. Wash and dry the bowl. Return the dough to the bowl. Cover the bowl with a damp dish towel and let rise at room temperature, away from drafts, until doubled in size, $1\frac{1}{2}$ hours.

In a small bowl, lightly mix together the diced butter and lard with your fingertips. Then divide it into three batches. Punch down the dough. Roll out the dough, rolling away from you, on a lightly floured surface with a lightly floured rolling pin, to an 18×6-inch rectangle, with a short side facing you. Dot the top two-thirds of the dough rectangle with one batch of the butter and lard mixture, leaving a $\frac{1}{2}$-inch border at the edges. Fold the uncovered bottom third of the rectangle up over half the fat, then fold the top third of the rectangle down to make a three-layer dough sandwich about 6 inches square, with the completely enclosed side at the top. Seal the side and bottom edges by pressing down with a rolling pin. Give the dough a quarter turn to the left so the completely enclosed side is to your left. Repeat the rolling and folding without adding fat at this time. Wrap the dough in plastic wrap and refrigerate for 30 minutes. Repeat the rolling, filling, folding, and chilling processes twice more. Each time, roll out the dough with the completely enclosed side to your left. After the last folding, tightly cover the dough. Then, for easiest handling, chill at least a day, or overnight, before cutting.

Roll out the dough to a circle about $\frac{3}{4}$ inch thick. Leave to rest, uncovered, for 5 minutes. Brush off the excess flour. Using a floured biscuit or cookie cutter, stamp out about twenty rounds or ovals. Place the cutouts, upside down and apart, on the prepared baking sheets. Cover with plastic wrap. Let stand until slightly risen, about 20 minutes. Meanwhile, heat the oven to 400F. Lightly brush the butteries with milk. Bake them for 25 to 30 minutes, or until golden brown and crisp. Transfer to wire racks. Serve warm.

MICHEL ROUX'S BRIOCHE

INGREDIENTS

Makes one large brioche.

- 1 cake compressed fresh yeast (0.6 ounce), or 1 envelope active dry yeast ($2\frac{1}{2}$ teaspoons) plus $\frac{1}{2}$ teaspoon granulated sugar
- $\frac{1}{4}$ cup lukewarm milk (95F to 105F)
- $1\frac{1}{2}$ teaspoons kosher salt or flaked sea salt
- $3\frac{1}{2}$ cups white bread flour (preferably unbleached and stone-ground)
- 5 large eggs, at room temperature, lightly beaten
- 1 cup (2 sticks) unsalted butter, softened
- 2 tablespoons granulated sugar
- 1 large egg yolk lightly beaten with 1 tablespoon milk, to glaze

one large brioche mold, $9\frac{1}{2}$ inches wide at the top and $4\frac{1}{2}$ inches wide at the base, buttered, or one deep 7-inch copper saucepan, buttered

"The perfect golden brioche has a delicious rich, buttery flavor, yet it does not leave a trace of butter on your fingers or an aftertaste on the palate," says Michel Roux (page 170).

He likes to use $1\frac{1}{2}$ cups of butter to $3\frac{1}{2}$ cups of flour when he makes brioche; pastry chefs vary the quantity from $\frac{1}{2}$ cup of butter right up to an extravagant $2\frac{1}{4}$ cups of butter without altering the quantity of flour, but these variations depend on how the brioche is to be used. The most common proportion is half the amount of butter to flour. But remember, the best, freshest unsalted butter is vital for good flavor, whatever quantity of butter you use.

The fine, sponge cake-like crumb of a brioche is achieved through three risings, two at normal room temperature and one in the refrigerator. (If the rising is done at too warm a temperature, the butter will melt and ooze out of the dough.) The soft, rich dough is then chilled before it is shaped, so the dough is firm enough to maintain its distinctive top-heavy shape.

Although brioches are usually eaten warm with butter and preserves for breakfast, firmer, plainer doughs are used for savory dishes such as Alyson Cook's Brie en Brioche (page 113), or for sweeter pastries such as the Fancy Ring Doughnuts (page 95). Richer brioches can be hollowed out and filled with sautéed wild mushrooms or seafood in a spicy or creamy sauce.

Michel Roux says, "For a real treat, cut the brioche into slices, sprinkle with confectioners' sugar, and glaze under a very hot broiler. Serve the slices by themselves for breakfast or, as a monstrous indulgence, warm, with chocolate mousse." He adds that brioche looks very impressive if braided or formed into a crown shape.

Brioche dough can be frozen, wrapped in a freezer bag, after it has risen and been punched down, but before it is shaped. To use, let the dough thaw gradually in the refrigerator for 4 to 5 hours, then proceed with the recipe.

Crumble the fresh yeast into the bowl of a large stationary electric mixer fitted with a dough hook or a large bowl, if mixing by hand. Stir in the lukewarm milk and salt until smooth. If using dry yeast, mix the granules and the $\frac{1}{2}$ teaspoon sugar with the lukewarm milk and let stand until foamy, 5 to 10 minutes (page 18). Stir in the salt.

Add the flour and eggs to the yeast mixture and beat with the dough hook to form a

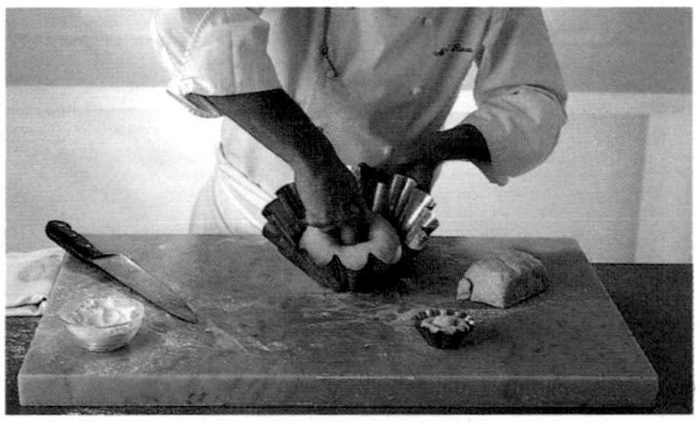

USING HIS FINGERS, MICHEL FORMS A DEEP INDENTATON IN THE LARGE PIECE OF DOUGH IN THE BRIOCHE MOLD.

THE INDENTATON SHOULD EXTEND ALMOST TO THE BOTTOM OF THE MOLD.

HE ROLLS THE SMALLER PIECE OF DOUGH INTO AN ELONGATED PEAR SHAPE.

HE GLAZES THE TOP OF THE RISEN BRIOCHE.

AFTER THE DOUGH HAS RISEN, USING SCISSORS THAT HAVE BEEN DIPPED IN COLD WATER, MICHEL SNIPS ALL AROUND THE EDGE.

WHEN UNMOLDED, BRIOCHE AND MINI BRIOCHE HAVE DISTINCTIVE SHAPES.

soft dough. Then knead the dough with the dough hook until it is smooth and elastic, about 10 minutes. Or, if mixing by hand, stir the flour and eggs into the yeast mixture. With a sturdy wooden spoon or your hand, beat until the dough is smooth and elastic, about 20 minutes.

Beat together the softened butter and sugar in a medium-size bowl until light and fluffy. Beating at low speed, add the butter mixture to the dough, a little at a time, making sure it is completely incorporated after each addition. If you are working by hand, or if the dough feels stiff and it takes a long time to add the butter with the mixer, squeeze the butter mixture into the dough with your hands. Then, continue beating with the dough hook for about 5 minutes, or by hand for 15 minutes, until the dough is perfectly smooth, glossy, shiny, and fairly elastic.

Cover the bowl with a damp dish towel. Let the dough rise at room temperature, away from drafts, until doubled in size, 1¾ to 2 hours.

Punch down the dough by flipping it over quickly with your fingertips not more than two or three times. Return the dough to the bowl. Cover with a damp dish towel and refrigerate for several hours, but not more than 24 hours.

Turn out the dough onto a lightly floured work surface and shape it into a large ball. To make the brioche in a mold, cut off one-fourth of the dough to make the topknot. Shape the larger piece of dough into a ball and place it in the prepared mold. Form a deep indentation in the center with your fingers, almost down to the bottom of the mold. With your palm held at an angle against the work surface, roll the smaller piece of dough into an elongated pear shape with a narrow neck.

Using lightly floured fingertips, gently press the narrow neck well down into the hole in the center of the large ball.

If you are using the saucepan, line it with a sheet of buttered parchment paper twice the height of the pan. Shape all the dough into a ball, then place in the pan. The brioche will bake into a tall, cylinder shape.

Lightly brush the top of the brioche with egg glaze, working from the outside inward. Take care not to let any glaze run into the crack between the main body of the dough and the topknot, or onto the edges of the mold, because it will prevent the dough from rising properly. Cover with plastic wrap.

Let the dough rise at room temperature, away from drafts, until almost doubled in size, 1½ to 2 hours; it may take an hour or so longer if the dough has been chilled 24 hours. During the last 15 minutes of rising, heat the oven to 425F.

Glaze the brioche again. Using scissors dipped in cold water, snip all around the edges so the dough doesn't stick to the pan to help it rise properly in the oven. Bake for 10 minutes. Reduce the oven temperature to 375F and bake 50 to 60 minutes longer until it is well browned and sounds hollow when tapped underneath. If the brioche is browning too quickly, cover loosely with foil. If you are unsure about doneness and do not wish to unmold the brioche, an instant-read thermometer inserted just to one side of the topknot will register 200F. Carefully unmold the brioche and transfer to a wire rack to cool.

VARIATION: MINI BRIOCHES You can use the same dough to make individual, mini brioches. Lightly butter twenty small brioche molds measuring 3¼ inches wide at the top and 1½ inches wide at the base (5 fluid ounce capacity). Weigh the dough and divide it into twenty equal pieces, or roll it into a fat rope and cut it into twenty equal pieces. Shape as for the large brioche, right. Glaze, cover with plastic wrap, and let rise at room temperature, away from drafts, until doubled in size, about 1 hour. Glaze again. Bake in a 425F oven for 5 to 7 minutes until they begin to brown. Then reduce the oven temperature to 375F and bake about 10 minutes longer, until the brioches are well browned and sound hollow when tapped on the bottoms. An instant-read thermometer inserted just to one side of the topknot will register 200F. If the brioches are browning too quickly, cover loosely with a sheet of foil. Carefully unmold the brioches and transfer to wire racks to cool.

BABAS AND SAVARINS

A very light, yeasty dough that produces a holey crumb is used to make babas and savarins because it soaks up sugar syrup like a bath sponge. The final result is a thoroughly sodden, cake-like dessert that is, nevertheless, light in texture, never heavy.

Babas are said to have been "invented" in the mid-17th century by Duke Stanislas of Lorraine, who dunked his stale kugelhopf in a rum syrup. He was so taken by his creation, according to the legend, he named it after Ali Baba, his favorite character in A Tale of a Thousand and One Nights. Dome-topped babas are usually baked in individual bucket-shaped baba or dariole molds, then soaked in syrup flavored with rum, although you can use other liqueurs. Kirsch is delicious, especially if you slice strawberries into the reserved syrup to serve with the babas.

Savarins, on the other hand, are ring shaped, large or small. They are made without the currants that are generally included in babas, although the savarin dough is often flavored with other fruit additions, such as grated lemon or orange rind or chopped candied fruit, which are added after the butter is incorporated. The soaking syrup is enhanced with grated lemon or orange rind and juice; spices, such as cinnamon or cardamom; or liqueurs, such as kirsch, rum, Grand Marnier, Cointreau, or Cognac.

A savarin is especially delicious served with a filling in the center of the ring. Try sweetened, vanilla-flavored whipped cream, fruit salad, or poached fruit. Savarins are usually decorated with glacéed cherries and angelica that has been cut into leaves, but I prefer to do without these ornamental extras.

Correct rising is vital when you make babas and savarins. Not enough time and the dough will be heavy; too much time and the dough will run over the top of the mold during baking. Also, make sure the dough rises in a spot that is warm, but not hot.

Babas and savarins keep well, tightly wrapped, for up to 24 hours. They can also be baked and stored in an airtight container for two or three days, or wrapped and frozen for one month. If frozen, unwrap them, place them still frozen on baking sheets, and reheat in a 350F oven for 10 to 12 minutes for babas, 15 to 20 minutes for savarins. Baste them with hot syrup shortly before serving.

Saturated with a lemon- or orange-flavored sugar syrup and filled with fresh fruit, a savarin makes a dessert that is as impressive looking as it is delicious. It is ideal to serve for a dinner party. I have filled this one with fresh strawberries and oranges but you can use any fruit.

JUST BEFORE SERVING, SPOON THE RUM OVER EACH BABA.

RUM BABAS

INGREDIENTS

Makes eight babas.

- 2 cups white bread flour (preferably unbleached and stone-ground)
- 1 teaspoon kosher salt or flaked sea salt
- 2 tablespoons granulated sugar
- 1 cake compressed fresh yeast (0.6 ounce), or 1 envelope active dry yeast ($2\frac{1}{2}$ teaspoons) plus $\frac{1}{2}$ teaspoon granulated sugar
- 3 tablespoons lukewarm milk (95F to 105F)
- 3 large eggs at room temperature, lightly beaten
- $\frac{1}{2}$ cup currants
- $\frac{1}{4}$ cup amber or dark rum
- $\frac{1}{2}$ cup (1 stick) unsalted butter, softened

FOR THE SYRUP:

- 2 cups granulated sugar
- $3\frac{3}{4}$ cups water
- 6 to 8 tablespoons amber or dark rum

- eight baba molds ($8\frac{1}{2}$ fluid ounce capacity)
- a baking sheet

This recipe is adapted from one taught at L'Ecole de Cuisine La Varenne, which is based at the Château du Fey, in France's Burgundy region.

Stir together the flour, salt, and sugar in a large bowl. Crumble the fresh yeast into a small bowl. Stir in the lukewarm milk until smooth. If using dry yeast, mix the granules and the $\frac{1}{2}$ teaspoon sugar with the lukewarm milk and let stand until foamy, 5 to 10 minutes (page 18). Make a well in the center of the flour. Add the yeast mixture to the well. Then mix the eggs into the yeast mixture. Using your hand or a wooden spoon, work in the flour from the bowl to make a smooth, sticky, very thick batter-like dough.

Work the dough in the bowl by beating it with your hand. Tilt the bowl slightly and, using your hand like a spoon with fingers together and palm upward, lift the dough and push it back into the bowl. Continue this motion for 5 minutes, or until the dough becomes very elastic, smooth, and somewhat looser.

Cover the bowl with a damp dish towel. Let rise in a warm place (about 75F), away from drafts, until doubled in size, 45 minutes to 1 hour. Meanwhile, warm the rum in a small saucepan. Add the currants and let them soak. Butter the molds and chill them in the freezer for 10 minutes. Butter them again. This double buttering helps prevent the soft, rich dough from sticking; the butter sets and does not get absorbed by the dough as it rises. If the kitchen is very hot and the butter starts to melt, put the molds in the refrigerator; otherwise, leave them at room temperature.

Punch down the risen dough in the bowl. Using your hand as before, gradually beat in the softened $\frac{1}{2}$ cup of butter until the dough, like a very thick batter, is smooth and even, not streaky. Drain the currants and work them into the dough.

Drop the dough from an ungreased metal spoon into the molds, filling each one-third full. Arrange the molds on a baking sheet and cover with a damp dish towel. Let rise at warm room temperature (about 75F), away from drafts, until the dough rises almost to the top of the molds, 30 to 50 minutes. Check to make sure the dough is not sticking to the cloth. During the last 15 minutes of rising, heat the oven to 400F.

Bake the babas on the baking sheet for about 20 to 30 minutes, or until they are golden brown and begin to shrink from the sides of the molds. Unmold them onto a wire rack and let cool.

To make the syrup, stir together the sugar and water in a medium-size saucepan over low heat until the sugar is dissolved. Bring to a boil and let boil for 2 to 3 minutes, or until the syrup becomes clear.

Remove the pan from the heat. Add the babas, one or two at a time, to the very hot syrup. Using a large slotted spoon, gently turn them over several times to make sure they absorb as much syrup as possible; they will swell and become very shiny. Using the slotted spoon, carefully lift the babas out of the syrup and onto a plate. Soak the remaining babas. Reserve the remaining syrup. Just before serving, spoon or brush the babas with the rum. Add any remaining rum to the reserved syrup and serve separately for spooning over the babas.

VARIATIONS: MINI RUM BABAS Grease about sixteen small baba molds ($4\frac{1}{2}$ fluid ounce capacity), dariole molds, or muffin pans. Make the baba batter as above. Butter and fill the molds as above. Cover with a damp dish towel. Let rise at warm room temperature (about 75F), away from drafts, until the dough has risen almost to the top of the molds, 20 to 45 minutes. Bake in a 400F oven for 20 to 30 minutes. Then cool and soak with the syrup and sprinkle with the rum as described above.

GRAND BABA In Alsace and Lorraine, whole giant babas are served at parties or celebration meals. Make the baba batter as above, but let it rise in a well-buttered 9-inch kugelhopf mold and then bake in a 400F oven for 40 to 45 minutes. Cool and soak with the syrup and sprinkle with the rum as described above.

SAVARIN

Make the Rum Baba batter as opposite, omitting the currants and their rum soak. Butter a large 4- to 5-cup ring or savarin mold or two smaller $1\frac{1}{4}$- to $1\frac{1}{2}$-cup ring molds, as described in the baba recipe. Fill the mold or molds one-third full with the batter. Let rise at warm room temperature, away from drafts, for 30 to 50 minutes, or until the dough is almost to the top of the mold. Bake in a 400F oven for 20 to 25 minutes until it is golden and shrinks from the sides of the mold. Unmold it onto a wire rack.

Make the sugar syrup as for Rum Baba (opposite) in a large, shallow pan, adding the finely grated rind and juice of 1 large lemon when the syrup is removed from the heat. If the savarin fits, place it in the very hot syrup in the pan and spoon the syrup over it until it is saturated. If the savarin is too big for the pan, put it on a wire rack set over a jelly-roll pan and spoon the hot syrup over it, reheating any syrup that drips onto the pan and spooning it over the savarin, until all the syrup is absorbed. The savarin will swell and look very shiny.

Just before serving, sprinkle 3 to 4 tablespoons amber or dark rum over the savarin. Fill the center with whipped cream that has been sweetened to taste and flavored with vanilla, or with fresh fruit salad.

THE DOUGH WILL RISE ALMOST TO THE TOP OF THE MOLD.

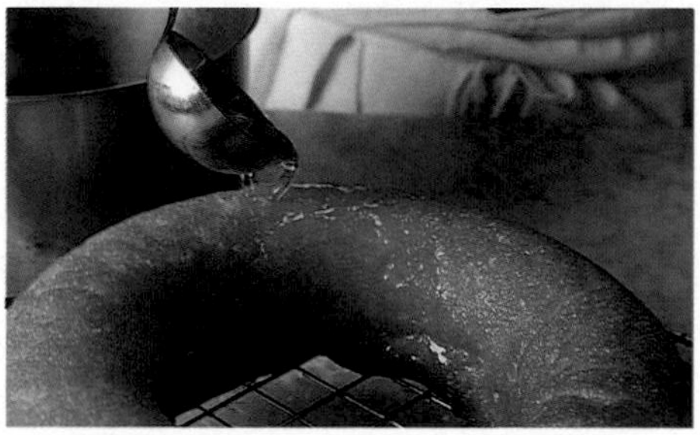

SPOON THE HOT SYRUP OVER THE FRESHLY BAKED SAVARIN.

LIST OF SUPPLIERS

EQUIPMENT

BRIDGE KITCHENWARE
214 E. 52nd Street
New York, NY 10022
800-274-3435
Professional bakeware, cookware, tools.
Catalogue available.

BROADWAY PANHANDLER
520 Broadway
New York, NY 10012
212-966-3434
Bakeware, cookware, tools.

DEAN & DELUCCA, INC.
MAIL ORDER DEPARTMENT
560 Broadway
New York, NY 10012
800-221-7714
Specialty bakeware, including brioche pans, cookware, tools.
Catalogue available.

KING ARTHUR® FLOUR BAKER'S CATALOGUE
P.O. Box 876
Norwich, Vermont 05055
800-827-6836
Specialty bakeware and tools.
Catalogue available.

KITCHEN KRAFTS
P.O. Box 805
Mount Laurel, NJ 08054
800-776-0575
Specialty bakeware.
Catalogue available.

LA CUISINE
323 Cameron Street
Alexandria, VA 22314
800-521-1176
Cookware and bakeware; baking ingredients.
Catalogue available.

MAID OF SCANDINAVIA
3244 Raleigh Avenue
Minneapolis, MN 55416
800-328-6722
Specialty bakeware and tools.
Catalogue available.

WILLIAMS-SONOMA
P.O. Box 7456
San Francisco, CA 94120-7456
800-541-2233
Bakeware, cookware, tools.
Catalogue available.

ZABAR'S
2245 Broadway
New York City, NY 10024
212-496-1234
Bakeware, cookware, tools.
Catalogue available.

FLOURS AND GRAINS

BRUMWELL MILLING
328 East Second Street
Sumner, IA 50674
319-578-8106
Stone-ground, certified organic bread flour, rye and spelt flours, cornmeal.
Price list available.

BUTTE CREEK MILL
P.O. Box 561
Eagle Point, OR 97524
503-826-3531
Stone-ground bread flour, pastry flour, buckwheat flour, cornmeal.
Price list available.

GRAY'S GRIST MILL
P.O. Box 422
Adamsville, RI 02801
508-636-6075
Stone-ground certified organic bread flour, rye and spelt flours, stone-ground cornmeal.
Price list available.

THE GREAT VALLEY MILLS
R.D. 3, Country Line Road
Box 1111
Barto, PA 19504
800-688-6455
Stone-ground bread flour, pastry flour, rye and semolina flours, steel-cut oats.
Catalogue available.

KING ARTHUR® FLOUR BAKER'S CATALOGUE
(see EQUIPMENT)
Stone-ground bread flour, pastry flour, white whole-wheat flour, amaranth, barley, semolina, and spelt flours, cornmeal, vital wheat gluten, cracked wheat, wheat flakes.

NEW HOPE MILLS
R.R. 2, P.O. Box 269A
Moravia, NY 13118
315-497-0783
Stone-ground bread flour, buckwheat, rye, and spelt flours, vital wheat gluten, cornmeal.
Catalogue available.

PETE'S SPICE AND EVERYTHING NICE
174 First Avenue
New York, NY 10009
212-254-8773
Bread flour, pastry flour, buckwheat, rye, semolina, and spelt flours, cornmeal.
Catalogue available.

SHILOH FARMS INC.
P.O. Box 97
Sulphur Springs, AR 72768
800-362-6832, for the West and Midwest on the East Coast.

GARDEN SPOT
438 White Oak Road
New Holland, PA 17557
800-829-5100
Certified organic, stone-ground bread flour and spelt flour.

STAFFORD COUNTY FLOUR MILLS Co.
P.O. Box 7
Hudson, KS 67545
316-458-4121
Hudson Cream unbleached white and whole-wheat flours.

WAR EAGLE MILL
Route 5, Box 411
Rogers, AR 72756
501-789-5343
Certified organic, stone-ground bread flour, buckwheat and rye flours, cornmeal.
Catalogue available.

DRIED AND CANDIED FRUIT AND CITRUS PEELS

DEAN & DELUCCA
(see EQUIPMENT)
Dried and candied fruit, candied citrus peels, in season.

PETE'S SPICE AND EVERYTHING NICE
(see FLOURS AND GRAINS)
Dried and candied fruit, candied citrus peel.

TIMBER CREST FARMS
4791 Dry Creek Road
Healdsburg, CA 95448
707-433-8251
Certified organic, no-sulphur-added dried apples, apricots, peaches, pears, prunes, raisins.
Catalogue available.

ACKNOWLEDGMENTS

Linda Collister and Anthony Blake would like to thank the following people:

IN THE UNITED STATES: Noah Alper, Caroll Boltin, Linda and Ken Busteed, Alyson Cook, Cindy Falk, Jeffrey Hamelman, Annette and Will Hertz, Lois and Jerry Keller, Hayley Matson, Ina McNeil, Susan Stephenson, Viola and Henry Unruh and Barbara Walker.

IN FRANCE: Clarisse and Jean Michel Deiss and Lionel Poilâne.

IN GREAT BRITAIN: Beverly LeBlanc, Janet Bligh, Sandra Bosuston, Betty Charlton, Julia Royden-Cooper, Brigitte Friis, Elaine Hallgarten, Kyle Hayes, Randolph Hodgson of Neals Yard Dairy, Pierre Koffmann, Barbara Levy, Joy Portch, Rachel Roskilly, Michel Roux, Joy Skipper, Louise Simpson, Jagdeesh Sohal, Anna, Rollo and Cosmo Sterk, Mike Thurlow of Letheringsett Mill, Jonathon Topps and Paul Welti.

IN IRELAND: Mary Curtis, Phoebe and Bill Lett, Veronica Steele of Milleens Dairy and Alice and Gerry Turner.

The authors also wish to express their appreciation to the Bulgarian Wine and Tourist Agency, Kansas Wheat Commission, Nuremberg Tourist Office, Sharwoods and Trustees Philipsburg Manor.

Sedgewood® Press would like to extend its thanks to the following for their generous assistance:

Rabbi Hershel E. Portnoy; Brinna Sands, King Arthur® Four; Teresa and Carol Scafuro, The Main Street Grainery, Chatham, New York; Donald Stinchcomb, Purity Foods, Okemo, Michigan.

INDEX

Page numbers in *italic* refer to the illustrations